Black Religion in America

I0091896

Black Religion in America is an introduction to the religious history of African Americans from the period of slavery to the twenty-first century. It analyses Black people's varying religious responses to W.E.B. Du Bois's notion of double consciousness, the experience of racial exclusion in America, of having "two souls, two thoughts, two unreconciled strivings, two warring ideals in one dark body."

The book traces the social justice thought and activism of Black Christians, conjurors, Muslims, Pentecostals, humanists, and various esoteric prophets across historical epochs, introducing students to major religious groups and innovators within African American religious history who have striven for full social inclusion. It offers a narrative interpretation of Black religion that engages this current generation of students grappling with enduring marginalization in the post-civil rights and post-Obama era. This is to say, despite the victories of the civil rights movement, culminating for some with the historic election of Barack Obama in 2008, Black religions have not provided a panacea for lingering social inequities. Still, throughout American history, Black people have continuously creatively employed religion to respond to changing oppressions.

The book underscores the intersectionality of Black religious women and examines their experience and resistance of racism, sexism, and classism. Featuring student-friendly pedagogy including discussion questions, the book is a must-read for all students of African American religion, religion in America, or African American history, interested in studying how Black religion has factored in the long struggle for social justice in America.

Jonathan Chism is Associate Professor of History at University of Houston–Downtown, USA.

Religion in America

Mexican American Religions
An Introduction
Brett Hendrickson

Hinduism in America
An Introduction
Michael J. Altman

Black Religion in America
An Introduction
Jonathan Chism

For more information about this series, please visit: https://www.routledge.com/Reli gion-in-America/book-series/RIA

Black Religion in America

An Introduction

Jonathan Chism

Routledge
Taylor & Francis Group

LONDON AND NEW YORK

Designed cover image: Getty Images

First published 2026
by Routledge
4 Park Square, Milton Park, Abingdon, Oxon OX14 4RN

and by Routledge
605 Third Avenue, New York, NY 10158

Routledge is an imprint of the Taylor & Francis Group, an informa business

© 2026 Jonathan Chism

British Library Cataloguing in Publication Data
A catalogue record for this book is available from the British Library

Library of Congress Cataloging-in-Publication Data
A catalog record has been requested for this book

ISBN: 9781032416717 (hbk)
ISBN: 9781032416724 (pbk)
ISBN: 9781003359197 (ebk)

DOI: 10.4324/9781003359197

Typeset in Sabon
by Taylor & Francis Books

Contents

Figures

Acknowledgements

This book is deeply indebted to the generations of intellectual giants of Black religion. Many are now with the ancestors, but their academic legacy lives. I am thankful for scholars and colleagues who are actively producing scholarship and enhancing understanding of the Black religious experience. I am most appreciative of Dr. Anthony Pinn, my mentor and former doctoral advisor at Rice University. He has inspired me from the first course I took with him as an undergraduate student at Rice University until the present.

I am grateful to the Office of Sponsored Research at the University of Houston–Downtown for granting me a semester of Faculty Funded Research leave and course releases to dedicate time to this project. I sincerely appreciate my alumni cohort and writing group colleagues in the National Center for Faculty Development and Diversity—Dr. Nadine Ross and Dr. Sabia McCoy-Torres. Our routine meetings have helped me to remain encouraged, focused, and dedicated.

I am thankful to friends and colleagues who were able to take time to review select chapters of the manuscript and to share feedback based on their areas of expertise. Special thanks to Stephen Finley, Jesse Esparza, and Biko Gray for their suggestions. I appreciate the multiple Routledge reviewers who offered constructive feedback. Any flaws in this work are my responsibility.

I am forever thankful for my parents—Elder Moses Chism Sr. and Missionary Forrestine Chism. Their devotion to the church undergirds my research interest and passion in religion. My wife, Courtney, has been a partner, friend, and supporter throughout my academic journey as we have reared our two adorable kids together—Jay and Jasmine. My mother-in-love and aunts have especially offered valuable support with childcare and enabled me to carve out the time needed to complete this project.

Introduction

"Of Our Spiritual Strivings"

Scholars of Black religion have devoted significant attention to how Black religions have fueled the social justice struggles of Black people from slavery to the present. Liberation has been a central thread or a "discursive 'burden' and cultural symbol" in Black religion for centuries because Black people have been constantly subject to systems of domination.[1] Indeed, Black religious history is not only about activism or the freedom struggle. Yet, oppression and the fight against it has been a unifying feature of Black people and religions. Anthony Pinn argues that Black religion is fundamentally "the quest for complex subjectivity" or "the creative struggle in history for increased agency, for a fulness of life."[2] Pinn's theory acknowledges how the historical and contemporary reality of racial oppression undergirds the variety of ways Black people have striven for life meaning in the United States of America. In line with Pinn's theory, this book acknowledges the racist and oppressive context in which Black religions have developed and aims to explore how Black people have employed religion to not only make sense of life but to counteract racism and other forms of discrimination—focusing on their various religious responses to living in a racist country and a modern world yet replete with white supremacy.

Sociologist Peter Berger's theory of religion also undergirds this book. In *The Sacred Canopy*, he defines religion as "the human enterprise by which a sacred cosmos is established."[3] He describes the sacred cosmos or canopy as the "powerful reality" beyond but intricately centered on humanity that humans continuously construct to give meaning to the world. He emphasizes that religion is "a human projection" that is firmly grounded in humans' beliefs about ultimate reality.[4] Humans construct sacred canopies to safeguard against living in a disordered and socially unstable world. Berger states, "Every society is engaged in the *never completed* enterprise of building a humanly meaningful world."[5] Erecting a "meaningful world" is always unfinished and shifting as the world is constantly changing. This especially ties to the history of Black people who have incessantly invented and remade religions to pursue meaning amid everchanging oppressive circumstances. This book devotes significant attention to founders and religious innovators who refashioned longstanding traditions or established new religions and movements in the United States of America.

Rather than ranking a given religion or orientation above another, this book highlights diverse ways Black people have negotiated race, nation, and religion throughout American history. One of the principal claims of this book is that Black religion centers on creatively striving for meaning, hope, and fulfillment in a country that has historically devalued Black life. Another claim is that Black people's spiritual strivings are not fixed but have evolved and changed with the times.

DOI: 10.4324/9781003359197-1

The Spiritual Strivings of Black People

William E.B. Du Bois examined the intersections between race, religion, and American political life in the early twentieth century.[6] Double consciousness is a central concept in his classic work *The Souls of Black Folk*. It is the identity crisis Black people have faced when seeking to reconcile the apparent contradiction of being Black and American. He explains:

> It is a peculiar sensation, this double-consciousness, this sense of always looking at one's self through the eyes of others, of measuring one's soul by the tape of a world that looks on in amused contempt and pity. One ever feels his twoness—an American, a Negro; two souls, two thoughts, two unreconciled strivings; two warring ideals in one dark body, whose dogged strength alone keeps it from being torn asunder ... The history of the American Negro is the history of this strife—this longing to attain self-conscious manhood, to merge his double self into a better and more accurate self.[7]

Besides experiencing exclusion because of their race, Black people have often been marginalized on account of their gender, sexual orientation, class, disability, and other intersecting identities. Though double consciousness neglects these other areas, the concept "captures the beauty of the interior" of Black life and reveals how Black folks from the antebellum era to the early twentieth century strove to "transform" the soul of the American nation that excluded them.[8] Du Bois held that the ultimate religious ideal was for Black people to refuse to accept their racialization as inferior, to break free of the veil of race, and to exert their creative capacity to transform "the nation's oppressive landscape" and establish a "truer world."[9]

In *The Souls of Black Folk*, he also adopted religious terms such as "souls" and "spiritual strivings." He refers to the soul broadly as "the thought and feeling, the thousand and one little actions which go to make up life."[10] For Du Bois, the concept of the soul is not based on the traditional Christian notion of innermost being or "a metaphysical substance that lies outside of time and human existence."[11] It constitutes what Black people are thinking and feeling individually and collectively within their oppressive situation.[12] It includes the collective sense of double consciousness and the longing to overcome racial exclusion. Du Bois describes the "spiritual strivings" of Black folks as "the travail of souls whose burden is almost beyond the measure of their strength."[13] As with the soul, for Du Bois, spiritual striving does not relate exclusively to the metaphysical dimension or to traditional modes of spirituality such as prayer. It more fully comprises the creative energy springing from Blacks' souls as they squeeze hope from despair and work to counteract forces of marginalization and exclusion. Some secular examples of spiritual strivings that Du Bois mentions include participating in electoral politics and pursuing higher education. Building on Du Bois's work, this book explores a wide array of creative initiatives religious Black people have developed to strive for meaning and inclusion in American society throughout American history.

A Note on Terms

I privilege the adjective Black throughout this book because it ties to historical and contemporary movements such as the Black Power, Black Consciousness, and the Black Lives Matter movements. I refer to Black people to accentuate the humanity of Black folks subject to dehumanizing assaults at the hands of white supremacist systems throughout American history. In essence, Black people are humans and not merely Blacks or racialized subjects.

As oppression is a global and pervasive phenomenon, freedom is also a comprehensive and expansive concept. The Black Freedom struggle includes the movement to abolish slavery in the nineteenth century, the resistance to lynching in the United States, the fight for the right to vote, the dismantling of the prison industrial complex, and struggles to advance equity in employment, housing, healthcare, education, and other social sectors. Though the Black Freedom Movement has an international scope and encompasses anticolonial resistance movements, our focus is on the North American context, particularly the United States. This book also adopts an intersectional understanding of freedom and acknowledges links between racism, sexism, classism, heterosexism, ableism, and other forms of oppression that Black people experience simultaneously.

Lastly, I employ the term Black religion instead of Black religions. Indeed, Black religion is not monolithic. There is a rich diversity of Black religious traditions and orientations in the United States and across the African Diaspora. However, I employ Black religion to stress how Black people have historically employed religion to grapple with being denied freedom and full citizenship in the United States, a democratic society. Black people have turned to religion to address the common experience of double consciousness. Similarly, there is no such singular institution as the Black Church. The term refers to the seven Protestant denominational churches that constitute the majority of Black Christians. Still, I occasionally refer to the Black Church throughout this book for the same reason that I employ Black religion. This is simply a reference to the common racialized identity and experience of Black Christians across denominations.[14]

Looking Ahead

Each chapter narrates Black people's spiritual strivings during a classic period in American history, including the colonial, antebellum, Reconstruction, Jim Crow, civil rights, post-civil rights, and post-Obama eras. Attention is focused on the spiritual strivings of a wide range of Black religious groups and figures, including those some researchers perceived as accommodationist and apolitical. I do not restrict spiritual strivings to the popular protest demonstrations led by Black religious leaders such as Martin Luther King Jr. Drawing on research produced by scholars of Black religion and primary sources, the book accentuates Black people's religious agency and numerous innovative responses to social oppression throughout American history. Each chapter includes further readings to inspire deeper study and analysis. The core chapters also include review questions to facilitate classroom discussion and reflection.

Notes

1 Sylvester A. Johnson, *African American Religions, 1500–2000: Colonialism, Democracy, and Freedom* (New York: Cambridge University Press, 2015), 404.
2 Anthony Pinn, *Terror and Triumph: The Nature of Black Religion* (Minneapolis, MN: Fortress Press, 2003), 173.
3 Peter L. Berger, *The Sacred Canopy: Elements of a Sociological Theory of Religion* (New York: Random House, 1967), 25.
4 Peter L. Berger, *The Sacred Canopy: Elements of a Sociological Theory of Religion* (New York: Random House, 1967), 180.

5   Peter L. Berger, *The Sacred Canopy: Elements of a Sociological Theory of Religion* (New York: Random House, 1967), 27.

6   Robert Wortham, *W.E.B. Du Bois and the Sociology of the Black Church and Religion, 1897–1914* (Lanham: Lexington Books, 2018), 1.

7   W.E.B. Du Bois, *The Souls of Black Folk: Essays and Sketches* (Chicago: A.G. McClurg, 1903. New York: Johnson Reprint Corp., 1968), 3.

8   Jonathan Kahn, *Divine Discontent: The Religious Imagination of W.E.B. Du Bois* (Oxford: Oxford University Press, 2009), 55.; Terrence L. Johnson, *Tragic Soul-Life: W.E.B. Du Bois and the Moral Crisis Facing American Democracy* (New York: Oxford University Press, 2012), 46.

9   Sylvester A. Johnson, *African American Religions, 1500–2000: Colonialism, Democracy, and Freedom* (New York: Cambridge University Press, 2015), 50; W.E.B. Du Bois, *The Souls of Black Folk: Essays and Sketches* (Chicago, IL: A.G. McClurg, 1903; New York: Johnson Reprint Corp., 1968), 150–151.

10 Jonathan Kahn, *Divine Discontent: The Religious Imagination of W.E.B. Du Bois* (Oxford: Oxford University Press, 2009), 65.

11 Jonathan Kahn, *Divine Discontent: The Religious Imagination of W.E.B. Du Bois* (Oxford: Oxford University Press, 2009), 65.

12 Jonathan Kahn, *Divine Discontent: The Religious Imagination of W.E.B. Du Bois* (Oxford: Oxford University Press, 2009), 65; Terrence L. Johnson, *Tragic Soul-Life: W.E.B. Du Bois and the Moral Crisis Facing American Democracy* (New York: Oxford University Press, 2012), 47–48.

13 W.E.B. Du Bois, *The Souls of Black Folk* (Chicago, IL: A.C. McClurg & Co., 1903), 5.

14 The seven major denominations are: the African Methodist Episcopal Church; the African Methodist Episcopal Zion Church; the Christian Methodist Episcopal Church; the National Baptist Convention, Incorporated; the National Baptist Convention of America, Unincorporated; the Progressive National Baptist Convention; and the Church of God in Christ. C. Eric Lincoln and Lawrence Mamiya, *The Black Church in the African American Experience* (Durham, NC: Duke University Press, 1990).

Further Readings

Berger, Peter L. *The Sacred Canopy: Elements of a Sociological Theory of Religion*. New York: Random House, 1967.

Du Bois, W.E.B. *The Souls of Black Folk: Essays and Sketches*. Chicago, IL: A.G. McClurg, 1903. New York: Johnson Reprint Corp., 1968.

Johnson, Sylvester A. *African American Religions, 1500–2000: Colonialism, Democracy, and Freedom*. New York: Cambridge University Press, 2015.

Johnson, Terrence L. *Tragic Soul-Life: W.E.B. Du Bois and the Moral Crisis Facing American Democracy*. New York: Oxford University Press, 2012.

Kahn, Jonathan. *Divine Discontent: The Religious Imagination of W.E.B. Du Bois*. Oxford: Oxford University Press, 2009.

Pinn, Anthony. *Terror and Triumph: The Nature of Black Religion*. Minneapolis, MN: Fortress Press, 2003.

Savage, Barbara D. *Your Spirit Walks Besides Us: The Politics of Black Religion*. Cambridge, MA: Harvard University Press, 2008.

Wortham, Robert. *W.E.B. Du Bois and the Sociology of the Black Church and Religion, 1897–1914*. Lanham, MD: Lexington Books, 2018.

1 "On Being Brought from Africa to America"
Spiritual Strivings in the Colonial Era

'Twas mercy brought me from my Pagan land,
Taught my benighted soul to understand
That there's a God, that there's a Saviour too:
Once I redemption neither sought nor knew.
Some view our sable race with scornful eye,
'Their colour is a diabolic die.'
Remember, Christians, Negros, Black as Cain,
May be refin'd, and join th' angelic train.
                    Phillis Wheatley, "On Being Brought
                        from Africa to America," 1773

Slavery in the New World was primarily driven by economic motives rather than divine providence. European nations, such as Portugal, Spain, and Britain, exploited the New World's resources, leading to a profitable environment for slavery. The fertile lands of the South became a prime location for cultivating crops like tobacco, rice, and indigo.[1]

Initially, Europeans sought labor from Native Americans and impoverished Whites, but these options proved unsustainable. By the early seventeenth century, African indentured servitude evolved into lifelong chattel slavery due to racial distinctions and economic advantages. Europeans rationalized the transition by insisting that they were saving Africans' souls through converting them to Christianity, as seen in the writings of slaveholders like Gomes Eannes De Azurara.[2] Gradually, slavery became a fixed institution and passed from one generation of enslaved Africans to the next. Enslavers treated enslaved Africans as property rather than human beings. They confined them in dungeons along the coast for weeks, months, or even up to a year before boarding a slave ship. Europeans branded them with a company mark to signify their status as property. Africans then endured a brutal six to eight-week journey across the Atlantic, known as the Middle Passage. Packed tightly in dense, overcrowded ships, Africans contracted diseases such as dysentery, typhoid, measles, smallpox, yellow fever, and malaria. Ship crewmen sexually assaulted captive women and girls. Many Africans died from disease, dehydration, starvation, and suicide.[3]

Survivors experienced further dehumanization when they were sold at auctions alongside animals and other inanimate objects. They suffered under brutal conditions on plantations. Numerous enslaved Black people yearned and prayed for Divine mercy and deliverance.

Formerly enslaved Africans provided detailed accounts of their horrible experiences during the slave trade. In his 1798 book, Olaudah Equiano vividly describes his capture,

DOI: 10.4324/9781003359197-2

Figure 1.1 Africans on the slave deck of the bark "Wildfire," brought into Key West on April 30, 1860. Courtesy Library of Congress Prints and Photographs Division Washington, DC

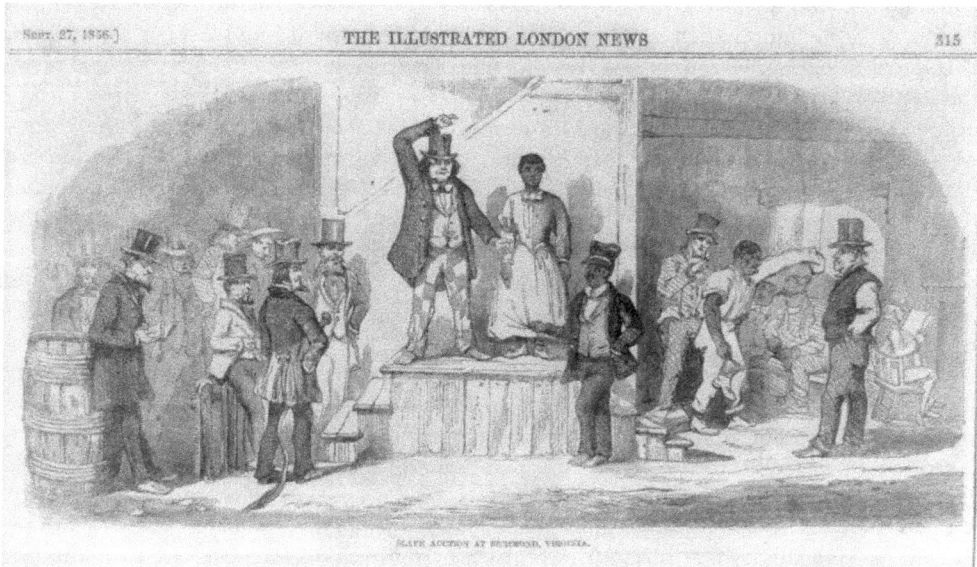

Figure 1.2 Slave auction at Richmond, Virginia. This is an illustration from the London News, September 17, 1856, of an African American woman being auctioned off in front of a crowd of men.
Courtesy Library of Congress Prints and Photographs Division Washington, DC

sale to traders, and journey to America in 1755. Although some evidence suggests Equiano may have been born in the United States, scholars generally regard his account as accurate. Another early narrative comes from Ayuba Suleiman Diallo (Job Ben Solomon), who detailed his experiences in the Atlantic slave trade.[4]

The end of the Transatlantic slave trade in 1808 did not halt the brutality; instead, conditions worsened, particularly with the rise of cotton as a cash crop. Africans in British North America, particularly in regions like the Lowcountry, endured long hours of hard labor under brutal conditions on rice and tobacco plantations. They were often barefoot, inadequately clothed, poorly housed and fed, and subjected to rape and abuse. The domestic slave trade continued to disrupt families and perpetuate the cycle of slavery throughout the South.[5]

Enslavers aimed to control and exploit enslaved people to maintain plantation capitalism. Scholars E. Franklin Frazier and Melville Herskovits debated the severity of the harm done to enslaved Africans' ability to transmit their cultures in the Americas. Frazier argued that enslavement severed the cultural heritage of the descendants of enslaved Black people. It left them with minimal retention of African traditions. He cited the West African tradition of dancing as a rare exception. Enslavers weakened cultural transmission and social cohesion among enslaved Africans in America by enforcing their culture on enslaved people and prohibiting them from openly speaking their native languages and practicing their ancestral religions.

The history of African people in America by no means began with Transatlantic slavery. Prior to their enslavement, Africans lived in a homeland characterized by a rich tapestry of religious and cultural diversity, which included religions such as Islam,

Christianity, and ancestral worship. The seventh century saw the arrival of Muslims in Egypt. Notable figures such as Mansa Musa, the Mali emperor, and Askiya Muhammad I, ruler of Songhay, were fervent Muslims who undertook pilgrimages to Mecca during the fourteenth and fifteenth centuries, respectively. Estevan, an enslaved African who accompanied Spanish explorers to Florida in 1527, is recognized as one of the earliest Muslims in North America.[6] Most Africans captured in the Atlantic slave trade practiced "ancestor worship" and believed their ancestors' spirits greatly influenced their lives.[7] They revered the spirit within a deceased relative and respected the spirit inhabiting family land, trees, rocks, and the "sky above their community."[8] Frazier argues that very little of enslaved Blacks' original culture was able to survive in the United States because of slavery and the inexorable efforts of Whites to convert enslaved Black people to Christianity.[9]

Conversely, Herskovits insisted that African cultural traits, or "Africanisms," persisted in the New World. The endurance of African religious beliefs is evident in practices like Candomble in Brazil, Santeria in Cuba, Shango in Trinidad, and Voodoo in Haiti, traditions where enslaved Black people merged their African beliefs with Christianity.[10] Herskovits also noted subtle African influences in the U.S., such as spirit possession beliefs, dancing, and music, where enslaved Blacks blended African and European styles. Despite prohibitions against traditional practices, they maintained African rhythms through expressions such as "hand-clapping," "foot-tapping," "rhythmic preaching," and "antiphonal (call and response) singing."[11]

Evidence suggests that neither slavery nor extensive missionary outreach to enslaved Black people did not completely erase Africanisms.[12] They maintained strong traces of their African cultural practices and cosmologies in the United States in areas like the Low Country where they were densely populated. Throughout the United States, moreover, they exerted cultural agency and reshaped Christianity, and other religious traditions based on their new social location, lived experiences, and spiritual needs.

Missionary Outreach to Enslaved Black People

Missionary outreach to enslaved Black people was generally sparse during the first 150 years of slavery in the United States because of several factors, including the general disinterest in religion in the South (where most enslaved people lived), the shortage of missionaries focused on outreach to enslaved Black people, and language and cultural barriers. Some enslavers resisted slave conversion because they feared that Christian conversion might inspire them to rebel against the slave system. They also believed Africans were too primitive, barbarous, and intellectually inferior to grasp theological concepts.[13] Missionaries such as Francis Le Jau, who served in South Carolina, explained, "Many Masters can't be persuaded that Negroes and Indians are otherwise than Beasts, and use them like such ... I endeavor to let them know better things."[14] Masters also frequently complained that Christianity would make enslaved individuals "saucy" or cause them to feel that they should be treated as equals to Whites.[15] Moreover, the primary concern among many masters was that enslaved people who proclaimed to be Christians would demand manumission and would deprive them of free labor and disrupt the newly established social hierarchy.

Court records from colonial Virginia document the debates White colonial Americans had about Christianity and slavery. In 1641, the Virginia court in *Re Graweere* ruled that a Black child could be freed to be raised as a Christian. To maintain the enslaved status of Christian Africans, in 1667, a Virginia court decided that Black Christians could be enslaved permanently. This 1667 law closed the loophole that freed some Black Christians. It clarified that baptism would not alter the freedom of enslaved Black Christians and quieted slaveholders' fears about sharing the gospel with them. Other colonial legislatures followed Virginia in passing similar laws.[16]

After this issue was resolved in the courts, many early colonial missionaries sought to persuade slaveholders that missionary outreach to enslaved Blacks could bolster the system of slavery. They argued that enslaved Black people who converted to Christianity would serve their masters with "Christian Love and Duty."[17] They strove to convince slaveholders that they should be permitted to share the gospel with enslaved Black people by contending that Christianity would create "better slaves" who were docile and more compliant with the slave system. Christian colonial organizations were by no means monolithic or of the same opinion when it came to evangelizing them.[18] Quakers such as George Fox and William Edmundson pushed for increased missionary outreach to the enslaved Black masses. The Quakers' antislavery stance influenced enslavers to restrict Quakers' access to slave quarters. This partly explains why few Black people joined the Society of Friends.[19]

During the colonial era, a minority of enslaved Black people joined Puritan churches. Puritans believed that Black people were indeed members of the human family with souls that needed to be saved. In the *Negro Christianized* (1706), Cotton Mather argued that enslaved Blacks were "Rational Creatures" and should be treated not as "Bruits but as Men."[20] Puritans welcomed enslaved Black converts to attend religious services and communal prayers. Still, New England Puritans forced them to sit in segregated areas during worship. They treated them as social inferiors, holding that God ordained White Europeans to civilize enslaved Blacks through Christianity.[21] Many Black folks recognized that Puritans did not see them as equal church or colonial society members. Puritans condoned and participated in the institution of slavery. Overall, the Puritans had limited success with evangelizing masses of enslaved Blacks in the northern colonies.

The Anglican Church, or the Church of England, ministered to enslaved Black people and indigenous Americans within the middle and southern colonies via the Society for the Propagation of the Gospel in Foreign Parts (SPGFP), founded in 1702. Unlike the Quakers, the SPGFP did not oppose slavery, and several of its ministers were even slaveholders. Thus, southern slaveholders allowed them to minister to enslaved people with fewer restrictions.[22] The SPGFP started organizing multiple schools in the colonies to help teach enslaved Black people Christian doctrines. However, society missionaries met increased resistance from slaveholders who were opposed to teaching enslaved people to read because they feared that education could influence enslaved people to become rebellious and organize revolts.[23] Some SPGFP missionaries questioned if enslaved people were capable of understanding the catechism. One observer wrote that native Africans' "rudeness of manners, variety, and strangeness of their language and shallowness and weakness of mind made it impossible to make progress in their conversion."[24] Many enslaved people who possessed a clear grasp of English and understood the message that SPGFP missionaries presented to them outright rejected Anglican Christianity because they preferred to maintain their traditional religious beliefs.[25]

Only a tiny segment of the enslaved population in British Colonial North America converted to Christianity and joined Christian fellowships such as the Quakers, Puritans, and Anglicans, with some achieving near-equal communion with White Christians.[26] Black people began to convert to Christianity in increasing numbers when the

First Great Awakening revivals swept across the northeastern colonies between the 1730s and 1750s.[27] The revival was characterized by powerful, emotionally charged, and dramatic preaching, which differed considerably from Puritan and Anglican ministers' expository and didactic sermons. Evangelists such as George Whitefield (1714–1770) and Jonathan Edwards (1703–1758) warned hearers of the suffering that awaited them in the afterlife if they did not repent of sin and follow Christ. For example, in "Sinners in the Hands of an Angry God," Edwards moved attendees to feel the weight of sin, envision the threats of Hell, and accept Christ as their Savior. Revivalist preachers emphasized immediate conversion for baptism and generally avoided convoluted doctrinal explanations. In contrast to Anglican missionaries who required new converts to undergo catechesis and ultimately demonstrate an understanding of critical tenants of the Christian faith, such as the Apostle's Creed, before being eligible for baptism, awakening revivalists made the process of becoming Christian more accessible for enslaved people who generally were prohibited from learning to read and write. Conversion requires individual repentance of sin and acceptance of Christ instead of demonstrating an understanding of Christian doctrine. Furthermore, White revivalists welcomed Blacks to their religious meetings and allowed them to participate in the service by singing hymns and taking part in the sacraments and various religious ceremonies.[28]

The Awakening revivals attracted masses of Black people for multiple reasons. First, there was a measure of theological alignment between evangelical and traditional African religions. For example, during Christian revivalist worship services, many worshipers experienced the movement of the Holy Spirit through shouting and fainting. This resembled the practice of spirit possession in traditional African religions, where similar dramatic physical manifestations and movements occurred. Scholars have also associated Methodists' and Baptists' emphasis on the sacrament of water baptism with traditional African water rituals and spiritual beliefs.[29] Second, the egalitarian impulses of evangelical faith were appealing to many enslaved Black people. During both revival periods, White ministers took the Great Commission seriously and were eager to share the gospel with all people—Whites, Blacks, and Native Americans. By focusing on inward conversion, the Awakenings downplayed outward social status. The revivalists stressed that all persons needed to repent of sin and personally accept the redeeming grace of Christ.[30] Once a person experienced salvation, they were extended the right hand of fellowship and welcomed into the life of the church. Besides welcoming Blacks into the church, White evangelicals permitted many Black folks to preach. The evangelical belief in the equality of all souls before God became evident when Blacks such as Harry Hoosier or "Black Harry," William Lemon, and "Uncle" Jack preached to Black and White audiences. Morte, a formerly enslaved person, recalled an instance when a sermon he preached on the porch of "the big house" moved his master and other Whites to tears. Morte communicated the traditional evangelical message of the need to experience the new birth and receive Jesus as Lord. He remembered that Whites on his southern plantation who heard his message were "all in tears."[31] Nevertheless, many lay and ordained Black Christians and ministers remained constrained by the slave system despite delivering moving sermons.

The fervor of the First Great Awakening largely bypassed the South, the region of colonial America that had the most enslaved people. Many White settlers on the Kentucky and Tennessee frontiers found themselves beyond the reach of established churches that emerged following the First Awakening. The revival reached the western frontier and the South during the Second Awakening, sweeping states such as Kentucky, Virginia, North Carolina, South Carolina, and Tennessee from the 1800s to 1830s.[32]

During the Second Great Awakening, southern ministers, such as Reverend James McGready (1763–1817), prayed for God to deliver southerners from "apostasy" and to stir their longing to experience Divine blessings. Eventually, a fire for Christian experience erupted across the American West and the South. Attracting crowds that many church buildings could not accommodate, religious leaders started holding outdoor revival meetings, known as camp meetings. The first camp meeting was held at Gasper River in Kentucky, with the largest at Cane Ridge in August 1801, drawing around 25,000 worshippers. During camp meetings, it was not uncommon for those gathered to experience intense physical and emotional reactions, including but not limited to fainting and involuntary convulsions and jerking while on the ground. Blacks and Whites also sang, prayed, and shouted together. As with the First Great Awakening, revivalist ministers emphasized heartfelt faith over theology. They stressed preaching that centered firmly on plainly interpreting and expounding the Scriptures and biblical stories to inspire sinners to surrender their lives to Christ. They viewed conversion as a personal matter between an individual and God. Second Awakening ministers embraced Arminianism, a doctrine advanced by Jacobus Arminius in the sixteenth century that holds that individuals can accept or reject Christ. This belief starkly contrasts with the Calvinism upheld by revivalists during the First Awakening. Pioneered by the French theologian John Calvin in the seventeenth century, Calvinism contends that God had already predestined who would be saved. The Second Great Awakening led to the revitalization of the Baptist, Methodist, and Presbyterian denominations in the South and laid the foundation for the South to emerge as the "Bible Belt."[33]

Both free and enslaved Black people attended revival meetings and joined Methodist and Baptist churches in large numbers after the Awakening revivals. Methodist records showed an increase of nearly 10,000 African members between 1786 and 1790. Though less meticulous with records, Baptist churches had about 20,000 African members. Though the Great Awakenings helped bring many Black people with minimal contact with Christianity into the Christian fold by the early nineteenth century, the revivals did not substantially impact rural areas, with a limited number of evangelical churches.[34] To share the gospel with rural folks (White and Black), Southern evangelical missionaries established plantation missions.

Advanced by the United Evangelical Front, plantation missions were a conglomerate of mission outreach societies that aimed to convert and teach Christianity to Southerners. Charles Colcock Jones, a Presbyterian minister who was a leading advocate of the southern plantation missions, wrote *Catechism of Scripture, Doctrine, and Practices for Families and Sabbath Schools: Designed also for the Oral Instruction of Colored Persons* (1837). In his catechism, Jones included a section entitled the "Duty of Servants." He cited Scriptures that encouraged enslaved people to be obedient to their masters and to serve them "with good will" as they served the Heavenly master. Jones's catechism even insisted that the Bible instructed them to obey cruel masters. Using biblical texts such as 1 Peter 2:18–21 and 1 Timothy 6:1–2, Jones endeavored to persuade enslaved Christians that accepting abusive treatment from Whites was noble and following the example of Christ, who honorably surrendered to being whipped and endured the pain of the cross. In submitting to suffering, Black people were being like Jesus Christ. Plantation missionaries hoped that enslaved Black individuals who received such instruction would submit to the slaveholding system.

Still, despite southerners' efforts to teach them "proper" beliefs and practices and their tight restrictions on Black ministers and independent Black churches, most enslaved

Black people reinterpreted Christianity and "redeployed Christian vocabularies."[35] According to Du Bois, by 1859, about 468,000 Black folks had joined churches in the South.[36] Jones reported that Black Baptist membership grew from 18,000 in 1793 to 40,000 in 1813. Though these numbers might be exaggerated, the increase in membership among Black and White Baptists and Methodists was remarkable.[37] Black people who shared their faith and communicated the gospel in light of their existential circumstances contributed to the growth of Christianity in the South, not merely the White plantation missionaries.

Though numerous enslaved Black people converted to Christianity during the antebellum era, the majority of the Black population remained outside the Church. Scholars estimate that only about twenty-two percent of them were Christian in 1861. Despite the evangelistic efforts of southern plantation missionaries, numerous Black people rejected Christianity. Some of them maintained their traditional African beliefs. Some continued to follow Islam, which they practiced before arriving in America via the slave trade. For example, some enslaved Black people from the Wolof, Serer, Mandinka, Bambara, Fulani, and Hausa tribes were Muslims. Many enslaved Muslims in the antebellum era, like Bilali, Salih Bilali, Job Ben Solomon, Yarrow Mahmoud, and Omar ibn Said, kept their Muslim names, attire, and practices. Charles Ball, a formerly enslaved Black man, described meeting a Muslim on his plantation who routinely followed Islamic daily prayer rituals. Allen Austin estimates that 15 to 25 percent of early enslaved people were Muslims.[38]

Other Black people scorned Christianity and traditional theistic beliefs altogether because of the hypocrisy of White Christian slaveholders. Some enslaved Black folks who were atheists and agnostics presented logical and philosophical arguments that justified their rejection of Christianity. Daniel Alexander Payne, an American Methodist Episcopal Church bishop, noted in 1839 that he had encountered enslaved African atheists who pinpointed the hypocrisy between Whites' Christianity and Black enslavement. Payne wrote:

> The slaves are sensible of the oppression exercised by their masters', and they see these masters preaching the gospel; they hear these masters praying in their families … they scoff at religion itself—mock their masters, and distrust both the goodness and justice of God. Yes, I have known them even to question his existence.[39]

Concerning the difficulty of converting them to Christianity, C.C. Jones expressed:

> He who carries the Gospel to them, encounters depravity entrenched in ignorance, both real and pretended. … He discovers deism, skepticism, universalism. He meets all the various perversions of the Gospel, and all the strong objections against the truth of God; objections which he may perhaps have considered peculiar only to the cultivated minds, the ripe scholarship, and profound intelligence of critics and philosophers! Extremes here meet on the natural and common ground of a darkened understanding and a hardened heart.[40]

In voicing his frustration with being unable to convert enslaved Black people successfully, Jones provides insight into the religious diversity that existed among enslaved Africans in the South during the antebellum era. Many of them did not find the Christian gospel compelling.

Though numerous enslaved Black people were not Christians leading up to the Civil War, it isn't easy to know with precise certainty the religious demographics of enslaved Blacks. This is because Black people often practiced their faith in secret. Black missionaries who came to the South to minister to recently freed Blacks encountered those who had a firm grasp on Christian doctrine and "church polity" and had become formal members of institutional churches. Still, they recognized that some formerly enslaved Blacks were practicing religions outside of the institutional churches.[41]

The "Invisible Institution"

Beyond merely accepting the doctrines of various White missionaries, enslaved Black people reinterpreted Christianity in light of their social location. They fused Christianity with folk religious beliefs and traditions.[42] The secret religious gatherings of enslaved Black people in the South are referred to as the "invisible institution." While an institution is typically a formal or established organization with a founder or founders, by-laws, or formal rules and procedures, the invisible institution was informal because slaveholders prohibited Black people from freely establishing formal religious institutions. They could be whipped for violating slaveholders' commands and attending clandestine religious services. The invisible institution was a common understanding among enslaved Black folks of the need for a separate space to hold religious services. A former enslaved Black individual reported, "When we had our meetings of this kind, we held them in our own way and were not interfered with by the white folks."[43] They met in concealed locations called "hush" harbors to avoid detection. According to Peter Randolph, a former enslaved Black man who was freed in 1847 before the Civil War:

> Not being allowed to hold meetings on the plantation, the slaves assemble in the swamp, out of reach of the patrols. They have an understanding among themselves as to the time and place of getting together. This is often done by the first one arriving breaking boughs from the trees, and bending them in the direction of the selected spot. Arrangements are then made for conducting the exercises.[44]

Randolph's description suggests that the invisible institution occurred in the brush of the backwoods.

The invisible institution was not restricted to forested areas. Some enslaved Black Christians also held private religious services after formal biracial worship services were complete. They conducted religious services in old barns or shacks away from Whites. In these structures, they aspired to reduce the noise level of the meetings. For example, they prayed into large containers filled with water to muffle loud sounds of praise and ecstatic spiritual moans or outbursts. They also turned the iron pots up to reduce noise as they sang and prayed.[45] Sister Shelly, a former enslaved Black woman, reported, "we would take pots and put them right in the middle of the floor to keep the sound in the room; yeah, keep the whites folks from meddling."[46]

Enslaved Black people who attended secret religious meetings boldly defied and disobeyed their masters' commands. They risked suffering consequences if caught. Additionally, enslaved Christians reflected on what the gospel meant to them and disputed racist biblical hermeneutics that deduced that they were cursed descendants of Ham (Genesis 9:24–25; Genesis 4:11–16). Proslavery apologists adopted the curse of the Ham myth to provide biblical justification for the involuntary servitude of Black people. The

Figure 1.3 A Black camp meeting in the South; *Harper's Weekly*, vol. 16 (August 10, 1872). This artistic image may reflect the nature of religious services in the Invisible Institution. Courtesy Library of Congress Prints and Photographs Division Washington, DC

myth circulated as early as the fifteenth century. It was drawn from a story in Genesis when Noah cursed his son for immodestly seeing his nakedness in his drunken condition (Genesis 9:20–25). Holding the Bible to be a source of Scriptural authority, proslavery apologists appealed to this text to cite biblical evidence to justify enslavement of Africans. In truth, nothing in this account identifies Ham with Africans, and the curse on Canaan most likely served to explain the Israelites' eventual enslavement of the Canaanites, who were the original occupants of the Promised Land.[47] Although it is likely that some enslaved Black folks potentially questioned if they were divinely cursed given the reality of their enslavement, evidence indicates that many Black Christians challenged White Christians' racist stereotypes and affirmed Black people's dignity as beloved sons and daughters of God made in the divine image.

Howard Thurman, a twentieth-century Black pastor and theologian, reported that his grandmother, Nancy Ambrose, who was born into slavery in Florida on the McGhee Plantation, told him that she despised hearing White plantation ministers use the words from the Apostle Paul to condone human bondage. She reflected:

> At least three or four times a year he used as a text: "Slaves, be obedient to them that are your masters ... as unto Christ." Then he would go on to show how it was God's will that we were slaves and how, if we were good and happy slaves, God would bless us. I promised my Maker that if I ever learned to read and if freedom ever came, I would not read that part of the Bible.[48]

She came to outright reject the letters of Paul as the authentic, inspired Word of God. Enslaved Black Christians often gravitated towards those parts of the Bible that gave them hope, such as the story of the children of Israel's liberation from Egyptian bondage.

The invisible institution was not merely a secret location for worship. It was also a place where enslaved Black people expressed their religious creativity. It is impossible to know precisely all that happened because the meetings were held in secret. There is little documentation beyond oral testimony from formerly enslaved people. It is safe to assume that Black people indubitably were creative and exercised their freedom of self-expression in these spaces.

During secret religious services, they engaged in folk practices they could or would not do in the presence of Whites. One example is the ring shout, which was practiced in the Lowcountry. A former enslaved Black reported:

> The shout takes place on Sundays or on praise nights through the week ... The benches are pushed back to the wall when the formal meeting is over, and old and young, men and women ... all stand up in the middle of the floor, and when the spiritual is struck up, begin first walking and by-and-by shuffling round, one after the other, in a ring. The foot is hardly taken from the floor, and the progression is mainly due to a jerking, hitching motion, which agitates the entire shouter, and soon brings out streams of perspiration.[49]

The ring shout is a tradition that has African origins. The Ekoi people of southern Nigeria and the West African Ibo, Yoruba, and Ibibio folk performed a similar dance as the ring shout. During their dance, they move every part of their bodies and do a "counterclockwise shuffle" until a "wave-like ripple ... runs down the muscles of back and along arms to the finger-tips."[50]

In addition to the ring shout, enslaved Black people experienced the movement of the Spirit via engaging in traditional Christian rituals. Randolph, a former enslaved Black attendee of a secret meeting, recalled that "twenty and thirty men and women" fainted under the influence of spirit as a result of Blacks' "preaching," "praying," and "singing."[51] They sang spiritual songs and prayed that God would help them to survive and experience liberation from slavery. One formerly enslaved person recalled praying intensely during the secret worship "for dis day of freedom." He reflected, "We come from four and five miles away to pray together to God dat if we don't live to see it, do please let our chillum live to see a better day and be free, so dat dey can give honest and fair service to de Lord and all mankind everywhere."[52] Unable to be fully transparent and share the deepest concerns of their hearts when praying aloud in White religious services, in the invisible institution, they disclosed their sincere longings to God and each other.

Enslaved Black people were eager to listen to Black ministers preach during the secret religious meetings. Black ministers preached sermons that drew on biblical stories they committed to memory. They learned to recite scriptures by hearing them repeated orally because Whites generally did not permit them to read. John Jasper (1812–1901), a Black Baptist minister with poor grammar skills, emerged as a powerful orator. He mastered the art of skillfully and emotionally engaging his audience. For instance, when telling the Exodus story, a passage familiar to many enslaved Black people, Jasper aspired to paint a clear picture of the children of Israel crossing the Red Sea. He pretended to speak to one of the lagging Israelites during his sermon. He urged him to keep moving and to cross over. Mesmerized by Jasper's narration, a Black elderly woman suddenly jumped from her pew and shouted to "the imaginary Israelite," "Hurry up brother, get across, they can't git at you there!"[53] Though Jasper likely delivered this sermon in a traditional church setting, it may reflect the type of "real preachin" that occurred in the invisible institution.[54] Enslaved Blacks were eager to hear sermons addressing their need for hope and courage against all odds.

It is unclear whether men or women primarily led worship service during secret religious meetings. Enslaved Black women were by no means absent or silent. They lifted their voices when praying, testifying, and praising God. A former enslaved Black woman recalled, "My mother could send up the most powerful prayer of anybody on the plantation." An enslaved man acknowledged that a Black woman called "Aunt Sylvia" supervised a weekly religious service in his slave quarter in Mississippi. Though she was likely illiterate and uneducated, he praised her as "a good thinker" who seemed to "know everything just from her mother wit."[55] White denominations such as the Anglicans, Baptists, and Methodists did not permit women to preach based on 1 Corinthians 14:34–35, which stated that women should be silent in church. The Methodist Bishop Francis Asbury allowed both White males from the lower classes and enslaved Black men such as Harry Hoosier to grace the pulpit and to travel with him when sharing the gospel throughout the South. However, Asbury denied this opportunity to White and Black women. Though some Black women preached in the Invisible Institution, they were likely prohibited from preaching in the mainline churches.[56]

Alexis Wells-Oghoghomeh's *The Souls of Womenfolk: The Religious Cultures of Enslaved Women in the Lower South* (2021) closely studies the conjuring tradition that was practiced among enslaved Black people in the Low Country region, namely in South Carolina and Georgia. Though enslaved women rarely led churches in the South during the antebellum period, they exercised their leadership in other ways. Enslaved women— "mothers, grandmothers, and community elders"—responded to the "dismembering effects of enslavement" by "re/member[ing] the medicinal and ritual cycles of their forebears" and developing "ceremonial responses" in their new context.[57] Blacks and Whites especially respected the older women in slave communities for their knowledge and power. Many women who were honored as "Aunts" were "seeresses," "plantation doctors," nurses, and midwives who affirmed the conjuring tradition and West African cosmology.[58]

Though some enslaved Black people who converted to Christianity came to denigrate conjure as a heathenish practice, the practice was common among enslaved folks in the South who often interchangeably used witch, witch doctor, conjuror, hoodoo doctor, rootworker, two-facer, and trick doctor. Conjurors were described as "two-facers" or "two-handed" because they employed magical spiritual power to serve practical ends, including "healing, protection, and defense."[59] For example, conjure doctors could address human misfortune, which some enslaved people believed was the result of hoodoo doctors who inflicted harm. Rasanha Frazier, a blind, formerly enslaved person from Mississippi, held that the loss of her vision was due to a conjuring. She explained, "When dey wants conjure you, dey sneak round and git de hair combin' or de finger or toenail, or anything natural 'bout your body and works de hoodo on it."[60]

Though some enslaved Black Christians repudiated conjure, many enslaved Black Christians pragmatically vacillated between conjure and Christianity to meet different needs. Some conjurors adopted Christian symbols such as crosses and charms with biblical verses written on them. An enslaved Black spiritual leader named William Webb distributed root bags to fellow Black Christians. He believed that both root bags and prayer could help Black people maintain peace among themselves and their masters and endure harsh working conditions on the plantations. Many Black people upheld both Christianity and conjure as systems that could permit them to access the supernatural world to serve practical ends. They drew on conjure when it benefitted them and on Christianity to address needs that conjure could not satisfy.[61]

Besides possessing a basic knowledge of how to deliver babies into the world, enslaved community midwives adopted conjuring folklore. They believed humans have a spiritual connection to the earth and that natural herbs have healing powers for bodies. Additionally, enslaved midwives, like their African women ancestors, understood childbirth to be a physical and spiritual phenomenon. Besides physically delivering babies, midwives perceived that they had the sacred task of guiding "new spirits into the embodied world," and they adhered to specific "protocols" and "rituals" to prevent "spiritual retribution."[62] Midwives advised expecting mothers to take special precautions to protect their babies from evil spirits. For example, in line with West African traditions, some midwives instructed pregnant mothers to avoid allowing folks to touch their bellies and to keep their pregnancy a secret as long as possible.[63]

Besides the midwife who used her powers to help women and children survive enslavement, the hag was an enslaved woman who used spiritual power for destructive ends. Enslaved Black people "feared" and tried to avoid hags who could shape-shift or enter a

Figure 1.4. Grave of Hackless Jenkins, 1878–1928, Sea Islands, Georgia, decorated with clocks, glassware, and other objects. Sea Islands, 1933. Photograph by Doris Ulmann. Jenkins is an example of a Black person who vacillated between conjure and Christianity. The artifacts on his grave indicate his embrace of conjure, yet the note "Asleep in Jesus" on the tombstone signals his possible conversion to the Christian faith.
Courtesy of the Library of Congress.

"trans-sense realm," defined as the "interstitial space between human and spirit."[64] Always a female, a hag could powerfully cross between "modes of embodiment and disembodiment" and manipulate her body into the form of an animal, such as a cat or buzzard, and "ride" victims during the night.[65] According to Wells-Oghoghomeh, the hag personified the oppressive reality of enslaved Black people. Hag mythology "expressed bondspeople's visualizations of uncontrollable violence in their midst: the externalization of the antagonistic and fatal forces that were constant specters in the community but could never be fully exorcised from it."[66] Somewhat similar to the destructive, violent, and overbearing slave system, the hag was a powerful entity that "even a skilled rootworker could not undo her conjure."[67] While an enslaved man named "Strickland" believed that saying "Lord have mercy" or "Jesus save me" could stop a hag, many enslaved Black people believed that once the hag started riding a victim, the "Christian language had no dominion."[68] The hag was an entity to be avoided through engaging in ritual practices such as "placing a Bible under one's pillow for protection," using Benne seed—a hag repellant, or "placing a broomstick, salt, sifter, or newspaper at the threshold of the door."[69]

White supremacy is the hag of American history. Though the system of slavery crumbled following a blood-soaked, death-tolling Civil War, and the walls of Jim Crow came tumbling down as a consequence of the mid-twentieth century civil rights movement, white supremacy has managed to keep riding Black victims. Despite various religious strategies Black people have employed, hag-like racist systems have demonstrated the capacity to shape-shift. Racism mutated from plantation slave patrols to police officers who looked suspiciously at Black bodies, stopping and frisking them in urban communities. It morphed from the old Jim Crow of the late nineteenth and twentieth century to what legal scholar Michelle Alexander called the New Jim Crow of the late twentieth and early twenty-first centuries. Like Strickland, many Black Christians across generations have exercised tremendous faith in the power of Christianity to defeat white supremacy. Yet it has continued to victimize Black folks despite the rebuke of numerous prayer warriors and the protest demonstrations of people of faith.[70] Upcoming chapters will explore Black people's diverse creative religious strivings against hag-like oppressive systems across American history. The next chapter focuses on their spiritual strivings in the nineteenth century, including Black independent churches, Black nationalism and Ethiopianism, Black religious protest literature, and the planning of insurrections.

Review and Discussion Questions

1   In what ways did economic interests, racial ideologies, and religious justifications contribute to the development of chattel slavery in the New World?
2   Why did Black people in colonial and antebellum America start to convert to Christianity in great numbers during the First and Second Great Awakenings?
3   For what reasons did many enslaved Black people reject Christian faith during the colonial era?
4   How did enslaved Black religious people exercise their agency and creativity in the "invisible institution"? How did enslaved Black people utilize Christianity and conjure to find meaning amid their experience of oppression?

Notes

1 This chapter primarily focuses on slavery in British North America, given the centrality of Britain to the history of the United States. I acknowledge evidence that Africans arrived as explorers, servants, and slaves in the New World before Christopher Columbus's expedition.

2 John Hope Franklin and Alfred A. Moss, Jr., *From Slavery to Freedom: A History of African Americans*, 7th edition (New York: McGraw-Hill, 1994), 29–56; Darlene Clark Hine, William C. Hine, and Stanley Harrold, *African Americans: A Concise History, Combined Volume* (New York: Pearson, 2014), 25; Gomes Eannes De Azurara, *Chronicle*, 1: 50–51, Cited in Albert J. Raboteau, *Slave Religion: The "Invisible Institution" in the Antebellum South*, updated edition (New York: Oxford University Press, 2004), 96; Anne H. Pinn and Anthony B. Pinn, *Fortress Introduction to Black Church History* (Minneapolis, MN: Fortress Press, 2002), 1–2.

3 Nell Irvin Painter, *Creating Black Americans: African American History and Its Meanings, 1619 to the Present* (New York: Oxford University Press, 2006), 35; John Hope Franklin and Alfred A. Moss, Jr., *From Slavery to Freedom: A History of African Americans*, 7th edition (New York: McGraw-Hill, 1994), 37; Darlene Clark Hine, William C. Hine, and Stanley Harrold, *African Americans: A Concise History, Combined Volume* (New York: Pearson, 2014), 34.

4 Olaudah Equiano, *The Interesting Narrative and Other Writings* (New York: Penguin, 1995).

5 John Hope Franklin and Alfred A. Moss, Jr., *From Slavery to Freedom: A History of African Americans*, 7th edition (New York: McGraw-Hill, 1994), 32, 57; Darlene Clark Hine, William C. Hine, and Stanley Harrold, *African Americans: A Concise History, Combined Volume* (New York: Pearson, 2014), 25; Walter Johnson, *Soul by Soul: Life Inside the Antebellum Slave Market* (Cambridge, MA: Harvard University Press, 2001). Cited in Henry Louis Gates, Jr. "What Was the Second Middle Passage?," *The Root*, January 28, 2013 Retrieved from www.theroot.com/what-was-the-2nd-middle-passage-1790895016.

6 Although Christianity had become established in Northern Africa in the seventh century and early church fathers such as Aurelius Augustinus Hipponensis (354–430), popularly known as Saint Augustine of Hippo, descended from the Berbers in North Africa, it is fair to say that the inhabitants had limited exposure if any at all to Christianity in West Africa. Prior to Portuguese missions in the sixteenth century, Christianity was largely unknown in densely populated West Africa where scholars estimate most enslaved Blacks derived their origins. John Hope Franklin and Alfred A. Moss, Jr., *From Slavery to Freedom: A History of African Americans*, 7th edition (New York: McGraw-Hill, 1994), 22.

7 Albert J. Raboteau, *Slave Religion: The "Invisible Institution" in the Antebellum South*, updated edition (New York: Oxford University Press, 2004), 7.

8 Albert J. Raboteau, *Slave Religion: The "Invisible Institution" in the Antebellum South*, updated edition (New York: Oxford University Press, 2004), 8–10; John Hope Franklin and Alfred A. Moss, Jr., *From Slavery to Freedom: A History of African Americans*, 7th edition (New York: McGraw-Hill, 1994), 20.

9 Edward Franklin Frazier, *The Negro Church in America* (New York: Schocken Books, 1964), 1–19, 86; Albert J. Raboteau, *Slave Religion: The "Invisible Institution" in the Antebellum South*, updated edition (New York: Oxford University Press, 2004), 52–54.

10 Albert J. Raboteau, *Slave Religion: The "Invisible Institution" in the Antebellum South*, updated edition (New York: Oxford University Press, 2004), 7–10, 16–17, 47–48.

11 Melville J. Herskovits, *The Myth of the Negro Past* (New York: Harper and Brothers, 1941), 232–235; Albert J. Raboteau, *Slave Religion: The "Invisible Institution" in the Antebellum South*, updated edition (New York: Oxford University Press, 2004), 65, 86.

12 Alexis Wells-Oghoghomeh, *The Souls of Womenfolk: The Religious Cultures of Enslaved Women in the Lower South* (Chapel Hill, NC: University of North Carolina Press, 2021), 235.

13 Albert J. Raboteau, *Slave Religion: The "Invisible Institution" in the Antebellum South*, updated edition (New York: Oxford University Press, 2004), 100, 125–126.

14 Le Jau to the Sec. of the S.P.G., March 22, 1708/9, printed in *The Carolina Chronicle of Dr. Francis Le Jau, 1706–1717*, edited by Frank J. Klingberg (Berkely and Los Angeles: University of California Press, 1956), 55; Cited in Albert J. Raboteau, *Slave Religion: The "Invisible Institution" in the Antebellum South*, updated edition (New York: Oxford University Press, 2004), 100–101, 125–126.

15 Albert J. Raboteau, *Slave Religion: The "Invisible Institution" in the Antebellum South*, updated edition (New York: Oxford University Press, 2004), 100–102.

16 Morgan, *Slave Counterpoint,* 11; Nell Irvin Painter, *Creating Black Americans: African American History and Its Meanings, 1619 to the Present* (New York: Oxford University Press, 2006), 49; John Hope Franklin and Alfred A. Moss, Jr., *From Slavery to Freedom: A History of African Americans*, 7th edition (New York: McGraw-Hill, 1994), 57–58; Albert J. Raboteau, *Slave Religion: The "Invisible Institution" in the Antebellum South*, updated edition (New York: Oxford University Press, 2004), 97–99.

17 Albert J. Raboteau, *Slave Religion: The "Invisible Institution" in the Antebellum South*, updated edition (New York: Oxford University Press, 2004), 103.

18 Anne H. Pinn and Anthony B. Pinn, *Fortress Introduction to Black Church History* (Minneapolis, MN: Fortress Press, 2002), 1–2; Albert J. Raboteau, *Slave Religion: The "Invisible Institution" in the Antebellum South*, updated edition (New York: Oxford University Press, 2004), 97.

19 Anne H. Pinn and Anthony B. Pinn, *Fortress Introduction to Black Church History* (Minneapolis, MN: Fortress Press, 2002), 3; Albert J. Raboteau, *Slave Religion: The "Invisible Institution" in the Antebellum South*, updated edition (New York: Oxford University Press, 2004), 111.

20 Anne H. Pinn and Anthony B. Pinn, *Fortress Introduction to Black Church History* (Minneapolis, MN: Fortress Press, 2002), 3; Albert J. Raboteau, *Slave Religion: The "Invisible Institution" in the Antebellum South*, updated edition (New York: Oxford University Press, 2004), 101.

21 Albert J. Raboteau, *Slave Religion: The "Invisible Institution" in the Antebellum South*, updated edition (New York: Oxford University Press, 2004), 109–110; Anne H. Pinn and Anthony B. Pinn, *Fortress Introduction to Black Church History* (Minneapolis, MN: Fortress Press, 2002), 4.

22 Albert J. Raboteau, *Slave Religion: The "Invisible Institution" in the Antebellum South*, updated edition (New York: Oxford University Press, 2004), 115.

23 Anne H. Pinn and Anthony B. Pinn, *Fortress Introduction to Black Church History* (Minneapolis, MN: Fortress Press, 2002), 6.

24 Michael A. Gomez, *Exchanging Our Country Marks: The Transformation of African Identities in the Colonial and Antebellum South* (Chapel Hill, NC: University of North Carolina Press, 1998), 246–247.

25 Michael A. Gomez, *Exchanging Our Country Marks: The Transformation of African Identities in the Colonial and Antebellum South* (Chapel Hill, NC: University of North Carolina Press, 1998), 246–247.

26 These were by no means the only Christian fellowships that slaves joined in colonial America. Anne H. Pinn and Anthony B. Pinn, *Fortress Introduction to Black Church History* (Minneapolis, MN: Fortress Press, 2002), 1–2; Albert J. Raboteau, *Slave Religion: The "Invisible Institution" in the Antebellum South*, updated edition (New York: Oxford University Press, 2004), 97, 126.

27 Harry Van Buren Richardson, *Dark Salvation: The Story of Methodism as it Developed among Blacks in America* (Garden City, NY: Anchor Press, 1976), 25; Albert J. Raboteau, *Slave Religion: The "Invisible Institution" in the Antebellum South*, updated edition (New York: Oxford University Press, 2004), 17.

28 Anne H. Pinn and Anthony B. Pinn, *Fortress Introduction to Black Church History* (Minneapolis, MN: Fortress Press, 2002), 6; Albert J. Raboteau, *Slave Religion: The "Invisible Institution" in the Antebellum South*, updated edition (New York: Oxford University Press, 2004), 132.

29 Albert J. Raboteau, *Slave Religion: The "Invisible Institution" in the Antebellum South*, updated edition (New York: Oxford University Press, 2004), 57–58.

30 Albert J. Raboteau, *Slave Religion: The "Invisible Institution" in the Antebellum South*, updated edition (New York: Oxford University Press, 2004), 148.

31 Albert J. Raboteau, *Slave Religion: The "Invisible Institution" in the Antebellum South*, updated edition (New York: Oxford University Press, 2004), 316–317.

32 John Boles, *The Great Revival: Beginnings of the Bible Belt* (Lexington, KY: University Press of Kentucky, 1996), xiv; Albert J. Raboteau, *Slave Religion: The "Invisible Institution" in the Antebellum South*, updated edition (New York: Oxford University Press, 2004), 11, 132.

33 John Boles, *The Great Revival: Beginnings of the Bible Belt* (Lexington, KY: University Press of Kentucky, 1996), 125–133.
34 Albert J. Raboteau, *Slave Religion: The "Invisible Institution" in the Antebellum South*, updated edition (New York: Oxford University Press, 2004), 133; John Boles, *Masters and Slaves in the House of the Lord: Race and Religion in the American South, 1740–1870* (Lexington, KY: University Press of Kentucky, 1988), 6–8; Harry Van Buren Richardson, *Dark Salvation: The Story of Methodism as it Developed among Blacks in America* (Garden City, NY: Anchor Press, 1976), 25; Anne H. Pinn and Anthony B. Pinn, *Fortress Introduction to Black Church History* (Minneapolis, MN: Fortress Press, 2002), 7. Alexis Wells-Oghoghomeh, *The Souls of Womenfolk: The Religious Cultures of Enslaved Women in the Lower South* (Chapel Hill, NC: University of North Carolina Press, 2021), 196; Albert J. Raboteau, *Slave Religion: The "Invisible Institution" in the Antebellum South*, updated edition (New York: Oxford University Press, 2004), 150.
35 Alexis Wells-Oghoghomeh, *The Souls of Womenfolk: The Religious Cultures of Enslaved Women in the Lower South* (Chapel Hill, NC: University of North Carolina Press, 2021), 196.
36 W.E.B. Du Bois, *The Negro Church* (Atlanta, GA: Atlanta University Press, 1903), 29; Cited in Albert J. Raboteau, *Slave Religion: The "Invisible Institution" in the Antebellum South*, updated edition (New York: Oxford University Press, 2004), 209.
37 Alexis Wells-Oghoghomeh, *The Souls of Womenfolk: The Religious Cultures of Enslaved Women in the Lower South* (Chapel Hill, NC: University of North Carolina Press, 2021), 199–201; Charles C. Jones, *A Catechism of Scripture Doctrine and Practice, For Families and Sabbath Schools, Designed Also for the Oral Instruction of Colored Persons*. Sixth Edition (New York: Leavitt, Trow and Company: 1837), 4, retrieved from https://babel.hathitrust.org/cgi/pt?id=njp.32101058495415&seq=5; Albert J. Raboteau, *Slave Religion: The "Invisible Institution" in the Antebellum South*, updated edition (New York: Oxford University Press, 2004), 131.
38 Alexis Wells-Oghoghomeh, *The Souls of Womenfolk: The Religious Cultures of Enslaved Women in the Lower South* (Chapel Hill, NC: University of North Carolina Press, 2021), 201; Albert J. Raboteau, *Slave Religion: The "Invisible Institution" in the Antebellum South*, updated edition (New York: Oxford University Press, 2004), 5, 209, 271–275; Turner, *Islam in the African-American Experience*, 11; Anne H. Pinn and Anthony B. Pinn, *Fortress Introduction to Black Church History* (Minneapolis, MN: Fortress Press, 2002), 11. Charles Ball, *A Narrative of the Life and Adventures of Charles Ball, a Black Man*, 3rd ed. (Pittsburgh, PA: John T. Skyrock, 1854), 143.
39 Daniel Alexander Payne, "Daniel Payne's Protestation of Slavery," in *Lutheran Herald and Journal of the Franckean Synod* (August 1, 1839), 114–115; cited in Anne H. Pinn and Anthony B. Pinn, *Fortress Introduction to Black Church History* (Minneapolis, MN: Fortress Press, 2002), 10.
40 Alexis Wells-Oghoghomeh, *The Souls of Womenfolk: The Religious Cultures of Enslaved Women in the Lower South* (Chapel Hill, NC: University of North Carolina Press, 2021), 201.
41 Albert J. Raboteau, *Slave Religion: The "Invisible Institution" in the Antebellum South*, updated edition (New York: Oxford University Press, 2004), 210.
42 Albert J. Raboteau, *Slave Religion: The "Invisible Institution" in the Antebellum South*, updated edition (New York: Oxford University Press, 2004), 149, 212; Edward Franklin Frazier, *The Negro Church in America* (New York: Schocken Books, 1964), 23.
43 Robert Anderson, *From Slavery to Affluence: Memories of Robert Anderson, Ex-Slave* (Hemingford, NE: 1927), 22–23; cited in John Hope Franklin and Alfred A. Moss, Jr., *From Slavery to Freedom: A History of African Americans*, 7th edition (New York: McGraw-Hill, 1994), 23.
44 Peter Randolph, *Sketches of Slave Life or, Illustrations of the Peculiar Institution* (Boston, MA: 1855) 30–31; cited in Albert J. Raboteau, *Slave Religion: The "Invisible Institution" in the Antebellum South*, updated edition (New York: Oxford University Press, 2004), 217.
45 Albert J. Raboteau, *Slave Religion: The "Invisible Institution" in the Antebellum South*, updated edition (New York: Oxford University Press, 2004), 215.
46 *Unwritten History of Slavery: Autobiographical Accounts of Negro Ex-slaves* (Washington, DC: Microcard Editions, 1968), 81–84; Cited in Milton C. Sernett, *African American Religious History: A Documentary Witness*, 2nd edition (Durham, NC: Duke University Press, 1999), 70.

47 Albert J. Raboteau, *Slave Religion: The "Invisible Institution" in the Antebellum South*, updated edition (New York: Oxford University Press, 2004), 318; Anne H. Pinn and Anthony B. Pinn, *Fortress Introduction to Black Church History* (Minneapolis, MN: Fortress Press, 2002), 2; Molly M. Oshatz, *Slavery and Sin: The Fight Against Slavery and the Rise of Liberal Protestantism* (New York: Oxford University Press, 2011).

48 Howard Thurman, *Jesus and the Disinherited* (Richmond, IN: Friends United Press, 1981), 30–35.

49 W.F. Allen, "The Negro Dialect," *Nation*, 1 (December 14, 1865): 744–745, reprinted in Bernard Katz, ed, *The Negro and His Folklore in Nineteenth-Century Periodicals* (Austin, TX: University of Texas Press, 1967), 79.

50 Walter Pitts, *Old Ship of Zion: The Afro-Baptist Ritual in the African Diaspora* (New York: Oxford University Press, 1993), 93.

51 Albert J. Raboteau, *Slave Religion: The "Invisible Institution" in the Antebellum South*, updated edition (New York: Oxford University Press, 2004), 217.

52 Ira Berlin, Marc Favreau, and Steven F. Miller, editors, *Remembering Slavery: African Americans Talk about Their Personal Experiences of Slavery and Emancipation* (New York: New Press, in association with the Library of Congress, Washington, DC, 1998), 195–196; cited in Anne H. Pinn and Anthony B. Pinn, *Fortress Introduction to Black Church History* (Minneapolis, MN: Fortress Press, 2002), 13.

53 Albert J. Raboteau, *Slave Religion: The "Invisible Institution" in the Antebellum South*, updated edition (New York: Oxford University Press, 2004), 239; Nancy B. Miner, "'All The World Was Shoutin': The Story of the Reverend John Jasper" Black and Christian.com, June 2003, retrieved from www.blackandchristian.com/articles/academy/miner-06-03.shtml; William E. Hatcher, *John Jasper: The Unmatched Negro Philosopher and Preacher* (New York: Fleming H. Revell Co., 1908).

54 Albert J. Raboteau, *Slave Religion: The "Invisible Institution" in the Antebellum South*, updated edition (New York: Oxford University Press, 2004), 214.

55 Catherine A. Brekus, *Strangers and Pilgrims: Female Preaching in America, 1740–1845* (Chapel Hill, NC: University of North Carolina Press, 1998), 129.

56 Catherine A. Brekus, *Strangers and Pilgrims: Female Preaching in America, 1740–1845* (Chapel Hill, NC: University of North Carolina Press, 1998), 63–64, 130–131.

57 Alexis Wells-Oghoghomeh, *The Souls of Womenfolk: The Religious Cultures of Enslaved Women in the Lower South* (Chapel Hill, NC: University of North Carolina Press, 2021), 134, 160, 194.

58 Alexis S. Wells-Oghoghomeh, "'She Comes Like a Nightmare': Hags, Witches and the Gendered Trans-Sense among the Enslaved in the Lower South," *Journal of Africana Religions*, vol. 5, no. 2 (2017): 259.

59 Yvonne P. Chireau, *Black Magic: Religion and the African American Conjuring Tradition* (Berkeley: University of California Press, 2003), 12, 20–21, 60; Alexis S. Wells-Oghoghomeh, "'She Comes Like a Nightmare': Hags, Witches and the Gendered Trans-Sense among the Enslaved in the Lower South," *Journal of Africana Religions*, vol. 5, no. 2 (2017): 246–247; Alexis Wells-Oghoghomeh, *The Souls of Womenfolk: The Religious Cultures of Enslaved Women in the Lower South* (Chapel Hill, NC: University of North Carolina Press, 2021), 183; Albert J. Raboteau, *Slave Religion: The "Invisible Institution" in the Antebellum South*, updated edition (New York: Oxford University Press, 2004), 277.

60 Albert J. Raboteau, *Slave Religion: The "Invisible Institution" in the Antebellum South*, updated edition (New York: Oxford University Press, 2004), 276–277.

61 Yvonne P. Chireau, *Black Magic: Religion and the African American Conjuring Tradition* (Berkeley: University of California Press, 2003), 15, 25–27; Albert J. Raboteau, *Slave Religion: The "Invisible Institution" in the Antebellum South*, updated edition (New York: Oxford University Press, 2004), 288.

62 Alexis S. Wells-Oghoghomeh, "'She Comes Like a Nightmare': Hags, Witches and the Gendered Trans-Sense among the Enslaved in the Lower South," *Journal of Africana Religions*, vol. 5, no. 2 (2017): 259; Alexis Wells-Oghoghomeh, *The Souls of Womenfolk: The Religious Cultures of Enslaved Women in the Lower South* (Chapel Hill, NC: University of North Carolina Press, 2021), 135–136, 160.

63 Alexis Wells-Oghoghomeh, *The Souls of Womenfolk: The Religious Cultures of Enslaved Women in the Lower South* (Chapel Hill, NC: University of North Carolina Press, 2021), 140.

64 Alexis S. Wells-Oghoghomeh, "'She Comes Like a Nightmare': Hags, Witches and the Gendered Trans-Sense among the Enslaved in the Lower South," *Journal of Africana Religions*, vol. 5, no. 2 (2017): 240–244, 249, 255.

65 Alexis S. Wells-Oghoghomeh, "'She Comes Like a Nightmare': Hags, Witches and the Gendered Trans-Sense among the Enslaved in the Lower South," *Journal of Africana Religions*, vol. 5, no. 2 (2017): 240–244.

66 Alexis S. Wells-Oghoghomeh, "'She Comes Like a Nightmare': Hags, Witches and the Gendered Trans-Sense among the Enslaved in the Lower South," *Journal of Africana Religions*, vol. 5, no. 2 (2017): 249, 260–261.

67 Alexis S. Wells-Oghoghomeh, "'She Comes Like a Nightmare': Hags, Witches and the Gendered Trans-Sense among the Enslaved in the Lower South," *Journal of Africana Religions*, vol. 5, no. 2 (2017): 249.

68 Alexis S. Wells-Oghoghomeh, "'She Comes Like a Nightmare': Hags, Witches and the Gendered Trans-Sense among the Enslaved in the Lower South," *Journal of Africana Religions*, vol. 5, no. 2 (2017): 254, 262.

69 Alexis S. Wells-Oghoghomeh, "'She Comes Like a Nightmare': Hags, Witches and the Gendered Trans-Sense among the Enslaved in the Lower South," *Journal of Africana Religions*, vol. 5, no. 2 (2017): 253.

70 A police officer fatally shot Sonya Massey, a thirty-six-year-old Black woman from Springfield, Illinois on July 6, 2024, for daring rebuke him "in the name of Jesus" while holding a hot boiling pot of water; Emma Tucker and Jillian Sykes, "Sonya Massey's mom called 911 to report her daughter was having a mental breakdown the day before she was killed," *CNN*, August 1, 2024, retrieved from www.cnn.com/2024/08/01/us/sonya-massey-mental-health-911-calls/index.html

Further Readings

Austin, Allan D. *African Muslims in Antebellum America: An Anthology.* Buffalo, NY: Prometheus Books, 1991.

Boles, John. *The Great Revival: Beginnings of the Bible Belt.* Lexington, KY: University Press of Kentucky, 1996.

Chireau, Yvonne Patricia. *Black Magic: Religion and the African American Conjuring Tradition.* Berkeley, CA: University of California Press, 2003.

Diouf, Sylvaiane. *Servants of Allah: African Muslims Enslaved in the Americas.* New York: New York University Press, 1998.

Equiano, Olaudah. *The Interesting Narrative and Other Writings.* New York: Penguin, 1995.

Gomez, Michael A. *Exchanging Our Country Marks: The Transformation of African Identities in the Colonial and Antebellum South.* Chapel Hill, NC: University of North Carolina Press, 1998.

Levine, Lawrence. *Black Culture and Black Consciousness: Afro-American Folk Thought from Slavery to Freedom.* New York: Oxford University Press, 1977.

Raboteau, Albert J. *Slave Religion: The "Invisible Institution" in the Antebellum South.* Updated ed. New York: Oxford University Press, 2004.

Washington Creel, Margaret. *A Peculiar People: Slave Religion and Community-Culture Among the Gullahs.* New York: New York University Press, 1989.

Wells-Oghoghomeh, Alexis. *The Souls of Womenfolk: The Religious Cultures of Enslaved Women in the Lower South.* Chapel Hill, NC: University of North Carolina Press, 2021.

Wilmore, Gayraud S. *Black Religion and Black Radicalism: An Interpretation of the Religious History of Afro-American People.* Maryknoll, NY: Orbis Books, 1983.

2 "Let My People Go"

Spiritual Strivings before the Civil War

> Go down, Moses, way down in Egypt's land,
> Tell old Pharaoh: Let my people go.
> The Lord told Moses what to do,
> Let my people go,
> To lead the Hebrew children through,
> Let my people go.
>
> "Go Down, Moses"
> (traditional spiritual song)

This chapter discusses four ways Black religious people pursued freedom during the antebellum era—the Independent Black Church Movement, Black Nationalism and Ethiopianism, Black Religious Jeremiads, and Slave Rebellions. Attention is devoted to a variety of Black religious leaders who creatively employed biblical figuralism to strive for liberation. Theophus Smith defines biblical figuralism as a "a hermeneutic tradition in which a person or place, object or event, is connected to a second entity in such a way that the first signifies the second and the second fulfills or encompasses the first."[1] For instance, early Christian writers engaged in figuralism when referring to Jesus as the return of Moses or David. They understood Jesus as extending the stories and legacies of figures from the Hebrew Bible. In a similar way, Black Christians have historically adopted the Bible as a conjure book, "a magical means" of striving to change their oppressive circumstances.[2] They saw themselves as fulfilling the stories of biblical heroes such as Moses, Joshua, Samson, Deborah, and Jesus. For example, Dr. Martin Luther King drew on Moses and the Exodus narrative during the civil rights movement when he told a packed audience at Mason Temple that he had seen the Promised Land of racial justice and equality in America (Deuteronomy 34:1–4).[3] He inspired Black people to believe that God would help them reach the Promised Land of freedom, equality, and justice in the United States just as God did for Israel. This chapter explores how Black antebellum Christians similarly engaged and interpreted a variety of biblical texts to challenge white supremacy.

The Independent Black Church Movement

Aside from fraternal organizations such as the Freemasons, most of the independent Black religious organizations during the antebellum period were Christian. Black Muslims were not "able to develop institutions to perpetuate their religion in the 19th century."[4] Though some Black Muslims such as Yarrow Mamount, Abd Al-Rahman

DOI: 10.4324/9781003359197-3

Ibrahima, Lamine Kaba, Omar Ibn Said, and others maintained ties to Islam and continued to practice Islam in the United States, it was a challenge for Black Muslims to form institutions to pass down their faith to their descendants in a "strange Christian land."[5] Omar Ibn Said, one of the most studied African Muslim slaves of the nineteenth century, engaged in "deceptive signification" and pretended to convert to Christianity. Still, there is evidence that he continued his Muslim faith. He kept an Arabic Bible and referred to Muhammad in many of his writings.[6] Some Black Muslims pretended to convert to Christianity and joined the American Colonization Society to return to Africa. Many enslaved Black Muslims practiced their religion privately. They were not able to freely form religious communities on the slave plantations. Subsequently, the Islam of "original African Muslim slaves" who brought their faith with them via the Middle Passage became "defunct over time."[7] It was immensely more difficult for enslaved Black Muslims to establish religious institutions than Black Christians.

Black people continued to join Methodist and Baptist churches, which became more institutionalized in the late eighteenth and early nineteenth centuries. The Northern Black independent church movement began because Black church leaders refused to accept White Christians' humiliating segregationist practices and customs. Northern and Southern White Methodist leaders endorsed the racial customs of their times. White Christians, for example, ordered Black parishioners to sit in separate areas during worship. They segregated themselves from Blacks when praying at the altar and partaking in the sacraments. They prevented Black ministers from serving in influential leadership offices.

Richard Allen (1760–1831) was the first Black Christian to establish an independent denomination. Born to enslaved parents, he joined the Methodist Church at seventeen and served in the Methodist Society. His second master allowed him and his brother to purchase their freedom after becoming convicted that slavery was wrong following his conversion to Methodism. Allen devoted his life to serving God in the Methodist Church. He became a traveling minister in states such as Delaware, New Jersey, and Philadelphia. He was present at the 1784 founding conference of Methodism in the United States, the "Christmas Conference" at Lovely Land Chapel in Baltimore, Maryland.[8]

When Allen returned to settle in Philadelphia, he attended St. George's Methodist Episcopal Church. He and Absalom Jones planned to share the Methodist faith with local Blacks. Allen and fellow Black Methodists became embittered with the ongoing racial discrimination and segregation they experienced during worship at the White Methodist Church they attended. On one occasion, White church leaders forcefully removed them from the altar as they were praying. Following this incident, several Black parishioners joined Allen in walking out of St. George's Methodist Episcopal Church in Philadelphia in 1787 because they refused to accept such blatant discrimination.[9]

Allen started conducting prayer meetings in his house and praying in the homes of other Blacks. Rather than immediately starting a separate church, he and other Black people in his circle founded the Free African Society on April 12, 1787. This mutual aid organization aimed to enable Black people to support each other and contribute to the abolitionist movement. Allen and Jones initially hoped to form the society as a religious organization. However, they abandoned this idea because Black people at the time were affiliated with different spiritual traditions that were not easily unifiable. Instead, they proposed forming an organization that welcomed persons of all religions committed to moral living and providing mutual support for Black people. The Free African Society did not merely provide a supportive network for free Black people in Philadelphia. It was an interreligious abolitionist organization that promoted freedom for enslaved African people throughout the South. As an abolitionist, Allen employed biblical figuralism. In "An Address to those who keep slaves, and approve the practice," he compared the plight of enslaved Black people to the enslaved Hebrews and noted how enslaved persons across both time periods had a proclivity to hate their oppressors (Deuteronomy 23:7). He argued that slavery was abhorrent to God, who "destroyed kings and princes, for their oppression of poor slaves." Allen also warned enslavers that if they maintained the system that there would be embittered enslaved Black people who would rebel. He insisted that God "hath from time to time raised up instruments for that purpose, sometimes mean and contemptable in your sight, at other times he hath used such as it has pleased him ..."[10] Inasmuch as Allen favored nonviolent abolitionism as a member of the Free African Society, he believed that God could and would use violent revolutionary leaders to overthrow the wicked system if White enslavers did not repent.

It displeased Allen when Free African Society members who were members of the Society of Friends started to incorporate features of Quaker polity, including seeking to commune with God in quiet meditation and private worship. Allen upheld congregational worship, corporate prayer, and the revivalist tenure of Methodist worship, which appealed to Blacks during the Great Awakening. He parted ways with the Free African Society and founded the Bethel Church in Philadelphia in 1794, despite opposition from White Methodists who wanted Blacks to remain in the White Methodist fellowship.[11]

Within three decades of separating from White Methodists, Allen, Daniel Coker, James Champion, and other Black Methodists convened a meeting in Philadelphia on April 9, 1816, to organize the African Methodist Episcopal (AME) Church as a separate Black denomination.[12] They did this because independent Black Methodist churches had to struggle vigorously to obtain rights to church properties controlled by the White Methodist denomination. White Methodists were also reluctant to relinquish control of church finances. Furthermore, bishops in the Methodist church rarely ordained or appointed Blacks as pastors. Subsequently, Black Methodist leaders established a separate denomination to obtain more control and autonomy.

Black Methodists in New York formed their church for a similar reason Allen and other Black Methodists in Philadelphia established Mother Bethel Church. John Street Methodist Church in New York had a small sanctuary that could not accommodate White and Black members. White Methodists forced the Black congregants to sit in the back of the church or in the balcony. To address their discriminatory treatment, Black members of New York's John Street Methodist Church, such as James Varick, Peter Williams, Abraham Thompson, William Miller, and June Scott, pressed Bishop Asbury to hold separate services at the church in 1796. Bishop Asbury permitted Black Methodists to have a separate service under the direction of a White-appointed minister, William Stillwell. The Black religious service grew in popularity among Black Methodists. They decided to pool their resources to build a separate church apart from John Street Church named Zion Chapel. The church maintained its affiliation with the White Methodist Church and followed its doctrines and polity. Although the church did not have a Black pastor, Black Methodist leaders had some authority. Zion Chapel had a Black Board of Trustees. Blacks controlled the property. Bishop Asbury ordained James Varick and a few other Black Methodists in the congregation as deacons in 1806. In 1820, Black Methodists affiliated with Zion Chapel and other recently formed local Black Methodist congregations decided to part ways with the White Methodist

Figure 2.1 Bishops of the A.M.E. Church, J.H. Daniels, *c*.1876.
Library of Congress Prints and Photographs Division Washington, DC

denomination. Desiring more power and control, Black trustees and deacons from Zion Chapel and other affiliated churches met in June 1821 to form a second Black independent Methodist denomination. James Varick became the denomination's first bishop. He was a free Black man, a licensed John Street minister, and a Zion Chapel deacon. During a general conference in 1848, the Black Methodists in the newly formed denomination decided to add Zion to their name to distinguish their denomination from the AME Church led by Allen, which they chose not to join. Both Black Methodist denominations established a solid organizational basis that enabled them to purchase new houses of worship. They developed a Book of Discipline, denominational manuals, and a system of governance that resembled the White Methodist churches from which they disaffiliated.[13]

Neither the AME Church nor the African Methodist Episcopal Zion (AMEZ) Church boasted a substantial membership. In 1860, the AME had a membership of about 19,963 members. The AMEZ Church had about 4,600 members. The institution of slavery prevented the AME or the AME Zion from attracting Southern Black Methodists. Southern plantation owners only permitted enslaved Black Methodists in the South to attend White Methodist churches or plantation mission churches.[14]

Around the same time, Black Methodists established churches; Black Baptists formed their own Baptist churches in the North and South. As with Black Methodists, Blacks of the Baptist faith attended biracial Baptist worship services on Southern plantations. Many early independent Black churches in the South were plantation mission churches. The Silver Bluff Church was the first independent Black Baptist Church in America under Black supervision. Founded in Silver Bluff, South Carolina, in 1775, it was led by David George. George Liele, an early Black missionary and licensed minister who preached at slave plantation missions in South Carolina and Georgia, also frequently ministered at Silver Bluff and helped organize the congregation. During the Revolutionary War, Liele received freedom for supporting the Loyalists. After the war, he relocated to the Caribbean, and he established a Black Baptist Church in Kingston, the Ethiopian Baptist Church of Jamaica. Liele also baptized Andrew Bryan, who founded the First Colored Baptist Church in Savannah in 1788, attended by hundreds of Black people. Bryan and other Black attendees were subject to intense harassment and persecution by White people who were suspicious that the Black worshippers might organize an insurrection. Bryan and many of his members were whipped, arrested, and forced to suspend their services. Bryan's master advocated for the Black congregation and permitted them to resume services in a shed on his plantation. Black Baptists established independent Baptist churches in the North, such as the Abyssinian Baptist Church of New York City, in 1808. The church had a nonsegregated membership. Free Black Baptists in Philadelphia organized a church in the city in 1809.[15]

In addition to racism among White Baptists, Baptist theology also inspired Black Baptists to separate from White Baptists. Black Baptist preachers affirmed biblical authority and upheld religious freedom and independence as hallmarks of the American way of life and the Baptist tradition. Unlike Methodist churches based on a connectional model, Baptist churches are marked by a solid commitment to the autonomy of the local congregation. Black Baptists from New York, New England, and a few other states in the country's northeastern region formed the American Baptist Missionary Convention in 1840. However, compared to Northern Black Methodists, Southern Black Baptists had more difficulty developing associations composed of numerous churches during the antebellum era.[16] Southern Black Baptist churches developed under the watchful eye of Southern slaveholders who restricted Blacks from growing churches and independent associations. After the Nat Turner rebellion of 1831, slaveholders intensified their effort to prevent Southern Black Baptists from worshipping separately. They made independent gatherings illegal in several parts of the South.

Not many independent churches were established among the Presbyterians and the Episcopalians during the early nineteenth century. As discussed in the previous chapter, most Black people found the enthusiastic evangelical worship experience attractive rather than the Presbyterians' and Episcopalians' polity, preaching, and formal worship style. Still, some Black people joined Presbyterian and Episcopalian churches. Blacks in these majority-White denominations formed independent churches for similar reasons as Black Methodists and Baptists. They felt excluded and restricted. They desired more independence and control over their religious lives. Many of the seminaries refused to admit Black Presbyterians and Episcopalian ministers. They made it difficult to receive the necessary educational credentials to become ordained ministers. Those who became ordained ministers often did not receive the same salary as their White counterparts. Some Black Presbyterians, Episcopalians, and Congregationalists established independent churches. However, they did not possess the same level of independence as Black

Methodists and Black Baptists because they remained connected to parent White denominations who controlled all church properties and pastors' salaries.[17]

Not all Black Christians were supportive of the establishment of independent Black churches. Some Black Christians held that Black believers should remain united with White Christians. Some free Blacks elected to stay with the White Methodist Episcopal Church. Less than five percent of the 42,304 Black Methodists joined the AME or AME Zion church when they initially formed. Some Black Methodists considered it outlandish for Black men who were formerly enslaved people and barely literate to refer to themselves with dignified titles such as presiding elder or bishop. They also desired to remain in-network with Whites for personal and social reasons. The notable abolitionist leader Frederick Douglass was initially unsupportive of the independent church movement. He believed God willed for churches to remain integrated along racial lines. However, Douglass later chose to join the AME Zion church because he came to recognize that all White Methodist churches were not supportive of freedom for enslaved Blacks. He accepted that independent Black churches provided Black Christians a means to support the abolition movement. The AME Zion Church was deeply involved in the Underground Railroad, a secret mechanism for helping enslaved people escape and secure their freedom. Black independent churches and denominations enabled Black Christians to prioritize the needs of Black people, which many White churches and institutions neglected. They also provided Black ministers an opportunity to develop leadership skills. Douglass became a local preacher in the Zion Methodist Conference. The church was instrumental in his development as an orator and abolitionist.[18] Black churches allowed Blacks to socialize and form communal bonds. According to Frazier, Black church gatherings permitted Blacks, disassociated from their African kinship ties, to develop solidarity and a "new basis of social cohesion."[19]

Black Women in Black Independent Churches

As Black people were dealing with racism in White churches, Black women experienced sexism in new independent Black churches. Black women could not "vote on church issues in their local churches" and in annual conferences until 1876, when the AME Zion granted them voting rights. By 1884, women could serve as "lay delegates" and could "discuss and vote on legislation affecting all churches in the denomination."[20] Jarena Lee's narrative illustrates Black women's struggles in Black churches. Lee was a free Black woman who converted to Christianity in 1804 while attending a White Methodist Church in Philadelphia. She accepted the call to ministry in 1809. Not feeling at home among the White Methodists, she joined Allen's Black Methodist congregation. Allen welcomed Lee to lead prayer services and to "exhort congregations after licensed ministers had delivered their sermons."[21] Allen recognized Lee's ministerial gifts, but he refused to license or ordain her. Lee continued in ministry, nonetheless, and believed God called her to preach. Interpreting Scripture to support women's liberation, she asked, "If the man may preach because the Savior died for him, why not the woman? Seeing he died for her also. Is he not a whole Savior, instead of a half one?"[22] She published her journal entitled *The Life and Religious Experience of Jarena Lee, a Coloured Lady, Giving an Account of Her Call to Preach the Gospel* in 1836.

Although Quakers ordained Black women such as Elizabeth and Zilpha Elaw to preach, Black denominations largely did not condone women's ordination in the nineteenth century. Black women shared their religious convictions through being "exhorters and evangelists." Exhorters could testify about their spiritual experience and lead prayer.[23] Evangelists were women commissioned to share the gospel among diverse churches in the community and during revival services rather than to a specific local congregation. Many early Black preaching women were evangelists in the northeastern sector of the country. Sophie Murray was a notable Black woman evangelist in Philadelphia in the early nineteenth century.[24]

Black Nationalism and Ethiopianism

Many early pioneers of classical Black nationalism, such as Edward W. Blyden and Martin Delaney, identified with the Exodus narrative and saw Black People as God's chosen and elect. Historian Wilson Jeremiah Moses defines classical Black nationalism as "the ideology that argued for the self-determination of African Americans within the framework of an independent nation-state."[25] Though the ultimate aim of Black nationalism has been the erection of a separate nation-state, historian Eddie Glaude explains that it also generally refers to Blacks' striving for racial solidarity and self-determination to contest racism and the perpetual threat of violence confronting free and enslaved Black people in the South and the North. Black nationalism intersects with Pan-Africanism, which is fundamentally concerned with fostering unity and racial pride among oppressed African people across the diaspora.[26]

Pan-Africanists such as Blyden and Delaney also embraced Ethiopianism, a Black literary religious tradition that developed in the late nineteenth century that accentuated the distinctiveness of Black people in the eyes of God. The biblical referent for Ethiopianism was Psalms 68:31, which states: "Princes shall come out of Egypt, and Ethiopia shall soon stretch forth her hands unto God."[27] Ethiopianists adopted figuralism by juxtaposing ancient Black Egyptians and Ethiopians with nineteenth century Black people. They connected biblical Ethiopians with the enslaved Hebrew people whom God delivered from Egyptian bondage. Ethiopianists prophetically interpreted "Ethiopia stretching out her hand to God" as a reference to the Divine redemption of enslaved Black people.[28] Because Ethiopia and Egypt are nations in Africa, Ethiopianists held that enslaved people of African descent were descendants of the ancient Black Ethiopians and Egyptians mentioned in Psalms 68:31. Ethiopianists reconfigured Egypt from being a place of bondage to an African place of affluence, culture, and civilization. They drew on this biblical reference ultimately to refute claims that Blackness was inherently inferior and to inspire Black people to take pride in their African heritage.[29]

Wilson Jeremiah Moses, a leading scholar on Black nationalism, determined that Ethiopianism was "mythic" because the majority of Black people in America do not have a direct lineage to ancient civilizations such as Ethiopia or Egypt. Most enslaved Black people's origins are connected to West African countries.[30] Nonetheless, many Black people embraced Ethiopianism because it encouraged Black people to be proud of their history and culture. Furthermore, Pan-Africanists desired to convince enslaved and free Black people that God willed them to unite to resist slavery and redeem Africa.

Some early Black Christian foreign missionaries who embraced Ethiopianism joined the American Colonization Society (ACS). In 1759, Reverend Samuel Hopkins, a White Congregationalist minister, proposed that Blacks should repatriate back to Africa to conduct missionary outreach in the region. Founded in 1817, the ACS was born out of Hopkins's missionary vision. The ACS held that repatriation was the means to wash America clean of the sin and stain of slavery.[31] The organization envisioned that the solution to the race problem was for free Black people to be sent back to Africa first, and then those who were enslaved would gradually be emancipated and returned to the Motherland.

The ACS's plan for repatriation of Blacks to Africa was different from a classical Black nationalist program, which aimed to establish an autonomous nation-state.[32] Edward W. Blyden (1832–1912) is an example of a Black Christian missionary who was drawn to the ACS because of his latent Black nationalist impulse to help Black people build independent churches in Africa. Born in St. Thomas, Virgin Islands or Danish West Indies, to free Black parents, Blyden migrated to New York in 1847. Although he grew up in the Dutch Reformed Church, became a minister as a teenager, and planned to devote his life to ministry in America, he seized the opportunity to join the ACS and to leave the United States because he feared the 1850 Fugitive Slave law. It gave the federal authorities the power to seize enslaved Blacks who escaped from the South to free Northern states. It caused terror among free Black communities and influenced free Blacks to consider emigrating to Africa or another country. The 1857 Dred Scott Supreme Court ruling also influenced his attraction to Black nationalism. The court ruled that enslaved Blacks who lived in free states were not citizens but property of their Southern owners. Blyden joined the ACS and endeavored to convince Black churches "to sponsor Liberian emigration" and to establish churches independent of White missionaries.[33]

Upon relocating to Liberia in 1851, Blyden excelled as a writer, educator, and statesman. While in Monrovia, in 1858 he became the principal of Alexander High School. He served as professor of Classics at Liberia College from 1862 to 1871. In addition to serving in the academy, he became the secretary of the State of Liberia and ran unsuccessfully for president. A prolific scholar, Blyden published several pamphlets over fifty years. In one of his notable works, *A Voice from Bleeding Africa* (1856), he denounced the system of slavery and discussed the humanity and potential of people of African descent. In *Christianity, Islam, and the Negro Race* (1887), he insisted that Islam had origins in Africa and had more positively impacted African peoples than Christianity, which had exploited Africans through colonialism, slavery, and imperialism. Though Blyden began his career as a Christian missionary, he came to embrace Islam as he studied the religion at Muslim centers in Liberia and Sierra Leone. He stressed that "West African Islam" could better bolster Pan-Africanism than European Christianity. Given his passion for Islam, leading Muslims from Fula town gave Blyden the Muslim name Abd-al-Kerim in 1871. Blyden helped link Pan-Africanism to the Black cultural "politics of global Islam," which will especially become a major force in the twentieth century (see Chapters 4 and 5).[34]

Martin Delany was perhaps the strongest proponent of Black nationalism during the early nineteenth century. Born in 1812 to free Blacks in Charleston, West Virginia, Delany became a journalist, physician, and abolitionist. He was a lay leader in the AME church and frequently conversed with Black clergy seeking to address the oppressive situation of Black people in America. He was also a member of the African Civilization Society, a missionary organization established in 1858 to bring "civilization and Christianization" to the African continent. Delany believed that Blacks could experience racial uplift through political and economic empowerment. He encouraged Black people to focus on helping themselves and held emigration as the only means to achieve "equality and social progress."[35] Though he believed Christianity could lead to the redemption of Africa, he was a staunch proponent of political black nationalism. He referenced Psalms

68:31 to bolster his arguments in *The Condition, Elevation, Emigration and Destiny of the Colored People of the United States, Politically Considered* (1852): "With the fullest reliance upon this blessed promise [Psalms 68:31], I humbly go forward in—I may repeat—the grandest prospect for the regeneration of a people that ever was presented in the history of the world."[36] Delany hoped to not merely Christianize Africa but to build a settlement in West Africa. He wrote, "Our race is to be redeemed; it is a great and glorious work, and we are the instrumentalities by which it must be done. But we must go from among our oppressors; it can never be done by staying among them."[37] Delany did not believe that America could be reformed. He led a convention in 1854, which promoted classical Black nationalism.[38]

Black Religious Jeremiads

Besides black nationalism, Black people challenged white supremacy through literature. Black religious persons used autobiographies, pamphlets, petitions, and various forms of protest writings to advance anti-racist religious arguments. Antislavery writings increased during the late eighteenth and early nineteenth centuries as activists strove to bring slavery to an immediate end. The invention of the cotton gin and improvement in the methods for harvesting and producing cotton made slavery more profitable in the South. As slavery was becoming a fixed feature of the Southern economy during the early national period, Black people wrote hundreds of pamphlets to make their case that slavery was inconsistent with the themes presented in the Declaration of Independence. A pamphlet is a form of literature between a broadside (a concise one-page document) and a book.[39] Robert Alexander Young, David Walker, and Maria Stewart wrote pamphlets that included scathing jeremiads that warned White people that God would judge America if she did not repent of slavery.

Derived from the prophet Jeremiah, a jeremiad is a lamentation, a call and cry for righteousness, directed toward those violating the divine covenant.[40] Jeremiah lamented the impending destruction of Israel after the people discounted his message and threatened to kill him (Jeremiah 11:21). Puritan preachers delivered jeremiads during the colonial period. They viewed England as the oppressive Pharaoh and believed God had chosen them to settle in New England to establish a "city upon a hill," a righteous nation. Puritan ministers preached to their congregations that members who remained faithful, obeyed God's commands, and adhered to the covenant terms would be blessed. However, those who became disobedient and disregarded the covenant would be subject to divine judgment. Throughout American history, Black people who employed the jeremiad viewed America as analogous to the oppressive Egyptian Pharaoh, who held the children of Israel in bondage. They used the jeremiad to condemn slavery, lynching, and various forms of oppression, especially at the hands of White Christians. The Black jeremiad pronounced impending divine judgment on oppressive White Southern slaveholders who feared the possibility of revolt among enslaved Black people.[41]

Robert Alexander Young was a free Black man from New York who published a pamphlet entitled "The Ethiopian Manifesto, Issued in Defense of the Blackman's Rights, in the Scale of Universal Freedom" in 1829.[42] His antislavery writing "inaugurate [d] black religious figuralism as a literary tradition."[43] Young also referenced Psalms 68:31 in stating, "surely hath the cries of the Black, a most persecuted people, ascended to my throne and craved my mercy; now, behold! I will stretch forth mine hand and gather them to the palm, that they become unto me a people, and I unto them their

God."[44] He boldly told White slaveholders that God had heard enslaved Blacks' moans and cries for help. He daringly asserted:

> Ah, doth your expanding judgment, base slaveholder, not from here descry that the shackles which have been by you so undeservingly forged upon a wretched Ethiopian's frame, are about to be forever from him unlinked ... Beware! Know thyselves [slaveholders] to be but mortal men, doomed to the good or evil, as your works shall merit from you ... Take warning, again we say, for a surety from this, God will give you signs to know, in his decrees he regards the fallen state of the sons of men.[45]

Instead of sending plagues as Yahweh did in Egypt, Young believed that "the Lord of hosts, the God of battles" would deliver Black people by sending a messiah to unite them "as a nation."[46] Young further employed biblical figuralism by perceiving himself to be like John the Baptist who proclaimed the coming of Christ (Matthew 3:1–3).[47] He did not pinpoint precisely who the Black Messiah would be. He explained, "How shall you know this man? By indubitable signs which cannot be controverted by the power of mortals, his marks being stamped in open visage, as equally so upon his frame, which constitutes him to have been particularly regarded in the infinite work of God to man."[48] Young believed the Messiah would help enslaved people develop discipline and teach them to live an ascetic life. The Messiah would influence global Black liberation through leading Black people to acquire such an intense thirst for freedom that they would be willing to die before tolerating enslavement.[49]

Young's manifesto accentuated millennialism themes. His work did not aim to spur Black people to rebel against the system. He wanted Blacks to trust that God would rescue them.[50] Young stated:

> So at this time, we particularly recommend to you, degraded sons of Africa, to submit with fortitude to your present state of suffering, relying in yourselves, from the justice of a God, there that time is at hand, when, with but the power of words and the divine will of our God, the vile shackles of slavery shall be broken asunder from you, and no man known who shall dare to own or proclaim you as his bondsman.[51]

Although several scholars have studied Young's work, it is difficult to know how widely read and received the tract was during its time. Young employed esoteric language. His meaning was mystical and not readily discernible to readers.

David Walker's *An Appeal to the Colored Citizens of the World* was more straightforward and widely read and circulated than Young's manifesto. The first edition, which was seventy-six pages, was printed in 1829. Born in 1785 in Wilmington, North Carolina, to a free mother and an enslaved father, Walker became one of the most influential antislavery writers of his time. He was a devout member of a local Methodist Church. He contributed to the abolitionist cause by sheltering runaway enslaved Black people in his home, supporting the *Freedom's Journal* in Boston, and delivering antislavery lectures. His *Appeal* was not merely a political or revolutionary document. It evidenced Walker's religious viewpoints regarding the political and social plight of Black people.[52] Walker scathingly excoriated the hypocrisy in White American churches and the nation in the nineteenth century. He insisted that immoral Christian slaveholders were willing to grasp power and wealth at any cost. He wrote, "If it were possible, would they not dethrone Jehovah and seat themselves upon his throne?"[53] His appeal was "a black jeremiad," a message of "indignation urgently challenging the nation to turn back to the ideas of its covenant."[54] He asserted:

> Oh Americans! Let me tell you, in the name of the Lord, it will be good for you, if you listen to the voice of the Holy Ghost, but if you do not; you are ruined!!! Some of you are good men; but the will of God must be done. Those avaricious and ungodly tyrants among you, I am awfully afraid will drag down the vengeance of God upon you. When God almighty commences his battle on the continent of America for the oppression of his people, tyrants will wish they were never born.[55]

The tone of his writing is replete with anger. Walker hoped to inspire Black people to become so disgusted with slavery to the point of taking up arms and violently overthrowing the system.

His work was "a summons" for them to defend their humanity and to use violence "to throw off the chains of slavery and fight in self-defense for freedom and dignity in the name of the Lord of hosts."[56] Walker warned that the nation would experience destruction if Whites did not repent of slavery. Whites who stood for justice and opposed slavery could potentially help save America from doom.[57]

Walker's *Appeal*, which circulated widely through states such as Virginia, Georgia, and South Carolina during the 1830s, alarmed and terrified political leaders in the North and South. Slaveholders would punish enslaved Black people whom they caught with the document in their possession. Though some friends and colleagues advised Walker to leave the country and relocate to Canada because slaveholders had threatened to take his life, Walker remained in Boston. He chose to continue his antislavery work in America despite the risks. Walker died on June 28, 1830, at forty-four years of age. Though the precise cause of his death is unknown, some persons suspect that fearful Whites poisoned him. Walker also had some enemies among Blacks who disagreed with his radicalism. Although no one can prove foul play regarding his death, he indeed died before the twilight years of his life. Given the politics and social climate in which he lived, it is conceivable that his prophetic rhetoric influenced him to die before his time.[58]

Although there is no precise record of how many copies were printed and disseminated, the *Appeal* circulated among free Blacks in the North and likely among enslaved Blacks in the South. The work potentially inspired Nat Turner and other Blacks who organized slave rebellions. Though slaveholders forbid the circulation of protest literature, abolitionists found ways to disseminate it clandestinely. Illiterate enslaved Blacks likely interacted with protest literature in a similar way as many unschooled enslaved Black people engaged the biblical text. Despite being forbidden from learning to read, enslaved Blacks accessed works of literature such as Walker's *Appeal* through the oral tradition.[59] They listened to literate abolitionists and free Black people read the material. Nat Turner's rebellion influenced increased scrutiny and suppression of protest literature and caused the pamphlet to be out of print for over a decade. Henry Highland Garnet and Maria Stewart recovered Walker's work and accented many of its themes in their writings in the mid-nineteenth century.[60]

Maria W. Stewart (1803–1879) was a teacher and abolitionist who called on Black women to exert their agency as women and activists. She wrote several articles for the *Liberator*, an antislavery periodical. In "Productions" (1835), she wrote, "Though

Walker sleeps, yet he lives and his name shall be had in ever-lasting remembrance."[61] In line with Walker's *Appeal*, she insisted that unity and education for Black people were the keys to overcoming enslavement and striving for civil and political rights.[62] Stewart also asserted that God would judge America for permitting the enslavement of Black people. She exclaimed:

> Oh, America, America, foul and indelible is thy stain! Dark and dismal is the cloud that hangs over thee, for thy cruel wrongs and injuries to the fallen sons of Africa. The blood of her murdered ones cries to heaven for vengeance against thee. Thou art almost become drunken with the blood of her slain; thou hast enriched thyself through her toils and labors; and now thou refuseth to make even a small return.[63]

Rather than being a moral beacon to the world or a "city upon a hill," Stewart castigated slaveholding America as being akin to the wicked ancient city of Babylon, which the Hebrew prophets predicted would fall because of sin. She criticized America for failing to respect divine law and the noble principles outlined in its Constitution. Yet, Stewart, like other Black writers who employed the jeremiad, believed that America could be spared from judgment if she repented.

Furthermore, in contrast to Walker, who believed Blacks should seize freedom by taking up arms, Stewart held that God would judge Whites. She wrote, "Then, my brethren, sheath your swords, and calm your angry passions. Stand still, and know that the Lord he is God. Vengeance is his, and he will repay."[64] Stewart's denunciation of a violent response from Black people may have helped her avoid backlash from Whites who, at the time, considered those who advocated violence as threats to the nation.[65]

Slave Rebellions

Biblical figuralism was a potent motivating factor undergirding slave plots and insurrections spearheaded by Black Christians. Besides the biblical Exodus narrative discussed at length, Black religious folks conjured the stories of biblical figures such as Samson, Joshua, and Jesus. When rebelling against the system, they saw themselves as reenacting the fights and battles of heroic biblical figures whom they studied. Furthermore, besides drawing on Scripture to justify violent rebellions, the revolt conspired by Denmark Vesey and Gullah Jack indicates that traditional West African cosmologies upon which the notion of conjure is grounded also gave some Blacks the courage and inspiration to challenge the slave system.

Motivated by Toussaint L'Ouverture's leadership of the Haitian Revolution (1791–1804) in Saint-Domingue, during which enslaved Blacks successfully defeated French and British forces and acquired independence from France, Gabriel Prosser and his brothers (Martin and Solomon) plotted the first large scale rebellion in North America in 1800. The brothers lived on the Brookfield plantation owned by Thomas Prosser, located near Richmond, Virginia.[66] At twenty-five years of age, Gabriel worked as a blacksmith. He stood about 6 feet 3 inches tall and possessed remarkable physical strength, literacy, intellectual prowess, and leadership skills.[67] He derived inspiration from Scripture, especially from the biblical figure Samson, a judge of Israel respected for his strength. In imitation of Samson, who derived strength from his long hair, Gabriel allowed his hair to grow long. He envisioned that God could use him to overcome well-armed White slaveholders with meager resources, as God gave Samson the strength to kill a thousand

Philistine soldiers with only the "jawbone of an ass" as a weapon. After defeating White slaveholders in Virginia, he hoped to emerge as the leader of independent Blacks in Virginia as General Toussaint rose as leader of Saint-Domingue (later Haiti).[68]

The plot Gabriel and his brothers devised was for enslaved Blacks to murder Virginia White enslavers, lay hold of their weapons and artillery, and loot the treasury, crippling the state of Virginia's economic base. Gabriel instructed fellow conspirators to spare antislavery Whites, including but not limited to Methodist and Quaker abolitionists. After freeing enslaved people in Richmond, Gabriel planned to negotiate the freedom of other enslaved Black people in Virginia and eventually throughout the South.[69]

Gabriel reported that he had organized an army of about ten thousand enslaved Blacks. The governor of Mississippi estimated that the numbers were as high as fifty thousand. Nearly one thousand enslaved people were at a designated place and prepared to attack on August 30. A storm arose and influenced them to postpone the insurrection. Some enslaved Blacks may have questioned if the storm was a sign from God that the rebellion should not occur. Tom and Pharaoh, two enslaved Blacks who participated in conspiracy talks, betrayed Gabriel and disclosed the plot to their owner, Mosby Sheppard. He urgently contacted the authorities, who sent the armed local militia to monitor the roads near the plantation where Gabriel lived and to defend the arsenal. Within days, the authorities began arresting conspirators. In about two weeks, roughly ten enslaved Black people received the death penalty. Nearly thirty-six enslaved Blacks who Whites believed to be associated with the conspiracy died. Gabriel temporarily evaded detection until a fellow enslaved person disclosed his location to the authorities, who arrested him on September 24, 1800. They executed him within two weeks. Following Gabriel's aborted rebellion, insurrections occurred in the early 1800s in other slave-holding states, including South Carolina, North Carolina, Georgia, Louisiana, and Mississippi. Many of the insurrections were planned and organized during religious meetings.[70]

Denmark Vesey, a Black Christian, likely met with fellow enslaved Blacks during a religious service when plotting his rebellion in South Carolina in 1822. In 1800, Vesey purchased his freedom from Captain Joseph Vesey, a slaveholder who conducted slave voyages during the Slave Trade. Denmark Vesey traveled across the world and served as Captain Vesey's assistant. After acquiring his freedom, he moved to Charleston and worked as a carpenter. Like Gabriel, Vesey was astute, learned, and possessed strong leadership traits. He was intrigued by abolitionist literature and incendiary pamphlets that arrived in Charleston from communities of free Black people. He was also a devoted student of the Bible. One of the passages that deeply inspired him was the story of the Battle of Jericho. It is a continuation of the Exodus narrative. Joshua, the successor of Moses, was responsible for leading the children of Israel to the Promised Land. Once the children of Israel crossed the Jordan, the city of Jericho was the barrier preventing them from entering the land of divine promise. Perceiving slaveholding America to be akin to Jericho, Vesey believed that God desired to use him to lead enslaved people to the Promised Land of freedom in America.[71]

Gullah Jack, an enslaved man who lived on Paul Pritchard's plantation and a member of the Gullah Society, was Vesey's close friend and co-conspirator who practiced conjure, an African-derived religious practice discussed in Chapter 1. As a conjuror, he developed a reputation as being invincible. Gullah Jack used a charm similar to Sandy Jenkins, a conjuror Frederick Douglass discussed in his autobiography. Jenkins gave Douglass a powerful root that inspired him to possess the courage to fight the slave breaker, Mr. Covey, and eventually escape his captivity. Jenkins's root was "an all-purpose charm" that "worked 'love,' physical strength, 'confidence', and protection."[72] William Wells Brown's narrative also referenced a conjurer named Dinkie who could avoid work because Whites feared his conjuring power. Dinkie warned an abusive overseer "dat if he lay his finger on him, he'd call de debble [devil] up to take him away."[73] Conjurors provided enslaved Blacks with roots that inspired them to oppose the slave system in the face of impossible odds. Marie Laveau, a well-known Voodoo Queen in New Orleans, "provided run-away slaves with charms to protect them on their journey north to liberty in Canada."[74] Roots inspired many enslaved Blacks to have confidence that they were invincible.[75]

In preparation for the insurrection, Gullah Jack told his followers to fast from all foods except for "parched corn and ground nuts," which they could eat on the day of the rebellion. He also instructed them "to keep a piece of crab claw in their mouths as protection against being harmed in the attack."[76] Though Vesey was a Christian, it is possible that he and other Christians collaborating with Jack were not outright dismissive of the power of conjure. While there were enslaved Blacks who practiced only traditional African religion or adhered to only Christianity, in the previous chapter, I discussed how many enslaved Black Christians adhered to both traditions and turned to conjure to satisfy everyday needs that Christianity left unmet.[77]

Both leaders likely worked out plans for the insurrection during religious services. Although there were some laws prohibiting religious meetings among Black people, those in authority did not tightly enforce the laws unless word or rumor spread that enslaved Blacks were contemplating and planning a rebellion. The relaxed and loose restrictions on Black religious meetings enabled Black Methodists, who had recently formed a denomination in 1816, to contribute to the planning of Vesey's revolt. The African Methodist Association disseminated information about the revolt through its Christian education program. Reverend Morris Brown, who rose to the rank of bishop in the Black Methodist Church, provided counsel to Vesey and other organizers of the rebellion.[78]

Vesey possibly recruited between three and nine thousand Black people to participate in the revolt, scheduled for Sunday, June 16, 1822. The organizers anticipated that additional enslaved Blacks and some Whites would join their ranks once the insurrection started. Leaders in Vesey's camp also asked the President of the free Republic of Haiti to support them in their struggle for liberation. Once the insurrection commenced, Vesey desired participants to spare only White allies. In line with biblical passages in the Old Testament in which God sanctioned total devastation of the property, insurrectionists were to kill all other Whites, destroy their property, and set the city ablaze.[79]

Like Gabriel's planned revolt, Vesey's rebellion was frustrated before it could materialize. William, one of the enslaved Black coconspirators, shared the plans with a house servant who revealed the plot to his White master. The authorities pressured and pushed William to disclose more precise details, including the scope and scale of the rebellion and the leaders involved. With the rebellion no longer a secret, the authorities could disperse the militia on the date of the scheduled revolt. Within weeks, authorities arrested Vesey and many of his lieutenants. Brown was forced to relocate to Philadelphia after authorities learned about the planned rebellion. Gullah Jack, the conjurer, was arrested and executed a few days later. Though most of the conspirators died as martyrs, they inspired other Blacks in South Carolina and in other slave states to resist the system—enslaved people who could not successfully rebel burned their masters' property. Many enslaved Blacks drew on conjure and used poison to resist the system.[80]

In 1831, a Baptist minister named Nat Turner organized a large-scale massive slave rebellion in Southampton, Virginia, that resulted in the deaths of 120 enslaved people and Whites. Born in 1800 to an enslaved woman named Nancy and to an unknown father, Turner was born with birthmarks that some Blacks believed to be indicative of those who possessed the gift to conjure. He emerged as a gifted child and was astute beyond his years. His grandmother was a devout member of Turner's Meeting House, a Methodist plantation church. Turner also acquired literacy and derived inspiration from reading Scripture, especially the Gospel of Luke. Turner interpreted Luke 12:31 as meaning that Jesus came to bring fire on earth instead of peace. Christians had a responsibility to disturb the slaveholding status quo. Like Jesus, Turner believed God called him to advance the kingdom through violence and taking up the sword. Rather than seeing Jesus as meek, soft, mild, and tolerant of oppression, Turner associated Christ with the fiery prophets of the Old Testament who warned wayward Israelites of God's wrath and impending judgment.[81]

Turner managed to escape plantation slavery for thirty days but decided to return to the slave plantation because he believed God wanted him to help eradicate the system of slavery. He quoted a passage from Luke 12:47, which says, "He who knows his master's will and does it not shall be beaten with many stripes, and thus I have chastened you." In his description of the rebellion in *The Southampton Insurrection* (1900), William Drewry wrongly perceived that Turner was referring to his White enslaver. It is most conceivable that Turner was referring to the will of his eternal or heavenly master. Turner believed God commissioned him to liberate his fellow enslaved Blacks and not merely secure freedom himself. Hence, he obediently returned to the plantation and accepted the divine calling.[82] After his return, Turner had a spiritual vision of "white and blacks' spirits" battling and saw tributaries of blood. A voice in the vision told him that his calling was to bear the burden of leading a rebellion and seeing blood spilled.[83]

In addition to accepting this divine calling, Turner received the call to preach and started to refer to himself as a minister after 1825. He preached to enslaved people on his nearby plantation and beyond. He continued having special revelations and mystical visions. For example, he once found blood on the ears of corn as he was working as a field hand. He interpreted this as Christ's blood "returning to earth again in the form of dew."[84] He also reported seeing odd "hieroglyphic characters on leaves in the woods" and "numbers with the forms of men in different attitudes, portrayed in blood."[85]

Turner interpreted a solar eclipse in February 1831 as a sign to move forward with the rebellion on July 4. He became sick before the scheduled date. The leaders then decided to postpone the uprising and take time to deliberate further. Turner viewed an extreme weather event as a sign from God that the time was ripe. Before the clock struck midnight, he led a group of enslaved people to the house of his master, John Travis. Using hand-to-hand combat munitions such as hatchets and axes, enslaved Blacks killed Travis and his family members. They confiscated his guns and weapons and used them to take the lives of nearly sixty Whites across the county. Turner and his followers planned to seize political control in the region and continue to gather more weapons. However, only able to obtain limited guns and ammunition, they were swiftly over-powered and were forced to retreat as more militia and law enforcement officials from a nearby county appeared. Turner hid out near Cabin Pond for several weeks. A White man eventually discovered him on October 30. He was arrested and swiftly tried and convicted. He received the death penalty. When talking with Thomas R. Gray during his confession, Turner was asked if he felt sorrowful for leading the rebellion. He responded, "Was not Christ crucified?"[86] Over one hundred enslaved people died during the uprising. Twenty Black insurrectionists were executed by hanging.[87] After the rebellion, slaveholders made Black religious gatherings illegal in several parts of the South. They tightened their restrictions on private religious meetings among enslaved people. Religion inspired Gabriel Prosser, Denmark Vesey, Gullah Jack, and Nat Turner's spiritual resistance.[88]

Enslaved Blacks who organized rebellions were not the only ones who considered violence as the necessary avenue for liberation. During the National Black Convention in 1843 in Buffalo, New York, Reverend Henry Highland Garnet, a free Presbyterian church pastor in Troy, New York, presented a radical proposal in his "Address to the Slaves of the United States of America."[89] Going against the grain of exodus theology, which typically admonished enslaved Blacks to trust that God would deliver them, he insisted that freedom would only come by enslaved Blacks taking matters into their own hands. He expressed:

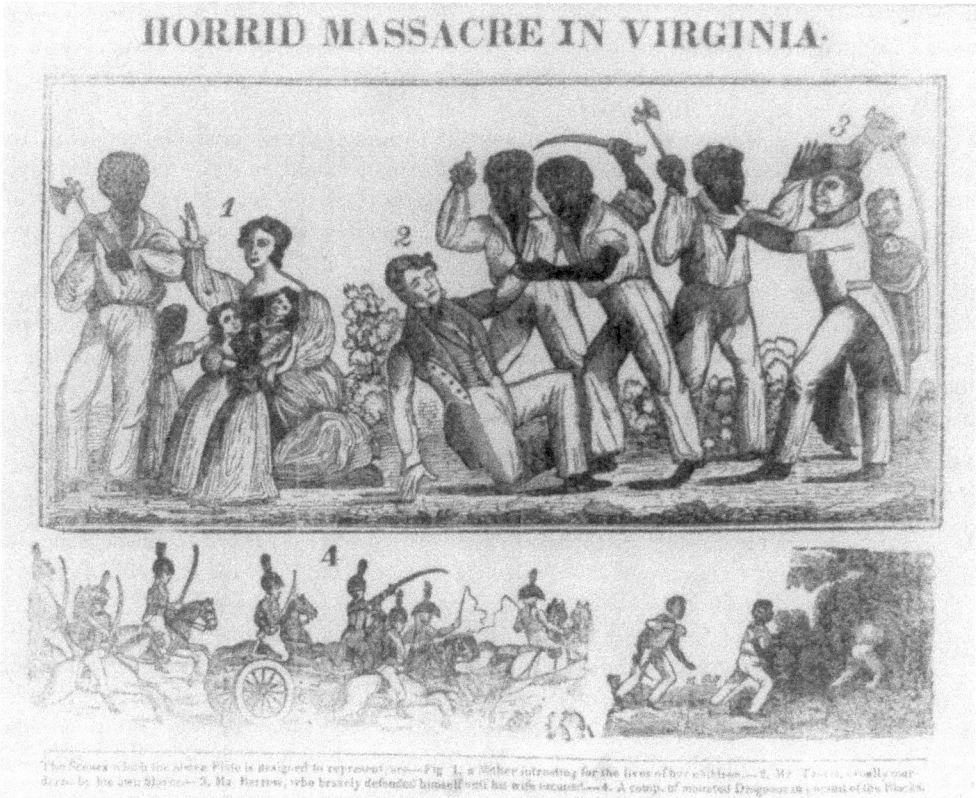

Figure 2.2 An artistic photograph depicting the horrid massacre in Virginia. Virginia South-ampton County, 1831.
Courtesy of the Library of Congress

You had far better all die—die immediately, than live slaves, and entail your wretchedness upon your posterity. If you would be free in this generation here is your only hope. However much you and all of us may desire it, there is not much hope of redemption without the shedding of blood. If you must bleed, let it all come at once, rather die freemen, than live to be the slaves. It is impossible, like the children of Israel, to make a grand exodus from the land of bondage. The Pharaohs are on both sides of the blood-red waters![90]

Reflecting on Garnet's figural interpretation of the Exodus story, Smith explains that Garnet is here striving to "break or redirect the power which the Exodus figure wields over the slaves insofar as it induces them to wait for the same providential deliverance that attended to the children of Israel."[91] Garnet held that enslaved Black people needed to be willing to take up arms and courageously confront White retaliatory violence to achieve liberation. They need not imitate Israel and wait for divine deliverance in the same fashion that the oppressed Hebrews did. His assertion that "pharaohs are on both sides of the blood-red waters!" was his manner of pinpointing the distinctiveness and complexity of Blacks' enslavement and racial oppression compared to the Israelites.[92] He understood that slavery was not merely a Southern concern. Many White Northerners were complicit in defending the institution. Indeed, the passage of the 1850 fugitive slave law, which empowered federal authorities to seize enslaved Black people who escaped to Northern states, upheld his analysis.

Frederick Douglass and other Garrisonian abolitionists considered Garnet's call for violence unfeasible. Garnet doubted that abolitionists could morally persuade slave-holding society to stop accruing economic and social benefits derived from the exploitation of Black bodies. Notably, a sizeable number of delegates found his argument tenable and accepted that enslaved Black people and their allies must be willing to put their lives on the line to abolish the institution of slavery. During the 1843 Convention, delegates barely favored Douglass's position by one vote—19 to 18.[93] Ultimately, the Civil War, the bloodiest war in the history of the United States, led to the crumbling of the slave system. Black people from the North and the South joined the Union Army to become agents of liberation.

Review and Discussion Questions

1   How does biblical figuralism accentuate the creative agency of Black religious people? What are examples of biblical figures, stories, and texts that Black people conjured during the antebellum era?
2   Why didn't Black Muslims establish independent organizations during this era? In what ways did the establishment of independent Black churches, such as the AME and AMEZ, facilitate community building and social activism among Black people?
3   What were the subtle differences between Robert Alexander Young, David Walker, and Maria Stewart's employment of the jeremiad? Which of these figures' writings did the establishment fear the most? Why might this have been so?
4   How did blending Christian and African spiritual practices influence the strategies and beliefs of rebellion organizers like Gullah Jack and Nat Turner?

Notes

1 Theophus H. Smith, *Conjuring Culture: Biblical Formations of Black America* (New York: Oxford University Press, 1994), 70.

2 Theophus H. Smith, *Conjuring Culture: Biblical Formations of Black America* (New York: Oxford University Press, 1994), 4. For additional analysis of ways African Americans have historically engaged and interpreted Scripture, see Cain Hope Felder, ed., *Stony the Road We Trod: African American Biblical Interpretation.* (Minneapolis, MN: Fortress Press, 2001).

3 Theophus H. Smith, *Conjuring Culture: Biblical Formations of Black America* (New York: Oxford University Press, 1994), 25, 68–70.

4 Richard Brent Turner, *Islam in the African-American Experience* (Bloomington, IN: Indiana University Press, 2003), 46.

5 Richard Brent Turner, *Islam in the African-American Experience* (Bloomington, IN: Indiana University Press, 2003), 25. See also Sylviane A. Diouf, *Servants of Allah: African Muslims Enslaved in the Americas.* New York: New York University Press, 1998.

6 Richard Brent Turner, *Islam in the African-American Experience* (Bloomington, IN: Indiana University Press, 2003), 38.

7 Richard Brent Turner, *Islam in the African-American Experience* (Bloomington, IN: Indiana University Press, 2003), 24, 46.

8 Richard S. Newman, *Freedom's Prophet: Bishop Richard Allen, the AME Church, and the Black Founding Fathers* (New York. New York University Press, 2009).

9 Richard S. Newman, *Freedom's Prophet: Bishop Richard Allen, the AME Church, and the Black Founding Fathers* (New York. New York University Press, 2009).

10 Richard Allen, *The Life, Experience, and Gospel Labours of the Rt. Rev. Richard Allen* (Philadelphia, Martin & Bolden, 1833), 45–47, retrieved from https://docsouth.unc.edu/neh/allen/allen.html#:~:text=Delegates%20from%20Baltimore%20and%20other,And%20proved%20himself%20a%20King.&text=That%20helpless%20church%20of%20thine,The%20God%20of%20Bethel%20heard.

11 Gayraud S. Wilmore, *Black Religion and Black Radicalism: An Interpretation of the Religious History of Afro-American People* (Maryknoll, NY: Orbis Books, 1983), 81–82; Milton C. Sernett, ed., *African American Religious History: A Documentary Witness* (Durham, NC: Duke University Press, 1999), 139.

12 Harry Van Buren Richardson, *Dark Salvation: The Story of Methodism as it Developed among Blacks in America* (Garden City, NY: Anchor Press, 1976), 7; Gayraud S. Wilmore, *Black Religion and Black Radicalism: An Interpretation of the Religious History of Afro-American People* (Maryknoll, NY: Orbis Books, 1983), 79.

13 Milton C. Sernett, ed., *African American Religious History: A Documentary Witness* (Durham, NC: Duke University Press, 1999), 155; Harry Van Buren Richardson, *Dark Salvation: The Story of Methodism as it Developed among Blacks in America* (Garden City, NY: Anchor Press, 1976), 12, 147.

14 Harry Van Buren Richardson, *Dark Salvation: The Story of Methodism as it Developed among Blacks in America* (Garden City, NY: Anchor Press, 1976), 64.

15 Albert J. Raboteau, *A Fire in the Bones: Reflections on African-American Religious History* (Boston, MA: Beacon Press, 1995), 22; Gayraud S. Wilmore, *Black Religion and Black Radicalism: An Interpretation of the Religious History of Afro-American People* (Maryknoll, NY: Orbis Books, 1983), 77; Leroy Fitts, *A History of Black Baptists* (Brentwood, TN: Broadman Press, 1985), 46.

16 Leroy Fitts, *A History of Black Baptists* (Brentwood, TN: Broadman Press, 1985), 43–67.

17 Gayraud S. Wilmore, *Black Religion and Black Radicalism: An Interpretation of the Religious History of Afro-American People* (Maryknoll, NY: Orbis Books, 1983), 89–91.

18 Harry Van Buren Richardson, *Dark Salvation: The Story of Methodism as it Developed among Blacks in America* (Garden City, NY: Anchor Press, 1976), 147–149; Gayraud S. Wilmore, *Black Religion and Black Radicalism: An Interpretation of the Religious History of Afro-American People* (Maryknoll, NY: Orbis Books, 1983), 95.

19 E. Franklin Frazier, *The Negro Church in America* (New York: Schocken Books, 1976), 14.

20 Bettye Collier-Thomas, *Daughters of Thunder: Black Women Preachers and Their Sermons, 1850–1979* (San Francisco: CA: Jossey-Bass Publishers, 1998), 22.

21 Bettye Collier-Thomas, *Daughters of Thunder: Black Women Preachers and Their Sermons, 1850–1979* (San Francisco: CA: Jossey-Bass Publishers, 1998), 44.

22 Bettye Collier-Thomas, *Daughters of Thunder: Black Women Preachers and Their Sermons, 1850–1979* (San Francisco: CA: Jossey-Bass Publishers, 1998), 45.

23 Bettye Collier-Thomas, *Daughters of Thunder: Black Women Preachers and Their Sermons, 1850–1979* (San Francisco: CA: Jossey-Bass Publishers, 1998), 19.

24 Bettye Collier-Thomas, *Daughters of Thunder: Black Women Preachers and Their Sermons, 1850–1979* (San Francisco: CA: Jossey-Bass Publishers, 1998), 20.

25 Joanna Brooks, *American Lazarus: Religion and the Rise of African-American and Native American Literatures* (New York: Oxford University Press, 2003), 118; Wilson Jeremiah Moses, ed., *Classical Black Nationalism: From the American Revolution to Marcus Garvey* (New York: New York University Press, 1996), 6.

26 Eddie S. Glaude. Jr., *Exodus!: Religion, Race, and Nation in Early Nineteenth-Century Black America* (Chicago, IL: University of Chicago Press), 10; Richard Brent Turner, *Islam in the African-American Experience* (Bloomington, IN: Indiana University Press, 2003), 48, 59.

27 Albert J. Raboteau, *A Fire in the Bones: Reflections on African-American Religious History* (Boston, MA: Beacon Press, 1995), 42; Joanna Brooks, *American Lazarus: Religion and the Rise of African-American and Native American Literatures* (New York: Oxford University Press, 2003), 118; St. Clair Drake, *The Redemption of Africa and Black Religion* (Chicago, IL: Third World, 1970).

28 Theophus H. Smith, *Conjuring Culture: Biblical Formations of Black America* (New York: Oxford University Press, 1994), 58–60.

29 Theophus H. Smith, *Conjuring Culture: Biblical Formations of Black America* (New York: Oxford University Press, 1994), 58–60.

30 Albert J. Raboteau, *A Fire in the Bones: Reflections on African-American Religious History* (Boston, MA: Beacon Press, 1995), 43.

31 Joanna Brooks, *American Lazarus: Religion and the Rise of African-American and Native American Literatures* (New York: Oxford University Press, 2003), 119.

32 Albert J. Raboteau, *A Fire in the Bones: Reflections on African-American Religious History* (Boston, MA: Beacon Press, 1995), 50.

33 Gayraud S. Wilmore, *Black Religion and Black Radicalism: An Interpretation of the Religious History of Afro-American People* (Maryknoll, NY: Orbis Books, 1983), 116–117.

34 Larry G. Murphy, J. Gordon Melton, and Gary L. Ward, eds., *Encyclopedia of African American Religions* (New York, NY: Garland Publishing, 1993), 97; Richard Brent Turner, *Islam in the African-American Experience* (Bloomington, IN: Indiana University Press, 2003), 50–57.

35 Gayraud S. Wilmore, *Black Religion and Black Radicalism: An Interpretation of the Religious History of Afro-American People* (Maryknoll, NY: Orbis Books, 1983), 111.

36 Martin Delany, *The Condition, Elevation, Emigration and Destiny of the Colored People of the United States, Politically Considered* (Philadelphia, PA: 1852), 38. Cited in Gayraud S. Wilmore, *Black Religion and Black Radicalism: An Interpretation of the Religious History of Afro-American People* (Maryknoll, NY: Orbis Books, 1983), 112–113.

37 Gayraud S. Wilmore, *Black Religion and Black Radicalism: An Interpretation of the Religious History of Afro-American People* (Maryknoll, NY: Orbis Books, 1983), 112.

38 The Civil War influenced Delany to shift his focus from building a separate nation in Africa to recruiting Black soldiers to support the Union army. After the Civil War, he served in the Freedmen's Bureau and supported the advancement of civil rights for newly freed Black people. Richard Newman, Patrick Rael, and Philip Lapsansky, eds., *Pamphlets of Protest: An Anthology of Early African-American Protest Literature, 1790–1860* (New York: Routledge: 2001), 17; Gayraud S. Wilmore, *Black Religion and Black Radicalism: An Interpretation of the Religious History of Afro-American People* (Maryknoll, NY: Orbis Books, 1983), 113.

39 Richard Newman, Patrick Rael, and Philip Lapsansky, eds., *Pamphlets of Protest: An Anthology of Early African-American Protest Literature, 1790–1860* (New York: Routledge: 2001), 2.

40 Bernard W. Bell, "President Barack Obama, the Rev. Dr. Jeremiah Wright, and the African American Jeremiadic Tradition," *The Massachusetts Review* 50, no. 3 (Autumn 2009): 337.

41 Valerie C. Cooper, *Word, Like Fire: Maria Stewart, the Bible, and the Rights of African Americans* (Charlottesville, VA: University of Virginia Press, 2012), 165.

42 Gayraud S. Wilmore, *Black Religion and Black Radicalism: An Interpretation of the Religious History of Afro-American People* (Maryknoll, NY: Orbis Books, 1983), 36.

43 Theophus H. Smith, *Conjuring Culture: Biblical Formations of Black America* (New York: Oxford University Press, 1994), 58.

44 Robert Alexander Young, *The Ethiopian Manifesto; Issued in Defence of the Black Man's Rights in the Scale of Universal Freedom* (New York: Printed for the author, 1829); Cited in Richard Newman, Patrick Rael, and Philip Lapsansky, eds., *Pamphlets of Protest: An Anthology of Early African-American Protest Literature, 1790–1860* (New York: Routledge: 2001), 88–89.

45 Gayraud S. Wilmore, *Black Religion and Black Radicalism: An Interpretation of the Religious History of Afro-American People* (Maryknoll, NY: Orbis Books, 1983), 37.

46 Thomas G. Poole, "What Country Have I? Nineteenth-Century African-American Theological Critiques of the Nation's Birth and Destiny." *The Journal of Religion* 72, no. 4 (1992): 536. www.jstor.org/stable/1204618.

47 Gayraud S. Wilmore, *Black Religion and Black Radicalism: An Interpretation of the Religious History of Afro-American People* (Maryknoll, NY: Orbis Books, 1983), 37.

48 Gayraud S. Wilmore, *Black Religion and Black Radicalism: An Interpretation of the Religious History of Afro-American People* (Maryknoll, NY: Orbis Books, 1983), 38.

49 Gayraud S. Wilmore, *Black Religion and Black Radicalism: An Interpretation of the Religious History of Afro-American People* (Maryknoll, NY: Orbis Books, 1983), 37–38.

50 Richard Newman, Patrick Rael, and Philip Lapsansky, eds., *Pamphlets of Protest: An Anthology of Early African-American Protest Literature, 1790–1860* (New York: Routledge: 2001), 84.

51 Robert Alexander Young, *The Ethiopian Manifesto; Issued in Defence of the Black Man's Rights in the Scale of Universal Freedom* (New York: Printed for the author, 1829).

52 Gayraud S. Wilmore, *Black Religion and Black Radicalism: An Interpretation of the Religious History of Afro-American People* (Maryknoll, NY: Orbis Books, 1983), 39–40.

53 Gayraud S. Wilmore, *Black Religion and Black Radicalism: An Interpretation of the Religious History of Afro-American People* (Maryknoll, NY: Orbis Books, 1983), 38–40.

54 Eddie S. Glaude. Jr., *Exodus!: Religion, Race, and Nation in Early Nineteenth-Century Black America* (Chicago, IL: University of Chicago Press), 34.

55 David Walker, *Appeal to the Coloured Citizens of the World, but in Particular, and Very Expressly, to Those of the United States of America* (New York: Hill and Wang, 1965), 13; cited in Eddie S. Glaude. Jr., *Exodus!: Religion, Race, and Nation in Early Nineteenth-Century Black America* (Chicago, IL: University of Chicago Press), 34.

56 Gayraud S. Wilmore, *Black Religion and Black Radicalism: An Interpretation of the Religious History of Afro-American People* (Maryknoll, NY: Orbis Books, 1983), 41.

57 Gayraud S. Wilmore, *Black Religion and Black Radicalism: An Interpretation of the Religious History of Afro-American People* (Maryknoll, NY: Orbis Books, 1983), 42.

58 Richard Newman, Patrick Rael, and Philip Lapsansky, eds., *Pamphlets of Protest: An Anthology of Early African-American Protest Literature, 1790–1860* (New York: Routledge: 2001), 4; Gayraud S. Wilmore, *Black Religion and Black Radicalism: An Interpretation of the Religious History of Afro-American People* (Maryknoll, NY: Orbis Books, 1983), 43.

59 Gayraud S. Wilmore, *Black Religion and Black Radicalism: An Interpretation of the Religious History of Afro-American People* (Maryknoll, NY: Orbis Books, 1983), 34–43.

60 Gayraud S. Wilmore, *Black Religion and Black Radicalism: An Interpretation of the Religious History of Afro-American People* (Maryknoll, NY: Orbis Books, 1983), 43; Richard Newman, Patrick Rael, and Philip Lapsansky, eds., *Pamphlets of Protest: An Anthology of Early African-American Protest Literature, 1790–1860* (New York: Routledge: 2001), 25, 90.

61 Richard Newman, Patrick Rael, and Philip Lapsansky, eds., *Pamphlets of Protest: An Anthology of Early African-American Protest Literature, 1790–1860* (New York: Routledge: 2001), 25.

62 Richard Newman, Patrick Rael, and Philip Lapsansky, eds., *Pamphlets of Protest: An Anthology of Early African-American Protest Literature, 1790–1860* (New York: Routledge: 2001), 15.

63 Maria W. Stewart, *Productions of Mrs. Maria W. Stewart, Presented to the First African Baptist Church & Society of the City of Boston* (Boston, MA: Friends of Freedom and Virtue, 1835), 18–19; cited in Marilyn Richardson, ed. *Maria Stewart, America's First Black Woman*

Political Writer: Essays and Speeches (Bloomington, IN: Indiana University Press, 1987), 39; Also cited in Valerie C. Cooper, *Word, Like Fire: Maria Stewart, the Bible, and the Rights of African Americans* (Charlottesville, VA: University of Virginia Press, 2012), 174.

64 Valerie C. Cooper, *Word, Like Fire: Maria Stewart, the Bible, and the Rights of African Americans* (Charlottesville, VA: University of Virginia Press, 2012), 169.

65 Valerie Cooper suggests that it is not clear whether Stewart's appraisal of "divine violence" was simply a "rhetorical" ploy to avoid placing herself at risk. Valerie C. Cooper, *Word, Like Fire: Maria Stewart, the Bible, and the Rights of African Americans* (Charlottesville, VA: University of Virginia Press, 2012), 169.

66 Gayraud S. Wilmore, *Black Religion and Black Radicalism: An Interpretation of the Religious History of Afro-American People* (Maryknoll, NY: Orbis Books, 1983), 53.

67 Susan DeFord, "Gabriel's Rebellion," *Washington Post*, February 6, 2000, retrieved from www.washingtonpost.com/archive/lifestyle/2000/02/06/gabriels-rebellion/33c9061a-e33d-4f18-b f02-fe3cd294f5df.

68 Gayraud S. Wilmore, *Black Religion and Black Radicalism: An Interpretation of the Religious History of Afro-American People* (Maryknoll, NY: Orbis Books, 1983), 54.

69 Gayraud S. Wilmore, *Black Religion and Black Radicalism: An Interpretation of the Religious History of Afro-American People* (Maryknoll, NY: Orbis Books, 1983), 54–55.

70 Gayraud S. Wilmore, *Black Religion and Black Radicalism: An Interpretation of the Religious History of Afro-American People* (Maryknoll, NY: Orbis Books, 1983), 54–55.

71 Gayraud S. Wilmore, *Black Religion and Black Radicalism: An Interpretation of the Religious History of Afro-American People* (Maryknoll, NY: Orbis Books, 1983), 57–58.

72 David H. Brown, "Conjure/Doctors: An Exploration of a Black Discourse in America, Antebellum to 1940," *Folklore Forum*, 23, no. 1/2 (1990): 14, https://hdl.handle.net/2022/2091; Frederick Douglass, *Narrative of the Life of Frederick Douglass: An American Slave* (Garden City, NY: Anchor Books, 1973, orig. 1845), 70–71.

73 William Wells Brown, *My Southern Home, or the South and Its People* (New York: n.p., 1880), 74. Cited in David H. Brown, "Conjure/Doctors: An Exploration of a Black Discourse in America, Antebellum to 1940," *Folklore Forum*, 23, no. 1/2 (1990): 12.

74 Ina J. Fandrich, *The Mysterious Voodoo Queen, Marie Laveaux: A Study of Powerful Female Leadership in Nineteenth Century New Orleans* (New York: Routledge, 2005), 163.

75 David H. Brown, "Conjure/Doctors: An Exploration of a Black Discourse in America, Antebellum to 1940," *Folklore Forum*, 23, no. 1/2 (1990): 7.

76 Gayraud S. Wilmore, *Black Religion and Black Radicalism: An Interpretation of the Religious History of Afro-American People* (Maryknoll, NY: Orbis Books, 1983), 59–60.

77 David H. Brown, "Conjure/Doctors: An Exploration of a Black Discourse in America, Antebellum to 1940," *Folklore Forum*, 23, no. 1/2 (1990): 4; Lawrence Levine, *Black Culture and Black Consciousness: Afro-American Folk Thought from Slavery to Freedom* (New York: Oxford University Press, 1977), 55–81.

78 Gayraud S. Wilmore, *Black Religion and Black Radicalism: An Interpretation of the Religious History of Afro-American People* (Maryknoll, NY: Orbis Books, 1983), 59–61.

79 Gayraud S. Wilmore, *Black Religion and Black Radicalism: An Interpretation of the Religious History of Afro-American People* (Maryknoll, NY: Orbis Books, 1983), 60–61.

80 Gayraud S. Wilmore, *Black Religion and Black Radicalism: An Interpretation of the Religious History of Afro-American People* (Maryknoll, NY: Orbis Books, 1983), 61–62.

81 Gayraud S. Wilmore, *Black Religion and Black Radicalism: An Interpretation of the Religious History of Afro-American People* (Maryknoll, NY: Orbis Books, 1983), 62–65.

82 Gayraud S. Wilmore, *Black Religion and Black Radicalism: An Interpretation of the Religious History of Afro-American People* (Maryknoll, NY: Orbis Books, 1983), 66.

83 Gayraud S. Wilmore, *Black Religion and Black Radicalism: An Interpretation of the Religious History of Afro-American People* (Maryknoll, NY: Orbis Books, 1983), 65–67.

84 Gayraud S. Wilmore, *Black Religion and Black Radicalism: An Interpretation of the Religious History of Afro-American People* (Maryknoll, NY: Orbis Books, 1983), 67.

85 Gayraud S. Wilmore, *Black Religion and Black Radicalism: An Interpretation of the Religious History of Afro-American People* (Maryknoll, NY: Orbis Books, 1983), 67–68.

86 Gayraud S. Wilmore, *Black Religion and Black Radicalism: An Interpretation of the Religious History of Afro-American People* (Maryknoll, NY: Orbis Books, 1983), 68–71.

87 Gayraud S. Wilmore, *Black Religion and Black Radicalism: An Interpretation of the Religious History of Afro-American People* (Maryknoll, NY: Orbis Books, 1983), 71.

88 Henry Louis Gates, Jr., "Did African-American Slaves Rebel?," PBS, www.pbs.org/wnet/africa n-americans-many-rivers-to-cross/history/did-african-american-slaves-rebel/

89 Black Convention meetings took place from 1831 to 1864. During these meetings, Black people debated various proposals for striving for liberation. Black Christians from different denominations (Methodists, Baptists, and Presbyterians) were delegates alongside Black abolitionists, writers, editors, and business professionals. Glaude discusses the Black Convention Meetings at length in *Exodus!: Religion, Race, and Nation in Early Nineteenth-Century Black America* (Chicago, IL: University of Chicago Press).

90 Eddie S. Glaude. Jr., *Exodus!: Religion, Race, and Nation in Early Nineteenth-Century Black America* (Chicago, IL: University of Chicago Press), 156.

91 Theophus H. Smith, *Conjuring Culture: Biblical Formations of Black America* (New York: Oxford University Press, 1994), 61.

92 Theophus H. Smith, *Conjuring Culture: Biblical Formations of Black America* (New York: Oxford University Press, 1994), 61–62.

93 Eddie S. Glaude. Jr., *Exodus!: Religion, Race, and Nation in Early Nineteenth-Century Black America* (Chicago, IL: University of Chicago Press), 158–159.

Further Readings

Callahan, Allen Dwight. *The Talking Book: African Americans and the Bible.* New Haven, CT: Yale University Press, 2008.

Cooper, J. Valerie. *Word, Like Fire: Maria Stewart, the Bible, and the Rights of African Americans.* Charlottesville, VA: University of Virginia Press, 2011.

Felder, Cain Hope, ed. *Stony the Road We Trod: African American Biblical Interpretation.* Minneapolis, MN: Fortress Press, 2001.

Glaude, Eddie S. *Exodus!: Religion, Race, and Nation in Early Nineteenth-Century Black America.* Chicago, IL: University of Chicago Press, 2000.

Greenberg, Kenneth S. *Nat Turner: A Slave Rebellion in History and Memory.* New York: Oxford University Press, 2004.

Howard-Pitney, David. *African American Jeremiad: Appeals for Justice in America.* Philadelphia, PA: Temple University Press, 2005.

Moses, Wilson J., ed. *Classical Black Nationalism: From the American Revolution to Marcus Garvey.* New York: New York University Press, 1996.

Newman, Richard S. *Freedom's Prophet: Bishop Richard Allen, the AME Church, and the Black Founding Fathers.* New York. New York University Press, 2009.

Pitts, Walter F. *Old Ship of Zion: The Afro-Baptist Ritual in the African Diaspora.* New York: Oxford University Press, 1993.

Smith, Theophus H. *Conjuring Culture: Biblical Formations of Black America.* New York: Oxford University Press, 1994.

Walker, David. *Appeal to the Coloured Citizens of the World, but in Particular, and Very Expressly, to Those of the United States of America.* New York: Hill and Wang, 1965. Originally published in 1829.

Young, Robert Alexander, *The Ethiopian Manifesto; Issued in Defence of the Black Man's Rights in the Scale of Universal Freedom.* New York: printed for the author, 1829.

3   "The Color Line Was Washed Away in the Blood"

Spiritual Strivings between Reconstruction and World War I

> It seemed that everyone had to go to "Azusa." … There were far more white people than colored coming. The "color line" was washed away in the blood … The Spirit is laboring for the unity of believers today, for the one body, that the prayer of Jesus may be answered, "that they all may be one, that the world may believe."
>
> Frank Bartleman, *How Pentecost Came to Los Angeles*, 1925

The Civil War ended in April 1865 after General Robert E. Lee and the Confederate Army finally surrendered at the Appomattox Court House in Virginia. During the Reconstruction era (1865–1877), which began soon after Lee's surrender and lasted for over a decade, political leaders grappled with how to help recently freed enslaved Black people secure civil rights and to reintegrate the former Confederate southern states back into the Union. The 13th, 14th, and 15th amendments to the United States Constitution and the Civil Rights Act of 1875 were notable constitutional and legislative victories that propelled civil rights for Black people. Yet, these Reconstruction amendments were not favored by Southern White Democrats, known as Redeemers, who strove to regain political power in the South and to re-establish pre-Civil War racist systems. In Mississippi, White Southerners employed violence or the threat thereof to discourage and dissuade recently enfranchised Black men from exercising their voting rights. The close presidential race of 1876 between the Democrat Samuel B. Tilden and the Republican Rutherford B. Hayes gave White southerners the prime opportunity to halt Republicans' Reconstruction efforts. Southern Democrats proposed to grant the Republican candidate victory only if the Republicans agreed to withdraw the remaining federal troops from the Southern states and allow Southern state governments freedom and autonomy. Republicans' acceptance of this bargain, referred to as the Compromise of 1877, helped spur the end of the Reconstruction era in the South. In addition, Supreme Court rulings also contributed to and confirmed the end of Reconstruction. For example, the Supreme Court ruled in 1883 that the 1875 Civil Rights Act was unconstitutional. In the 1896 *Plessy vs. Ferguson* ruling, the Supreme Court essentially sanctioned racial segregation in the South by arguing that separate but equal facilities were constitutional.

The end of Reconstruction set the stage for the emergence of the Jim Crow era (1870s to 1960s), a period marked by legally sanctioned segregation in the South, brutal racial violence, and the suppression of Black people's civil and political rights. Black people had to persist in striving for social justice as the period of Reconstruction ended too soon, and the Jim Crow era began. The majority of Black Christians continued to favor moral suasion and respectability politics. Black Baptists stressed that Black people should develop educational and economic initiatives to uplift the Black race. Black

DOI: 10.4324/9781003359197-4

Holiness-Pentecostalism also emerged as a significant religious tradition alongside the Baptist and Methodist faiths. Although some early scholars overlooked the socio-political thrust of this religious tradition, the movement endeavored to advance social change by stressing the power of holiness and spiritual experience for racial reconciliation and unity in the Christian community amid the rise of Jim Crow. The interracial Pentecostal movement did not endure long. The color line resurfaced, and American Pentecostal churches came to mirror the larger American society. During this time, Black church women also struggled for increased autonomy and agency in Baptist, Methodist, and Holiness-Pentecostal denominations.

Black Churches During Reconstruction

Despite the freedom and rights newly freed Black Americans gained during Reconstruction, most were still economically impoverished. Though some Black people received free land due to General William Tecumseh Sherman's Special Field Order No. 15, the Johnson administration seized the land and restored the titles to former Confederate owners. This disappointed many free Blacks hoping for economic security and independence through agricultural work. Numerous recently freed enslaved Black people worked as sharecroppers or tenant farmers and were perpetually in debt as White merchants charged them excessive interest rates and rents. Black ministers encouraged Black people to remain optimistic amid economic struggles. James C. Embry, an AME minister from Bowling Green, Kentucky, praised Black folks in his community for persevering against the odds and obtaining property despite "the tightness of the class of whites they have to deal with."[1] To seek better opportunities many recently freed Black people moved from rural areas to cities. Black farm laborers struggled to find jobs in cities. In an editorial entitled "Advice from the Editors of This Paper to the Many Freedmen throughout the South," Elisha Weaver, an editor for the *AME Christian Recorder*, advised freedmen that they would be better off remaining in rural areas and maintaining their positions as sharecroppers and tenant farmers.[2]

Besides leaving the plantations, numerous formerly enslaved people withdrew from biracial churches because they desired autonomy and did not want to be treated as inferiors. Former slave plantation ministers established churches such as the Sixth Mount Zion Church in Richmond, Virginia, founded by John Jasper. Black churches of various denominations bourgeoned throughout the South after the Civil War. Freedom also afforded Black Baptists the opportunity to consolidate their influence through forming associations such as the Shiloh Association, a small association among seven Baptist churches in Richmond, Virginia, Gray's Association, the Eastern Missionary Baptist Association, the Middle District Association, the Zion Association, and several Baptist state conventions in the South. Black Baptists organized the National Baptist Convention in 1880 and the American National Baptist Convention in 1886.[3]

Black Methodist churches also grew in the South after the Civil War. Numerous Black Methodists left biracial Methodist churches and joined the AME, increasing the denomination's membership by more than fifty thousand by 1866. Membership in the South Carolina Conference of the AME more than doubled between 1866 and 1867. In 1866, there were 22,388 members. By 1867, there were 47,891 members. The AME Zion church also formed several annual conferences in the Southern states, including conferences in Louisiana, Alabama, Georgia, Florida, Texas, North Carolina, and Kentucky between 1865 and 1870.[4] Southern Black Methodists, William H. Miles, Richard H.

Vanderhost, Lucius H. Holsey, and Isaac Lane, founded a third Black Methodist denomination named the Colored Methodist Episcopal Church (CME) in 1870.[5]

Black people leaned heavily on Black churches for support and relief during Reconstruction. They could not depend entirely on the Bureau of Refugees, Freedmen, and Abandoned Lands, also known as the Freedmen's Bureau. Because the organization extended support to impoverished Southern Whites, it was limited in the aid it offered recently freed Black people. Hence, Black churches, especially Black churchwomen, were at the forefront of many social service programs and relief initiatives during Reconstruction. Many of the schools for freed people were associated with Black churches. Black teachers were often church members. The churches funded schoolbooks and supplies.[6]

Black ministers and churches were also deeply involved in Reconstruction politics. A White Georgian observed that Black ministers often preached political sermons. One Black minister admitted that the church had become so politicized that "revival or religious work for a while began to wane."[7] Black ministers attended Freedmen's Conventions and participated in state constitutional conventions in 1867 and 1868. Some ministers were even elected to seats in the state legislatures. For instance, Charles H. Pearce, a former missionary in the AME Church and a formerly enslaved person, was elected to the Senate in Florida, serving from 1868 to 1872.[8] Reverend Henry M. Turner won a seat in the state legislature in Georgia in 1868. He initially catered to the interests of White Southerners and backed proposals to protect "the rights of property owners" while supporting efforts to ensure that only qualified voters participated in the democratic process.[9] He even endorsed requiring voters to pay a poll tax and pass a literacy test to demonstrate their competency to vote. Turner eventually changed course and began to use his political power to advance the interests of Black people. For instance, he supported legislation advocating for government protection against physical violence and employment discrimination for Blacks. He also endorsed a bill that increased funding for public education programs for Black students. In 1870, he was among a group of Black politicians in Georgia whom White political leaders banished from the legislature. After expulsion, Turner embraced Black radicalism and became a strong proponent of Black nationalism.[10]

As Turner became radicalized during the 1870s, racial justice became less of a primary concern among federal politicians.[11] Although Radical Republicans advanced significant civil rights legislation during Reconstruction, they started to focus on other priorities and placed the goal of establishing a racially inclusive society on the back burner. Indeed, Blacks had received some political rights. Yet, the end of Reconstruction caused many of these rights to be compromised.

Once federal troops left the South and white supremacists stripped many Southern Blacks of political power, Black churches struggled to respond. Many Black ministerial politicians renewed their focus on religious work instead of politics. A minority of Black ministers turned toward Black nationalism during the end of Reconstruction. Although the church "embodied many of the basic ingredients of a nationalist movement," there were not enough Black nationalist Christians to persuade Black churches to adopt Black nationalism.[12] Henry M. Turner and Henry Highland Garnet were "a minority" among Black Christian ministers.

During the late nineteenth century, the more popular approach among Blacks was conservative moral suasion and respectability politics. Black Baptists stressed that Black people should develop educational and economic initiatives to uplift the Black race. Resisting White paternalism, they held that Black people should teach and train each other on how to carry and conduct themselves in a dignified manner to become fully included in American society. Black Baptists advocated for Black teachers in White schools and pushed for the establishment of independent Black schools and colleges.[13]

Many Black Baptist women who embraced respectability politics also advocated for social justice through protest measures such as signing petitions and participating in boycotts.[14] Black Baptist women opposed lynching when racial violence against Black people reached its highest point in American history during the nadir of race relations. They supported Black women activists such as Ida B. Wells and Anna Julia Cooper. Wells was an investigative journalist, a founding member of the NAACP, a women's rights advocate, and a leading activist against lynching in the South. Her works such as *Southern Horrors: Lynch Law in All its Phases* and *The Red Record* exposed and interrogated the roots of racial violence against Blacks. Cooper was a prominent educator and a pioneering Black feminist during the nineteenth century. Her first book, *A Voice from the South* (1892), stressed the value of Black women's voices, perspectives, and insights:

> The colored woman of to-day occupies, one may say, a unique position in this country. In a period of itself transitional and unsettled, her status seems one of the least ascertainable and definitive of all the forces which make for our civilization. She is confronted by both a woman question and a race problem, and is as yet an unknown or an unacknowledged factor in both.[15]

Cooper articulated Black women's experience with both sexism and racism in society. Black church women experienced resistance and discrimination from Black men on account of their sex within Black religious spaces and White women on account of their race within American society at large.

Inspired by Cooper and other women's rights movement activists who typified the "new woman" era because they demanded suffrage, equality, and more independence, Black church women pushed for more autonomy and control in the church during the late nineteenth century.[16] Black Baptist women formed the Women's Convention, an auxiliary of the NBC. Higginbotham explains, "Black women found themselves in the unique position of being at one separated and allied with Black men in the struggle for racial advancement while separated and allied with white women in the struggle for gender equality."[17] Mary Cook and Lucy Wilmot Smith, two women leaders in the convention, insisted that God ordained women to help men and not to be subservient to them.[18] Founded in 1900, the Women's Convention (WC) enabled Black Baptist women to have enhanced agency and influence in the denomination. Nannie Helen Burroughs was the "genius" behind the WC. During the inaugural meeting, she delivered a speech in Richmond, Virginia, entitled "How the Sisters are Hindered from Helping."[19] She expressed "righteous discontent" regarding the inequality Black Baptist women experienced in church.[20] She led the WC from 1900 until 1961. Sessions of the WC occurred concurrently with the NBC each year.

Black church women continued the long struggle to access the pulpit as preachers and ordained elders. The three dominant Baptist denominations—NBC USA, Inc., NBC of America Unincorporated, and PNBC—have deferred to local congregations and "have not taken a formal position on the issue of ordination."[21] Local Black Baptist churches have tended to be "conservative" and resistant to ordaining women in ministry.[22] Black male ministers appealed to scriptures such as 1 Peter 3:7 and 1 Corinthians 14:34 and to

Figure 3.1 Nine African-American women posed, standing, full length, with Nannie Burroughs
        holding banner reading, "Banner State Woman's National Baptist Convention."
Courtesy Library of Congress Prints and Photographs Division Washington, DC

traditional gender Victorian norms and customs of the period to argue against the
ordination of women as elders. Many nineteenth-century Blacks upheld the cult of
domesticity. They perceived that women's proper sphere in society was at home and
that men should be providers and leaders in public institutions.

   None of the Black denominations ordained women until the latter part of the twentieth century. The AME Zion ordained Julia A.J. Foote as a deacon in 1895 and Mary
Small as an elder in 1898. Small's ordination sparked debate within her denomination.
Still, Foote and Small's ordinations opened pathways for more women to be ordained in
the AME Zion. The AME General Conference of 1884 resolved women could be
licensed but not ordained. The AME North Carolina Annual Conference ordained Sarah
Ann Hughes as a deacon and took away her ordination two years later following
objections among male clergy. Legislation supporting women's ordination in the AME
was not passed until 1948, following much activism among AME church women.[23] The
CME denomination was rather unsupportive of women in ministry during the nineteenth century. Ida E. Roberts and Georgia A. Mill were ordained in 1915 in Charlotte,
North Carolina. Besides them, no other CME women were ordained into the ministry
until 1943.

The Emergence of Black Holiness-Pentecostalism

Though the Black Holiness Movement emerged in the 1870s, especially in the Midsouth region of the country, states such as Kentucky, Mississippi, Tennessee, and Arkansas, the roots of the holiness extend to the seventeenth century. John Wesley, the founder of Methodism, was an early pioneer of holiness, the teaching that God wills Christians to live free from sin and to experience Christian perfection. His teaching spread to other Methodists such as Timothy Merritt and Phoebe Palmer and was strongly advocated by the Presbyterian minister, Charles. G. Finney, during the Second Great Awakening in the early nineteenth century. Holiness teachers began to teach that sanctification was an additional experience, a second blessing or a second experience of divine grace, that believers should seek after receiving salvation. During sanctification, the believer is washed of original sin and empowered to live free of sin.

Amanda Berry Smith (1837–1915) was a Black Holiness minister who contributed to advancing the Holiness movement among Black and White people throughout the globe. She was reared in slavery in Long Green, Maryland, and received her freedom just before the start of the Civil War. She converted to Christianity in 1856 after her first marriage to Calvin Devine, who died when fighting in combat in the Civil War. She experienced sanctification after hearing a stirring sermon about the second blessing from Reverend John S. Inskip. She says, "I felt so wonderfully strange, yet I felt glorious ... I felt the touch of God from the crown of my head to the soles of my feet, and the welling up came, and I felt I must shout."[24] After this experience, Smith says that the Spirit clarified to her the meaning of Galatians 3:28, which states, "There is neither Jew nor Greek, there is neither bond nor free, there is neither male nor female, for ye are all one in Christ Jesus."[25] She wrote, "And as I looked at white people that I had always seemed to be afraid of, now they looked so small. The great mountain had become a molehill."[26] After her experience of sanctification, she said that she was freed from her fear of White people. She started to minister to White Christians increasingly. She preached "more often at white revival meetings than among black colleagues."[27]

Besides preaching to Blacks and Whites in the United States, Smith shared the gospel and holiness teachings in other countries, including ministering to congregations in England, Ireland, Scotland, and India. She was a missionary and elementary teacher in Liberia and Sierra Leone from 1881–1889.[28] When she returned to the United States in 1890, she completed her autobiography, published in 1893.[29] Her autobiography details her spiritual experience and is a rich repository of her ingenious theological mind as a Black woman in the holiness tradition at the turn of the nineteenth century. Her book helped advance holiness doctrines across racial and denominational lines.

Charles H. Mason's reading of Smith's *Autobiography* moved him to affirm sanctification in his personal life and preaching. During a revival meeting in Preston, Arkansas, he told persons attending the meeting that "sin was destroying them, their churches, and all that they possessed" and that "sin was the cause of all their sickness and disease."[30] While pastoring a church in Jackson, Mississippi, Mason befriended a local Baptist leader, Charles Price Jones. The two men organized Holiness meetings among Baptist members in Mississippi in 1896. After Baptist association leaders excommunicated Mason and Jones from the Baptist fellowship for preaching holiness during Baptist meetings, Mason, Jones, J.A. Jeter, W.S. Pleasant, and others established the Church of God in Christ as a holiness church committed to sanctification in 1897.[31]

Black Holiness Christians' emphasis on Christian perfectionism and living a holy life should not be lumped into the accommodationist politics advanced by Booker T.

Washington, which encouraged Blacks to accept segregation in the short term and prioritize Black economic self-improvement and vocational education as a means to achieve social progress. Though sanctified Christians committed to living according to Christian ethical standards, their aim was not simply to accommodate middle-class White America. According to ethicist Cheryl Sanders, Black holiness Christians viewed themselves as exiles in the "North American Babylon" and understood themselves as "in the world, but not of it."[32] They were adamant that sanctified persons must not compromise their moral standards nor "their peculiar liturgies of song, speech, and dance."[33] Like early Black Muslims who preserved their Muslim faith and names, sanctified Christians were intent on maintaining and preserving their folk religious identity by not assimilating into bourgeois Christian America at the beginning of the twentieth century. Wrongly classifying Black Holiness Christians as accommodationist overlooks their unique response to social injustice.

Race and Black Pentecostalism

The 1906 Azusa Street revival attracted people of various nationalities to Los Angeles, California, to experience spiritual baptism. Black Pentecostalism spread nationwide and gained traction globally. Though Charles Parham became the pioneer of the Pentecostal doctrine of initial evidence based on Acts 2, which posits that speaking in tongues is evidence of receiving the gift of the Holy Spirit, William H. Seymour was also a critical influencer in the global Pentecostal Movement. Parham introduced Seymour to Pentecostal doctrine while Seymour was his student at a small Bible School in Houston, Texas. However, Seymour did not experience Spirit baptism until he attended a small Bible and prayer group meeting at the home of Richard and Ruth Asberry at 214 Bonnie Brae St. in Los Angeles. After growing frustrated with not receiving spiritual baptism following intense prayer and meditation, Seymour sent a letter to Parham requesting help. Parham responded by sending Lucy Farrow and Joseph Warren from Houston to Los Angeles to aid Seymour. When they arrived, they joined the prayer meeting and laid hands on the persons assembled. Soon, the Pentecostal outpouring happened, and attendees at the prayer meeting, including Seymour, received the Holy Spirit with the gift of tongues.[34] Afterwards, the revival at Bonnie Brae St. began to burgeon, and the house could not accommodate the considerable numbers of visitors from diverse racial and ethnic groups, including Blacks, Hispanics, and Whites. The intense foot stomping and ecstatic dancing compromised the wooden porch, causing it to buckle and fold under the pressure.[35] Seymour and other leaders found a more accommodating place for worship to be an abandoned, dilapidated Methodist church at 312 Azusa Street that had incurred some damages from a small fire. After purchasing and renovating the building, Seymour and other volunteers opened their mission and formerly incorporated it as "the Azusa Street Apostolic Faith Mission of Los Angeles."[36]

Similar to the antebellum era's First and Second Awakening revivals, the Azusa revival was racially diverse. A *Los Angeles Daily Times* reporter described the demographics of the congregation and the scene at Azusa:

> Colored people and a sprinkling of whites compose the congregation, and night is made hideous in the neighborhood by the howling of the worshipers, who spend hours swaying forth and back in a nerve-racking attitude of prayer and supplication.[37]

The attendees were rekindling the spirit of the upper room discussed in Acts. They were aggressively tarrying and seeking to experience the baptism of the Holy Spirit. The Los Angeles Azusa revival became the launch pad of the Pentecostal movement.[38]

Many attendees read reports about the revival in *The Apostolic Faith*, a newspaper established by Clara Lum (a White member) and Seymour. Upon reading reports people traveled to Los Angeles from distant states to seek to experience the third blessing, divine healing, and unity in the Spirit that transcended race, gender, and class. Seymour and his ministerial coworkers welcomed all. They fostered an egalitarian and interracial atmosphere, stating, "God makes no difference in nationality; Ethiopians, Chinese, Indians, Mexicans, and other nationalities worship together."[39] The interracial dynamics of the revival influenced some to perceive that the spiritual baptism at Azusa not only resulted in persons speaking in tongues but also cleansed believers of racial bigotry and particularly enabled Blacks and Whites in Jim Crow America to worship together in genuine Christian fellowship. Frank Bartleman, a White Pentecostal who attended the Azusa Street Mission, asserted that the color line "was being washed away in the blood."[40]

Worshippers at Azusa also accepted Black folk religious practices that some Christians considered to be unrespectable, uncivilized, and unchristian derivatives of African religion. When Parham accepted Seymour's invitation to attend the revival, he denounced the "heathenish" expressions of worship he witnessed. He asserted that the religious fervor of Blacks and Whites present was a "freak imitation of Pentecost."[41] He castigated Azusa worship as "animalistic" and unchristian and categorized worshippers' glossolalia as "jabbering, not a tongue at all."[42] Upon seeing persons dancing uncontrollably, yelling, and frantically screaming, Parham concluded that many of the revival participants were seers or were possessed by demonic spirits, not the Holy Spirit. Parham insisted that the Holy Spirit does not cause a person to shake violently, to become exhausted from physical movement, and to become tired from praying in tongues. The truth of the matter is that Azusa reflected the folk religion of enslaved Black

Figure 3.2 Interracial members of the Azusa Street Mission, 1907 (Los Angeles, CA). Photographer unknown.
Courtesy of the Flower Pentecostal Heritage Center

people, which some White and Black mainline Christians disparaged as "heathenish" remnants from Africa. Attendees syncretized West African communal religion with holiness polity through singing spirituals and congregational praise and worship songs without accompanying hymnals, through using material objects for healing purposes such as anointing oil and prayer cloths, and through openness to spiritual possession.[43]

Leaders of the holiness Church of God in Christ, including C.H. Mason, J.A. Jeter, and D.J. Young, received news of the Azusa revival and trek to Los Angeles in 1907 to seek spiritual baptism. Mason provided a vivid description of his experience of the third blessing with the evidence of tongues: "When I opened my mouth to say glory, a flame touched my tongue, which ran down in me. My language changed and no word could I speak in my own tongue. Oh, I was filled with the glory of the Lord."[44] Mason's embrace of Pentecostalism caused a fissure between him and Jones, who did not accept the Pentecostal doctrine of initial evidence. Mason invited ministers who believed in Pentecostal doctrines to a conference in Memphis, Tennessee. The leaders decided to organize COGIC as a Pentecostal denomination, albeit they maintained their commitment to holiness teachings.

Mason became the most influential Black Pentecostal leader who attended the Azusa Street Revival. Of all the denominations that trace their roots to Azusa, the Church of God in Christ (COGIC) grew to become the largest, with more than six million members in the twenty-first century. Mason's organizational acumen and capacity to share authority and develop and empower new church leaders enabled COGIC to grow tremendously. While serving as the Senior Bishop and Chief Apostle of the denomination, Mason developed an episcopal polity and hierarchy that consisted of an intricate network of state bishops, superintendents, local pastors, ordained elders, and licensed ministers. Jurisdictional state bishops supervised matters in their respective states, including judging which ministerial candidates met the criteria for ordination, appointing elders to serve as pastors, as well as coordinating with state mothers who led women's departments and governed the licensing of women evangelists, missionaries, and church mothers.

As leader of COGIC, Mason imbibed the radical interracial ethos of Azusa.[45] For a few decades, COGIC had a significant number of White pastors and congregations. Since COGIC was the only incorporated Pentecostal denomination within the Pentecostal Movement, he was the only bishop who could ordain Pentecostal ministers and provide them with legitimate certificates of ordination that gave ministers the legal authority to perform marriages, funerals, and other Christian ceremonies; in addition, the certificates enabled ministers to receive discounts for railroad travel. In contrast to White Methodist bishops, who were reluctant to ordain Black ministers, Mason ordained more than 350 White ministers. There were several White COGIC churches between 1909 and 1913.[46] Mason declared in *A Brief Historical and Doctrinal Statement,* "The Church of God in Christ recognizes that all believers are one in Christ and all its members have equal rights. Its overseers, both colored and white, have equal power and authority in the church."[47]

Although several Whites associated with Mason and were ordained by him, Whites separated from the COGIC and established a new majority White denomination, the Assemblies of God, in 1914 in Hot Springs, Arkansas. In contrast to the Methodist story in which Black Methodists left White churches due to racial discrimination, numerous Whites departed the COGIC primarily to worship with people of their race and because of their prejudice against serving under a Black bishop. Some historians assert that

Durham's finished work doctrine was a driving wedge for the relationship. Many White Pentecostals came to perceive Mason's third blessing teaching to be in error and separated for theological reasons. However, Pentecostal scholars suspect that race was a central factor. Though White Pentecostals admired and respected Mason's ministry and welcomed him to preach at their churches, they still harbored racial biases and desired power and control. White Pentecostal leaders who organized the convocation to form the AOG extended invitations primarily and nearly exclusively to Whites. Whereas Mason ordained numerous White Pentecostal leaders, the AOG accommodated Southern mores and only ordained a few Black elders and pastors.[48]

Though many White Pentecostals left the COGIC and joined the AOG, some remained affiliated with the church. There were predominantly White congregations in Tennessee, Kentucky, California, Nevada, Washington, Oregon, Utah, Arizona, New Mexico, and Texas.[49] James Delk and William Holt were White pastors who maintained ties to COGIC and led congregations for several years. Delk mentioned an occasion when one of his White friends disparaged Black folks, telling him, "I love a negro in his place." Delk sarcastically asked him: "Do you love a white man out of his place?", and he further insisted: "Whenever we get Jesus in our hearts, nick-naming people and hating people, segregation and Jim Crow vanish away like the smoke of the hour."[50] Holt served as an aid to Mason, as the supervisor to the "Spanish mission in California," and as the denomination's first General Secretary.[51] Holt was arrested with Mason and spent time in jail in Paris, Texas, in 1918 after the Bureau of Investigation (BI), which today is known as the Federal Bureau of Investigation, accused Mason and other COGIC leaders of espionage and of seeking to dissuade Black people from dodging the draft during World War I. The BI suspected that Mason held similar sentiments as Marcus Garvey, who condemned World War I as the White man's war. Mason's open violation of segregation customs also aroused the BI's suspicion.

Though interracialism persisted in the COGIC years after the formation of the AOG and Whites served in high-ranking positions, COGIC gradually became a majority Black denomination. In 1933, Holt had a dispute with fellow Black leaders in the denomination, forcing him and the denomination to agree to part ways.[52] After Holt's departure, entire White congregations in the denomination diminished, and COGIC became quintessentially Black with a sprinkling of White members.

Class and Black Pentecostalism

Besides upholding the interracial spirit of early Pentecostalism, Mason affirmed the folk religion of enslaved Blacks that he witnessed from his mother, who was a formerly enslaved person. For example, he embraced the holy dance, a bodily expression of praise and worship that is generally unrehearsed and improvisational. During the dance, members experience an emotional breakthrough or comforting spiritual release of tension and energy. Vera Boykin, a COGIC woman evangelist who attended Kennerly Temple in St. Louis, Missouri, received much ridicule from her contemporaries for performing sacred dances. Instead of joining the chorus of those who condemned her for dancing, Mason performed the holy dance with her. COGIC stressed that holy dancing is biblically grounded, noting that David danced before God (2 Sam. 2:16).[53] The holy dance is typically performed in a sanctified church with music. In line with West African cultures, which integrated dance with music, sanctified Christians innovatively brought musical instruments into the folk church, including tambourines, guitars, and the keyboard. COGIC meetings resounded with spirited expression, dancing, and engaging rhythmic music. COGIC members contested class snobbishness by openly celebrating the "beauty" of Blackness and not kowtowing to "White interpretations" of Black religious culture.[54] This likely contributed to the denomination's growth among working-class Black folks.

In addition to embracing many folk religious expressions connected to West African traditions, Black Pentecostals have exhibited an affinity with the conjuring tradition discussed in Chapter 1. According to religious scholar Yvonne Chireau, "Pentecostal belief revolved around invisible forces, beings, and powers in the spiritual realm." Like conjurers, Pentecostals interpreted "unusual" occurrences in the physical world with a spiritual lens.[55] Mason possessed oddly shaped objects, including roots, branches, and vegetables, that he viewed as "sources of spiritual revelations" and signs of God's "strangeness" and wonder.[56] During the early nineteenth and twentieth centuries, many conjurors believed that material items were magical and could be utilized for healing.[57] Mason collected unusual artifacts. He used them to share spiritual revelations and invite members to reflect on God's wondrous works in nature and their lives. COGIC secretary C.G. Brown explained: "When scriptural texts seem to fail, and audiences seem to tire of the monotony of sermons, the Spirit directs Elder Mason's mind to a sign. God's mystery comes out of it as he turns it over and from side."[58] Because of Mason's use of objects in worship and the numerous persons who testified of being healed during his ministry, some accused him of being a conjuror.[59] Unlike some Black people who vacillated between Christianity and conjure, Mason was not a conjuror. He was a Christian leader who held that the Scriptures validated healing and spiritual experience. Yet, his mystical employment of material objects is comparable to conjurors.

Gender and Black Pentecostalism

Besides men such as Seymour and Mason, Black women also contributed to the development and growth of the Pentecostal movement. Black women Pentecostal pioneers, who came from the working class ranks and often served as domestics, such as Lucy Farrow, Neely Terry, and Jenny Evans Moore Seymour, also factored prominently in the Azusa Street Revival narrative. They helped birth the Azusa revival and were co-leaders of the Movement. They led altar prayers and preached the Word.[60] Farrow introduced Seymour to Parham and traveled to California to help initiate the revival. Terry informed Seymour about the opportunity to co-pastor a church in Los Angeles. Seymour's wife, Jenny Evans Moore Seymour, was a co-pastor at Azusa. Upon his death in 1922, she led the congregation for nearly a decade. It is hard to imagine that the Azusa revival would have spread as far and wide as it did without the contributions of numerous women.

Azusa had a diverse leadership, consisting of a team of twelve elders, seven women, and five men during its early years.[61] It started as rather gender inclusive. Seymour affirmed women in ministry, openly welcoming them to serve in leadership roles. However, over time, he capitulated to patriarchal gender hierarchies by restricting women "to lower ranks with less ministerial privilege."[62] He chauvinistically held that men should be at the front.

Women in the COGIC were also subject to patriarchal norms. The 1924 COGIC doctrinal statement explained that women should be "helpers" within the church and stressed that 1 Timothy 2:12 insisted that a woman should not "usurp the authority over the man." Mason and other leaders interpreted this scripture to mean that women should permit men to lead them and be in charge of the church. Additionally, some who opposed women serving as elders and pastors argued that Jesus did not explicitly call women disciples to follow him or appoint them to build the church as he did with figures like Peter, James, and John.[63] Still, under Mason's leadership, the COGIC welcomed women to work within their separate departments, similar to the Women's Convention in the National Baptist Convention. Mason invited Elizabeth "Lizzie" Woods Robinson (1860–1945) to found and serve as the first leader of the National COGIC Women's Department. During her long tenure as supervisor, Robinson established the Prayer and Bible Band, the Sewing Circle, the Children's Sunshine Band, and the Home and Foreign Mission Board.

Regarding the issue of women's ordination and preaching, Robinson sternly admonished women under her charge to adhere to the denomination's rules and regulations. She revoked the missionary and evangelist licenses of women who violated the rules and declared themselves elders or pastors. She encouraged women who felt a call to ministry to work within the church's parameters and fulfill their calling through their roles as teachers, evangelists, church mothers, or local or foreign missionaries. Although the denomination officially prohibited women from being ordained as elders and pastors, COGIC women unofficially preached through their roles as teachers, evangelists, and missionaries. Many women evangelists and missionaries' messages were as influential and convicting as their male ministerial colleagues. Yet, women were often restricted from preaching from the pulpit, an elevated platform designated for ordained clergy. Some COGIC women disregarded the official rules and publicly preached in pulpits and pastored churches. For example, E. Lane led two different congregations in Missouri in 1931. She succeeded her husband as pastor after his death. COGIC women who managed to pastor typically served under the jurisdiction of rare state bishops who were more liberal on the issue and disagreed with the denomination's stance.[64]

Instead of serving as pastors or ordained elders, most COGIC women exercised their influence and authority by serving as church mothers, Sunday school teachers, missionaries, and evangelists. Church mothers imparted wisdom and guidance to younger clergy and evangelists. Women were "agents of tradition" and helped to defend and preserve sanctified religious rituals.[65] COGIC women faithfully attended and orchestrated prayer meetings, Bible studies, revival meetings, and other church programs. COGIC women helped advance the mission of their local churches, state jurisdictions, and the national denomination.

Despite their dedication and faithful service, COGIC women could not rise to the highest rank in the denomination because of their sex. Since Richard Allen founded the AME church, men occupied the highest position in subsequent Black denominational hierarchies. Mary Magdalena Lewis Tate (1871–1930) was the first Black woman to break the glass ceiling. She founded a denomination and became the presiding bishop.

Born in Vanleer, Tennessee, to Belfield Street and Nancy (Hall) Street, Tate experienced Spirit baptism and spoke in tongues in 1908 following being healed of a terrible illness; she became a traveling evangelist and shared the holiness message in multiple states, including but not limited to Tennessee, Kentucky, and Illinois. She founded and established the Church of the Living God, the Pillar and Ground of the Truth, after holding a revival in Greenville, Alabama, in 1908. Nearly "one hundred" persons professed experiencing the baptism of the Spirit during the revival service.[66]

Figure 3.3 Portrait of Bishop Mary Magdalena Lewis Tate holding a Bible.
Courtesy of the Church of the Living God (public domain image)

The official church manual described Tate as "Saint Mary Magdalena, who is an apostle Elder of Jesus Christ, by the will of God and chiefly an Elder of the Church, a mother, a light to the nations of the earth ... the First Chief Overseer and true Mother in True Holiness."[67] She stressed that the Pentecostal outpouring happened first in her religious meeting before the Azusa revival led by Seymour. She taught her followers that their church marked the beginning of the true holiness revival.[68] Tate also emphasized that the denomination's name was distinctive and reflected the "true name" for "God's latter day house."[69] She accused other denominations and Pentecostal Holiness groups of having illegitimate names.

In contrast to many holiness and Pentecostal churches of her era, Tate permitted women to preach and pastor churches. Some male pastors in her holiness denomination separated from the church over this issue and formed the First Born Church of The Living God in 1913 and the House of God, Pillar and Ground of the Truth, Inc. in 1916. Nevertheless, she refused to capitulate to men in her denomination who disagreed with her position on the ordination of women. Despite schisms in her denomination, she still had roughly one hundred churches with small congregations under her supervision during her tenure as bishop, which lasted until her death.[70] The denomination had small churches across multiple states, including Georgia, Kentucky, Tennessee, and Florida.

As her denomination spread to Northern states and cities during the Great Migration, Tate encouraged her regionally diverse membership to remember their links to each other "instead of their connections—formal and otherwise to outside observers."[71] She expressed in the *General Decree Book*:

> There shall never be a Mason-Dixon Line, nor a middle wall of petition, nor any division or separation or difference of any description between the Saints and Churches herein named. North, South, East and West, home or foreign in the United States of America or in the Isles thereof or in any and all other lands and countries and Isles thereof ... There shall never be anticipated, or indulged or otherwise practiced or in any way at all acts of state or sectional prejudices and differences among any of the members.[72]

While Tate explicitly referred to unity among members in her church, the Great Migration influenced cultural interchange among Southern and urban Black Christians across denominational lines. The migration provided fertile soil for the rise of gospel music, a new style of music that became popular in Black churches. Furthermore, Black urbanites developed dynamic religions with creative approaches to striving for racial justice during the Migration and Depression era.

Review and Discussion Questions

1   Why was respectability politics popular among Black Christians during the late nineteenth century? How did Black Baptist church women use this approach to strive for social inclusion?

2   How did Black Baptist and Methodist women navigate the intersection of racism and sexism within both the church and society during this historical era? What strategies did they use to assert their leadership and influence?

3   In what ways did the Azusa Street Revival and the Church of God in Christ chal-
     lenge racial and class divisions in early Jim Crow America? Why was Pentecostal
     interracialism short-lived?
4   How did Black Pentecostal women challenge gender restrictions on their ministry in
     creative ways?

Notes

1   William E. Montgomery, *Under Their Own Vine and Fig Tree: The African-American Church in the South, 1865–1900* (Baton Rouge, LA: Louisiana State University Press, 1993), 140.
2   William E. Montgomery, *Under Their Own Vine and Fig Tree: The African-American Church in the South, 1865–1900* (Baton Rouge, LA: Louisiana State University Press, 1993), 137.
3   William E. Montgomery, *Under Their Own Vine and Fig Tree: The African-American Church in the South, 1865–1900* (Baton Rouge, LA: Louisiana State University Press, 1993), 96–100, 112.
4   William E. Montgomery, *Under Their Own Vine and Fig Tree: The African-American Church in the South, 1865–1900* (Baton Rouge, LA: Louisiana State University Press, 1993), 117–18.
5   William E. Montgomery, *Under Their Own Vine and Fig Tree: The African-American Church in the South, 1865–1900* (Baton Rouge, LA: Louisiana State University Press, 1993), 117–18.
6   William E. Montgomery, *Under Their Own Vine and Fig Tree: The African-American Church in the South, 1865–1900* (Baton Rouge, LA: Louisiana State University Press, 1993), 138, 147–148.
7   William E. Montgomery, *Under Their Own Vine and Fig Tree: The African-American Church in the South, 1865–1900* (Baton Rouge, LA: Louisiana State University Press, 1993), 163.
8   William E. Montgomery, *Under Their Own Vine and Fig Tree: The African-American Church in the South, 1865–1900* (Baton Rouge, LA: Louisiana State University Press, 1993), 163.
9   William E. Montgomery, *Under Their Own Vine and Fig Tree: The African-American Church in the South, 1865–1900* (Baton Rouge, LA: Louisiana State University Press, 1993), 163–180.
10 William E. Montgomery, *Under Their Own Vine and Fig Tree: The African-American Church in the South, 1865–1900* (Baton Rouge, LA: Louisiana State University Press, 1993), 180.
11 William E. Montgomery, *Under Their Own Vine and Fig Tree: The African-American Church in the South, 1865–1900* (Baton Rouge, LA: Louisiana State University Press, 1993), 192.
12 William E. Montgomery, *Under Their Own Vine and Fig Tree: The African-American Church in the South, 1865–1900* (Baton Rouge, LA: Louisiana State University Press, 1993), 252.
13 Evelyn Brooks Higginbotham, *Righteous Discontent: The Women's Movement in the Black Baptist Church, 1880–1920* (1923), 5.
14 Evelyn Brooks Higginbotham, *Righteous Discontent: The Women's Movement in the Black Baptist Church, 1880–1920* (1923), 187.
15 Manning Marable and Leith Mullings, eds., *Let Nobody Turn Us Around: Voices of Resistance, Reform, and Renewal: An African American Anthology* (New York: Rowman and Littlefield Publishers, 2009), 161.
16 Bettye Collier-Thomas, *Daughters of Thunder: Black Women Preachers and Their Sermons, 1850–1979* (San Francisco, CA: Jossey-Bass Publishers), 17.
17 Evelyn Brooks Higginbotham, *Righteous Discontent: The Women's Movement in the Black Baptist Church, 1880–1920* (1923), 80.
18 Evelyn Brooks Higginbotham, *Righteous Discontent: The Women's Movement in the Black Baptist Church, 1880–1920* (1923), 12.
19 Evelyn Brooks Higginbotham, *Righteous Discontent: The Women's Movement in the Black Baptist Church, 1880–1920* (1923), 158.
20 Evelyn Brooks Higginbotham, *Righteous Discontent: The Women's Movement in the Black Baptist Church, 1880–1920* (1923), 15.
21 Bettye Collier-Thomas, *Daughters of Thunder: Black Women Preachers and Their Sermons, 1850–1979* (San Francisco, CA: Jossey-Bass Publishers), 27–28.
22 Bettye Collier-Thomas, *Daughters of Thunder: Black Women Preachers and Their Sermons, 1850–1979* (San Francisco, CA: Jossey-Bass Publishers), 27–28.
23 Bettye Collier-Thomas, *Daughters of Thunder: Black Women Preachers and Their Sermons, 1850–1979* (San Francisco, CA: Jossey-Bass Publishers), 22–27.

24 Amanda Smith, *An Autobiography: The Story of the Lord's Dealings with Mrs. Amanda Smith the Colored Evangelist* (New York: Oxford University Press, 1988, orig. 1893), 79.

25 Amanda Smith, *An Autobiography: The Story of the Lord's Dealings with Mrs. Amanda Smith the Colored Evangelist* (New York: Oxford University Press, 1988, orig. 1893), 80.

26 Amanda Smith, *An Autobiography: The Story of the Lord's Dealings with Mrs. Amanda Smith the Colored Evangelist* (New York: Oxford University Press, 1988, orig. 1893), 80.

27 Estrelda Alexander, *Black Fire: One Hundred Years of Black Pentecostalism* (Cleveland, OH: The Pilgrim Press, 2005), 77.

28 Estrelda Alexander, *Black Fire: One Hundred Years of Black Pentecostalism* (Cleveland, OH: The Pilgrim Press, 2005), 87–88.

29 Vinson Synan, *The Holiness-Pentecostal Tradition: Charismatic Movements in the Twentieth Century* (Grand Rapids, MI: Eerdmans, 1997, orig. 1971), 27.

30 *Charisma*, November 2007, 44; J.O. Patterson, German R. Ross, and. Julia Mason Atkins, eds. *History and Formative Years of the Church of God in Christ with Excerpts from the Life and Work of Its Founder-Bishop C.H. Mason* (Memphis, TN: Church of God in Christ Publishing House, 1969), 16.

31 J.O. Patterson, German R. Ross, and. Julia Mason Atkins, eds. *History and Formative Years of the Church of God in Christ with Excerpts from the Life and Work of Its Founder-Bishop C.H. Mason* (Memphis, TN: Church of God in Christ Publishing House, 1969), 16; Charles H. Pleas, *Fifty Years Achievement from 1906–1956* (Memphis, TN: Church of God in Christ Press, 1906), 4–5; Mary Mason, *The History and Life Work of Elder C.H. Mason, Chief Apostle, and His Co-Laborers* (n.p., 1924), 25.

32 Cheryl J. Sanders, *Saints in Exile: The Holiness-Pentecostal Experience* (Oxford: Oxford University Press, 1996), 71, 146.

33 Cheryl J. Sanders, *Saints in Exile: The Holiness-Pentecostal Experience* (Oxford: Oxford University Press, 1996), 143.

34 Stanley Frodsham, *With Signs Following, the Story of the Pentecostal Revival in the Twentieth Century*. Revised edition (Springfield, Missouri: Gospel Publishing House, 1941), 31; Sarah Parham, *The Life of Charles Parham, Founder of the Apostolic Faith Movement* (New York: Garland Publishing, 1930), 155–156; *The Apostolic Faith*, September 1906, column 4, p. 1.

35 Keri Day, *Azusa Reimagined: A Radical Vision of Religious and Democratic Belonging* (Stanford, CA: Stanford University Press, 2022), 4.

36 Estrelda Alexander, *The Women of Azusa Street* (Cleveland, OH: The Pilgrim Press, 2005), 42; Frank Bartleman, *Azusa Street* (Plainfield, NJ: Logos International, 1980), 180; *The Apostolic Faith*, September 1906, column 4, p. 1; Keri Day, *Azusa Reimagined: A Radical Vision of Religious and Democratic Belonging* (Stanford, CA: Stanford University Press, 2022), 4.

37 "Weird Babel of Tongues," *Los Angeles Daily Times*, April 18, 1906, Part II, 1.

38 *The Apostolic Faith*, January 1907, column 2, p. 1; *The Apostolic Faith*, September 1906, column 4, p. 1.

39 Frank Bartleman, *Azusa Street* (Plainfield, NJ: Logos International, 1980), 48; Robert Anderson, *Vision of the Disinherited* (New York: Oxford University Press, 1979), 69.

40 Bartleman, *Azusa Street*, 48; Robert Anderson, *Vision of the Disinherited* (New York: Oxford University Press, 1979), 69.

41 Cecil M. Robeck Jr., *The Azusa Street Mission and Revival: The Birth of the Global Pentecostal Movement* (Nashville, TN: Thomas Nelson, Inc. 2006), 141.

42 Keri Day, *Azusa Reimagined: A Radical Vision of Religious and Democratic Belonging* (Stanford, CA: Stanford University Press, 2022), 54; Sarah Parham, *The Life of Charles Parham, Founder of the Apostolic Faith Movement* (New York: Garland Publishing, 1930), 169.

43 Sarah Parham, *The Life of Charles Parham, Founder of the Apostolic Faith Movement* (New York: Garland Publishing, 1930), 144; Estrelda Alexander, *Black Fire: One Hundred Years of Black Pentecostalism* (Cleveland, OH: The Pilgrim Press, 2005), 48.

44 J.O. Patterson, German R. Ross, and. Julia Mason Atkins, eds. *History and Formative Years of the Church of God in Christ with Excerpts from the Life and Work of Its Founder-Bishop C.H. Mason* (Memphis, TN: Church of God in Christ Publishing House, 1969), 19.

45 Several other Pentecostal groups emerged following the Azusa Revival. For example, the Pentecostal Assemblies of the World (PAW) was one of the largest and oldest Oneness Pentecostal

groups. Estrelda Alexander, *Black Fire: One Hundred Years of Black Pentecostalism* (Cleveland, OH: The Pilgrim Press, 2005), 120–123, 206.

46 Michael Wilkinson and Steven M. Studebaker, ed., *A Liberating Spirit: Pentecostals and Social Action in North America* (Eugene, OR: Pickwick Publications, 2010), 67–68; Theodore Kornweibel Jr., "Bishop C.H. Mason and the Church of God in Christ during World War I: The Perils of Conscientious Objection" *Southern Studies: An Interdisciplinary Journal of the South.* 26, Fall 1987: 277.

47 Elton H. Weaver III, *Bishop Charles H. Mason in the Age of Jim Crow: The Struggle for Religious and Moral Uplift* (New York: Lexington Books, 2020), 195.

48 Elton H. Weaver III, *Bishop Charles H. Mason in the Age of Jim Crow: The Struggle for Religious and Moral Uplift* (New York: Lexington Books, 2020), 195–97.

49 Elton H. Weaver III, *Bishop Charles H. Mason in the Age of Jim Crow: The Struggle for Religious and Moral Uplift* (New York: Lexington Books, 2020).

50 James Delk, "When I First Met Senior Bishop C.H. Mason," in Smith, "Lest We Forget: Sermons in Part by Elder CH Mason," Special Collections, n.p. I also present the material regarding Delk in a previously published journal article: Jonathan Langston Chism, "'The Saints Go Marching': Black Pentecostal Critical Consciousness and the Political Protest Activism of Pastors and Leaders in the Church of God in Christ in the Civil Rights Era," *Pneuma* 35 (2013), 7.

51 Estrelda Alexander, *Black Fire: One Hundred Years of Black Pentecostalism* (Cleveland, OH: The Pilgrim Press, 2005), 179.

52 Theodore Kornweibel Jr., "Bishop C.H. Mason and the Church of God in Christ during World War I: The Perils of Conscientious Objection" *Southern Studies: An Interdisciplinary Journal of the South.* 26 (Fall 1987): 277; Estrelda Alexander, *Black Fire: One Hundred Years of Black Pentecostalism* (Cleveland, OH: The Pilgrim Press, 2005), 180.

53 Estrelda Alexander, *Black Fire: One Hundred Years of Black Pentecostalism* (Cleveland, OH: The Pilgrim Press, 2005), 51; Elton H. Weaver III, *Bishop Charles H. Mason in the Age of Jim Crow: The Struggle for Religious and Moral Uplift* (New York: Lexington Books, 2020), 149; J.O. Patterson, German R. Ross, and. Julia Mason Atkins, eds. *History and Formative Years of the Church of God in Christ with Excerpts from the Life and Work of Its Founder-Bishop C.H. Mason* (Memphis, TN: Church of God in Christ Publishing House, 1969), 36.

54 Craig Scandrett-Leatherman, "Rites of Lynching and Rights of Dance: Historic, Anthropological, and Afro-Pentecostal Perspectives on Black Manhood After 1856," in *AfroPentecostalism: Black Pentecostal and Charismatic Christianity in History and Culture*, edited by Amos Yong and Estrelda Alexander (New York: New York University Press, 2011), 109.

55 Yvonne Patricia Chireau, *Black Magic: Religion and the African American Conjuring Tradition* (Los Angeles, CA: University of California Press, 2003), 109.

56 Yvonne Patricia Chireau, *Black Magic: Religion and the African American Conjuring Tradition* (Los Angeles, CA: University of California Press, 2003), 111.

57 Yvonne Patricia Chireau, *Black Magic: Religion and the African American Conjuring Tradition* (Los Angeles, CA: University of California Press, 2003), 117.

58 Lelia Mason Byas, *Bishop C.H. Mason, Church of God in Christ Founder* (Memphis, TN: Church of God in Christ Publishing House, 1995), 23. C.G. Brown, *C.H. Mason, A Man Greatly Used of God* (Memphis, TN: Church of God in Christ Publishing House, 1926), 12, 52–53; Yvonne Patricia Chireau, *Black Magic: Religion and the African American Conjuring Tradition* (Los Angeles, CA: University of California Press, 2003), 111.

59 David M. Tucker, *Black Pastors and Leaders: Memphis, 1819–1972* (Memphis, TN: Memphis State University Press, 1975), 92.

60 Keri Day, *Azusa Reimagined: A Radical Vision of Religious and Democratic Belonging* (Stanford, CA: Stanford University Press, 2022), 100; Estrelda Alexander, *Black Fire: One Hundred Years of Black Pentecostalism* (Cleveland, OH: The Pilgrim Press, 2005), , 295.

61 Keri Day, *Azusa Reimagined: A Radical Vision of Religious and Democratic Belonging* (Stanford, CA: Stanford University Press, 2022), 5.

62 Keri Day, *Azusa Reimagined: A Radical Vision of Religious and Democratic Belonging* (Stanford, CA: Stanford University Press, 2022), 6; Estrelda Alexander, *Black Fire: One Hundred Years of Black Pentecostalism* (Cleveland, OH: The Pilgrim Press, 2005), 295–296.

63 Elton H. Weaver III, *Bishop Charles H. Mason in the Age of Jim Crow: The Struggle for Religious and Moral Uplift* (New York: Lexington Books, 2020), 157–158.

64 Elton H. Weaver III, *Bishop Charles H. Mason in the Age of Jim Crow: The Struggle for Religious and Moral Uplift* (New York: Lexington Books, 2020), 158–159.

65 Elton H. Weaver III, *Bishop Charles H. Mason in the Age of Jim Crow: The Struggle for Religious and Moral Uplift* (New York: Lexington Books, 2020), 164; Cheryl Townsend Gilkes, *If It Wasn't for the Women: Black Women's Experience and Womanist Culture in Church and Community* (Maryknoll, NY: Orbis Books, 2001), 10.

66 Estrelda Alexander, *Black Fire: One Hundred Years of Black Pentecostalism* (Cleveland, OH: The Pilgrim Press, 2005), 187, 301.

67 Estrelda Alexander, *Black Fire: One Hundred Years of Black Pentecostalism* (Cleveland, OH: The Pilgrim Press, 2005), 191.

68 Estrelda Alexander, *Black Fire: One Hundred Years of Black Pentecostalism* (Cleveland, OH: The Pilgrim Press, 2005), 191, 301; Elton H. Weaver III, *Bishop Charles H. Mason in the Age of Jim Crow: The Struggle for Religious and Moral Uplift* (New York: Lexington Books, 2020), 51.

69 Estrelda Alexander, *Black Fire: One Hundred Years of Black Pentecostalism* (Cleveland, OH: The Pilgrim Press, 2005), 190; Mary Lena Lewis Tate, *The Church of the Living God, the Pillar and Ground of the Truth, Inc., Constitution and General Decree Book* (Nashville, TN: The Living Way Publishing Company, 1924), 74–75, cited in Elton H. Weaver III, *Bishop Charles H. Mason in the Age of Jim Crow: The Struggle for Religious and Moral Uplift* (New York: Lexington Books, 2020), 50–51.

70 Estrelda Alexander, *Black Fire: One Hundred Years of Black Pentecostalism* (Cleveland, OH: The Pilgrim Press, 2005), 189–191, 301.

71 Clarence Hardy, "Church Mothers and Pentecostals in the Modern Age," in *Afro-Pentecostalism: Black Pentecostal and Charismatic Christianity in History and Culture*, edited by Amos Yong and Estrelda Alexander (New York: New York University Press, 2011), 89.

72 Mary Magdalena Tate, *The Constitution Government and General Decree Book of the Church of the Living God, the Pillar and Ground of the Truth* (Chattanooga, TN: New and Living Way, 1924), 58–59, cited in Clarence Hardy, "Church Mothers and Pentecostals in the Modern Age," in *Afro-Pentecostalism: Black Pentecostal and Charismatic Christianity in History and Culture*, edited by Amos Yong and Estrelda Alexander (New York: New York University Press, 2011), 90.

Further Readings

Alexander, Estrelda. *Black Fire: One Hundred Years of Black Pentecostalism.* Downers Grove, IL: Intervarsity Press, 2011.

Butler, Anthea. *Women in the Church of God in Christ: Making a Sanctified World.* Chapel Hill, NC: University of North Carolina Press, 2007.

Collier-Thomas, Bettye. *Daughters of Thunder: Black Women Preachers and Their Sermons, 1850–1979.* San Francisco, CA: Jossey-Bass Publishers, 1998.

Day, Keri. *Azusa Reimagined: A Radical Vision of Religious and Democratic Belonging.* Stanford, CA: Stanford University Press, 2020.

Griffith, R. Marie and Barbara D. Savage, eds. *Women and Religion in the African Diaspora: Knowledge, Power, and Performance.* Baltimore, MD: Johns Hopkins University Press, 2006.

Higginbotham, Evelyn Brooks. *Righteous Discontent: The Women's Movement in the Black Baptist Church, 1880–1920.* Cambridge, MA: Harvard University Press, 1993.

Montgomery, William E. *Under Their Own Vine and Fig Tree: The African-American Church in the South, 1865–1900.* Baton Rouge, LA: Louisiana State University Press, 1993.

Sanders, Cheryl J. *Saints in Exile: The Holiness-Pentecostal Experience in African American Religion and Culture.* New York: Oxford University Press, 1996.

Smith, Amanda. *An Autobiography: The Story of the Lord's Dealings with Mrs. Amanda Smith the Colored Evangelist.* New York: Oxford University Press, 1988. Originally published 1893.

Weaver, Elton H. III. *Bishop Charles H. Mason in the Age of Jim Crow: The Struggle for Religious and Moral Uplift.* New York: Lexington Books, 2020.

4 "Now We Have a Righteous Government"
Spiritual Strivings during the Great Migration and Depression

During congregational services held in 1936, Peace Mission members sang, "Now we have a righteous Government, For God is reigning now."[1] Although this song's chorus sounds like a traditional Christian hymn, it was not an ode to the Triune God. It was a reference to Major Jealous Divine, also known as Father Divine, a Black man who founded the Peace Mission Movement in New York. Divine had an interracial following that accepted him as the incarnate God who would establish a "righteous government" that would eradicate racial division and social injustice—heaven on earth.

Divine's Peace Mission was only one of many religions Black people created during the First Great Migration (1916–1930) and the Great Depression (1929–1941). During the migration, Southern Blacks and Black immigrants migrated in droves to northeastern and midwestern cities such as Detroit, Cleveland, Chicago, New York, Philadelphia, and Cincinnati, dramatically increasing the Black population. Influenced by stories in Robert Sengstacke Abbot's *Chicago Defender*, many Southern Black Americans left the South to protest and escape racial violence and persecution. Ninety-two percent of the 754 lynchings that occurred in the United States between 1900 and 1909 were in the South. Additionally, wartime job opportunities motivated scores of Black migrants from the South and the Caribbean to relocate to cities. The enlistment of Whites in the war and the draft accelerated the demand for replacement workers. World War I also slowed the flow of European immigrants to the United States and created a demand for unskilled laborers in the auto, railroad, and food industries. Furthermore, agricultural disasters in 1915, including severe floods in Mississippi and Alabama and a horrendous boll weevil infestation, wreaked havoc on the agricultural southern sector and prevented many tenant farmers and sharecroppers from working, influencing them to migrate to cities.[2]

The Great Migration persisted until the Great Depression "slowed" its pace.[3] Rural Southern Whites who migrated to cities competed with urban Black Americans for menial jobs such as garbage workers and custodians. Many middle-class Northern families could no longer afford to hire Black women as domestics. Black unemployment was often more than double that of Whites in many urban locations. For example, the unemployment rate in Chicago was 40 percent in 1934. It was 48 percent in Pittsburgh, soaring as high as 60 percent in Detroit. Many Southern Black migrants who had secured stable manufacturing jobs were laid off from work and struggled to secure employment.[4]

Black religions helped Black people find meaning and hope amid the difficulties they faced during these times. This chapter explores how Black religious groups creatively catered to the needs of Black Americans during the first wave of the Migration and Depression. For example, some Northern Black Protestant churches developed social outreach programs to strive to meet the needs of folks adjusting to life in the cities and

DOI: 10.4324/9781003359197-5

Black people who were struggling amid the Great Depression.[5] Black Protestant Christians also innovated the gospel blues during these periods, offering Black people a cathartic release amid economic hardship and ongoing racial injustice. Thomas Dorsey's song "The Lord Will Make a Way Somehow" moved Black Christians to maintain their faith. This chapter also explores original religious institutions Black people established to respond to the spiritual and social needs of Black people during these times such as the Eternal Life Christian Spiritualist Church and the House of Innocent Blood, the Moorish Science Temple of America (MSTA), the Nation of Islam (NOI), and the Peace Mission Movement (PM). The chapter concludes with a discussion of how Bishop Ida Robinson, the founder of the Mt. Sinai Holiness Church, broke new ground in the struggle for women's equality in the church and society.[6]

Black Northern Protestant Churches' Responses to Socio-economic Challenges

In *Black Religion and Black Radicalism*, historian Gayraud Wilmore argued the Black Church became deradicalized during the Great Migration era. He defines Black radicalism as an assault on "the roots" of structural racism, which undergirds the oppression of Black people.[7] Black radicalism was not equivalent to communism, an economic ideology that called for the dismantling of capitalism. Although there were exceptions, most Black Americans were reluctant to embrace communism and socialism because White Americans viewed these movements as radical and disloyal to the country. Alexander Clark admonished Black people in an article published in the *AME Review* (1886) to "remember their historic allegiance to God and country" and to reject "the plots of anarchists."[8] Furthermore, many Black Christians also rejected Marxism because the movement upheld atheism. Because Black socialists risked experiencing further marginalization, during the nineteenth century, most Black people were more apt to focus on dismantling white supremacy instead of class oppression.

Wilmore contended that Bishop Henry M. Turner was one of the last religious torchbearers of Black radicalism before Black churches became largely deradicalized. Turner condemned Booker T. Washington's accommodationism, called for reparations, and admonished Blacks to defend themselves against white supremacist violence. No prominent Black radical leader arose after Turner's death in 1915 until Reverend Dr. Martin Luther King Jr. became the leader of the civil rights movement during the 1955 Montgomery Bus Boycott.[9] Between 1915 and 1955, Black Christians were members of the NAACP, a social justice organization founded by Northern Whites and Blacks in 1909. Yet, the NAACP was essentially a moderate civil rights group. Many Black ministers were conservatives who adopted the middle class values of White "mainline Protestants" who helped shape the organization during its inception.[10] Many Blacks in the organization embraced gradualism rather than an aggressive, radical assault on white supremacy.

Rather than radicalism, most Black churches adopted "moralistic, revivalistic Christianity" during the 1920s and 1930s. They favored racial uplift approaches based on White middle-class ethics, otherworldliness, and emotionalism. They encouraged Blacks to change their behaviors instead of challenging structural racism directly. Black churches essentially cared more about particular issues affecting the life of their congregations rather than the broader concerns affecting local Black communities during the period of deradicalization, which lasted throughout the migration and the Depression era. Wilmore acknowledged that some pastors and churches were actively involved in social outreach; however, he explains this "was always the exception rather than the rule."[11]

The Black Social Gospel

During the Great Depression and Migration, there were some Black pastors who embraced the social gospel, a movement spearheaded by figures such as Washington Gladden and Walter Rauschenbusch that stressed Christians had a moral responsibility to address social ills perpetuating economic inequality in industrial America. Social gospelers strove to oppose systemic causes of poverty. They collaborated with labor unions that fought for workers' rights, called for the government to protect vulnerable groups, and participated in the settlement house movement. However, many leading White social gospel leaders such as Josiah Strong failed to address racial inequity and often condoned white supremacy.

Adam Clayton Powell, Jr., the pastor of Abyssinian Baptist Church in Harlem, embraced the black social gospel. His church organized a variety of ministries to meet the social needs of the local Harlem community and to strive for racial justice during the Great Depression. Powell led peaceful boycotts to force White businesses in Harlem to hire Black managers and professionals. He helped form the Greater New York Coordinating Committee (GNYCC) for Employment. He was an outspoken advocate for fair and affordable housing. He directly addressed and condemned white supremacy during sermons. Besides being a pastor, Powell served on the New York City Council in 1941. He won a seat in the United States House of Representatives in 1945. He used his political power to fight for civil rights for Black people in Harlem and throughout the country. He exemplified the spirit of the black social gospel, which boldly responded to Black people's social and political needs.

A Oneness Pentecostal pastor, Reverend Robert Lawson, was another leader who embraced the social gospel and served the socio-economically impoverished in Harlem during the Great Migration era. His Refuge Church of Our Lord opened multiple small businesses to serve the community, including funeral homes, a nursery and childcare program, and a Refuge Grocery Store.[12] Inspired by the Harlem Renaissance and the New Negro Movement, Lawson stressed the importance of educating Black people about their African heritage. Black intellectuals like Arturo Alfonso Schomburg, Langston Hughes, and Zora Neale Hurston encouraged Black people to define themselves and to affirm their African past. They celebrated the innovative and cultural richness of Black people from lower social classes and disdained middle class Blacks' acculturation to White normative culture. In line with the Harlem Renaissance, Lawson's ministry established a library because many local libraries had inadequate holdings on Africa and Black history. He also founded two schools such as the Church of Christ Bible Institute, a school to train clergy, in 1916 and the Industrial Union Institute and Training School for inner-city youth in Southern Pines, North Carolina in 1931.[13]

Though Wilmore acknowledged exceptional Black men social gospel pastors during the period, he overlooked women's activism in the National Baptist Convention USA and other denominations during the Migration era (see Chapter 3). Decades before the 1963 March in Washington for Jobs and Freedom, Nannie Burroughs, president of the Women's Convention, insisted that "Negroes must have Jesus, Jobs, and Justice." She encouraged Black women to fight for freedom through the "weapons of education, improvement of home and family life, and Christian living."[14] During the Progressive era, NBC Women established settlement houses, employment training initiatives, and daycare programs, and schools. They collaborated with the National Association for Colored Women, which strove to protect the rights of women and children throughout the country.[15]

Historians Milton Sernett and Wallace Best provide examples of Northern Black churches that offered social services and charitable programs for newly arrived Southern, working-class migrants. Instrumentalist pastors believed churches should "redirect a greater proportion of denominational resources" toward the community instead of the local church.[16] During the Great Migration, multiple Black urban churches collaborated with local Urban Leagues, business professionals, and social service agencies to support incoming migrants. Even small churches with limited resources often had referrals to direct incoming migrants to needed social services.

Beyond simply being kind-hearted and charitable, instrumentalist pastors established social programs for migrants to attract new church members. For example, the Olivet Baptist Church experienced an increase of 11,000 members between 1916 and 1921. This membership boost was tied to the social programs that the church offered migrants.

In contrast to Olivet and other Black Baptist churches, AME churches were not as successful in boosting their membership because they were reluctant to adjust their church mission to meet migrants' needs. Some AME ministers, such as Mary Evans, who served as pastor of St. John AME, departed the denomination and founded churches committed to community engagement. In 1932, Smith accepted an invitation from Dr. John Russel Harvey to become the pastor of the Cosmopolitan Community Church, which began as a storefront ministry in the 1920s and conducted worship at a location that was formerly a funeral home before erecting a formal sanctuary.[17] Storefronts are defined as small vacant commercial properties in economically depressed communities that pastors transformed into sanctuaries to conduct religious meetings. Storefronts provided many ministers with the opportunity to experiment with planting a church.

Elder Lucy Smith's All Nations Pentecostal Church, based in Chicago, Illinois, started small but grew to nearly 3,000 members and became a hub where Chicago citizens of diverse races could obtain basic necessities during the Great Depression. Smith met the spiritual needs of persons in Chicago by leading healing services in which numerous persons testified of being healed of various ailments and conditions. However, her church was equally devoted to ensuring members' material needs were met, especially Southern migrants.[18]

Certainly, charitable ministries are not equivalent to radical ministry programs that aim to attack the roots of white supremacy. It may be argued that charitable ministries merely helped poor Blacks survive oppression a little longer instead of eradicating it. Yet, Black churches that committed time and limited resources to help Blacks survive the challenges of the Great Migration and Depression eras were direly needed. Charitable social ministries and social justice programs are not mutually exclusive. It is not a matter of either choosing to protest white supremacy or help Blacks survive it. Both have always needed to exist concurrently.

The Black Blues Gospel and Mixed Sermons

Internal classism was also a concern among Black Christians during the Great Migration era when poor Southern Black migrants worshipped and intermingled with elitist Black Christians. Bishop Daniel Alexander Payne of the AME church criticized the ring shout and other African folk traditions performed by some AME members as primitive and uncouth. He disparaged slave spirituals as "cornfield ditties."[19] Some AME churches in Chicago embraced the "decorous worship practices" affiliated with mainline White churches because they believed this would help Black people assimilate into American society. AME churches were particularly reluctant to embrace Southern migrants' expressive and emotional style of worship, which many Black Holiness-Pentecostals esteemed (see the discussion in Chapter 3).

Southern migrants influenced many mainline Protestant churches to become more accepting of Black folk cultural practices. Thomas Dorsey, a Black Southerner who relocated to Chicago, helped popularize blues gospel in urban mainline churches. Although scholars have noted that Charles Tindley performed gospel in Northern churches in the late 1800s, Dorsey synthesized "elements of the blues" with gospel music. He transformed the sound of gospel music during the early twentieth century.[20] Born in Villa Rica, Georgia, Dorsey attended Mount Prospect Church. The "improvised spirituals" that he heard in his church likely derived from the religion of enslaved Blacks and the "shaped-note hymnody" that traced to Southern White folk religious culture.[21] While serving as music minister at Pilgrim Baptist Church in Chicago, he performed Black gospel music using the improvisation technique he witnessed growing up in the South. He described improvisation as being open to going off script and following the guidance of the Spirit when singing a song or playing an instrument. Improvisation is a derivative and survival of West African musical traditions. Dorsey's improvised performance of his gospel songs moved his listeners. His most famous song was "Take My Hand, Precious Lord." Though the song's tune originated from George Nelson Allen's hymn "Must Jesus Bear the Cross Alone," Dorsey wrote the lyrics addressing Blacks' longing for a present and this worldly God who could help them deal with the challenges they faced during the Interwar period. When performing the song, he improvised as the Spirit moved him.[22]

In addition to improvisation, another feature of gospel music is the diversity of instruments that accompany singing. Mahalia Jackson acknowledged her exposure to gospel music in Black Southern sanctified churches. Jackson recognized the influence that a sanctified church near her New Orleans home had on her formation as a gospel musician. She reflected,

> The people had no choir or organ. They used the drum, the cymbal, the tambourine, and the steel triangle. Everybody in there sang and they clapped and stomped their feet and sang with their whole bodies. They had a beat, a powerful beat … I believe the blues and jazz and even rock and roll stuff got their beat from the Sanctified Church.[23]

The sound and the beat reflected in the array of musical instruments resonated with Jackson.

Though many early Black mainline churches initially spurned gospel music, it became common in African American Protestant churches by the 1930s. It fed Blacks' spirits, appealed to their emotions, and entertained Blacks of various classes. Black people enjoyed listening to the likes of Dorsey and Jackson. Radio station disc jockeys played gospel music on newly emerging Black radio stations.[24] Over time, other famous singers and groups emerged, such as Clara Ward, Aretha Franklin, Marion Williams, James Cleveland, the Five Blind Boys of Alabama, the Staple Singers, and Shirley Caesar.

Figure 4.1. An image of Mahalia Jackson singing, by Don Cravens.
Courtesy of Getty Images

Southern migrants also induced Black pastors of Northern urban churches to modify their method of preaching to appeal to their newly mixed Southern and Northern congregants. Southern migrants were accustomed to hearing preachers employ "vernacular" or accessible and conversational language when delivering sermons to the congregation. Southern Black preachers were typically less formal than their Northern counterparts. To accommodate their integrated audience of Southern and Northern Blacks, Black pastors began to preach "mixed-typed sermons" that catered to both groups. To satisfy native Northern members, ministers would start by reading their manuscripts and presenting a well-structured, organized, coherent argument with clear points. To engage Southern migrants, the minister would go off script, speak extemporaneously from the heart, and strive to inspire members to feel the Spirit until they were overcome with ecstasy and emotion.[25]

Urban Black Esoteric Religious Movements

Black people also turned to a wide array of religions besides Protestant Christianity to find meaning during the Migration.[26] In *Black Gods of the Metropolis*, anthropologist Arthur Huff Fauset described several new religious groups such as the Mount Sinai Holy Church of America, Inc., United House of Prayer for All People, Church of God (Black Jews), the Moorish Science Temple of America, and the Father Divine Peace Mission Movement as cults. He studied many of these religious groups in Philadelphia, where he lived. Though many early scholars of Black religion viewed non-Christian Black religious groups as "cults" or "sects," Fauset does not use the descriptor "cult" derisively.[27] His employment of the term underscores how the new religions offered Black people an alternative response to the physical and mental anguish they experienced during the Migration and Depression eras.[28] Rather than using the term cult, recent scholars of Black religion have classified many of the religious groups Fauset studied as esoteric. This means they were committed to promulgating secret and mystical knowledge. Though esotericism has roots in the West, African American religious innovators turned toward this form of spirituality during the Migration and Depression to meet Blacks' spiritual needs for life meaning in their oppressive context.

Many early Black esoteric religious prophets, especially leaders of Black Muslim traditions, had strong ties to the Universal Negro Improvement Association (UNIA), founded by Marcus Garvey in 1914. Though Garvey was a Roman Catholic and George Alexander McGuire, an Episcopal Priest, attempted to make his African Orthodox Church "the official religion" of the UNIA, Garvey was adamant that the UNIA was a "nondenominational multi-dimensional movement" that aimed to address "all the wants and needs of the Negro."[29] The organization was attractive to Blacks across faith traditions and had hundreds of thousands of members and several chapters in diverse towns and cities throughout the United States and in locations outside the country during the early twentieth century.[30] The UNIA gave numerous urban Black Americans disillusioned with white supremacy in the South and the North the confidence that Black people could use their agency to create thriving businesses independent of White people. Most of all, Garvey inspired Black people to believe they could collaborate globally to establish a separate nation uncontrolled by white supremacy. In 1919, the UNIA established the Black Star Line, a shipping company, to facilitate the emigration of Black people to Africa. Garvey's imprisonment and eventual deportation by President Coolidge in 1927 following his conviction of mail fraud prevented the organization from fulfilling its ultimate vision of building a separate Black nation. The dismantling of the organization left a religious void and vacuum to be filled by a wide range of esoteric religious traditions, including but not limited to the founders of Black Spiritual Churches, Black Muslim traditions, and the International Peace Mission.[31]

Black Spiritual Churches

Faucet excluded Black spiritualists or spiritual churches from his study, deeming that there was a minuscule population of spiritualist churches in urban areas compared to other new religious groups. Researchers who completed their studies after Fauset suggest that he overlooked the numbers of urban Black people attracted to spiritual churches. According to Mays and Nichols, 7.6 percent of Black churches in major Northern urban centers were Spiritual churches. Drake and Dayton noted that Black Spiritual churches constituted 10.7 percent of Black religious groups in Chicago. By 1938, about 51 Black spiritualist churches were in Chicago, and at least one Chicago spiritual church had more than 2,000 members.[32]

Spiritual churches employed "magico-religious rituals and esoteric knowledge" to help adherents manipulate their "present condition."[33] They link to the history of spiritualism, a religious movement that swept through the United States in the early nineteenth century. Spiritualists were essentially religious persons who believed that living persons could communicate with the deceased via a medium.[34] Black spiritualist churches changed their name from spiritualist to spiritual due to the tendency for some to associate the former with evil or with magic employed for harmful intentions. They desired to avoid the negative "stigma" associated with spiritualism, particularly the view that it was demonic and dangerous. Many Black leaders of spiritual churches desired to distinguish themselves from hoodoo, voodoo, or several African-derived religions. Still, the spiritual tradition has roots in West African religions. Black spiritual churches synthesized multiple traditions, including but not limited to Black Pentecostalism, Roman Catholicism, voodoo, New Thought metaphysics, Islam, Judaism, and others. A central distinctive component of the spiritual worship service is the séance, a part of the religious service during which participants engage the departed family and friends as well as a host of intermediaries such as popular Catholic saints such as the Virgin Mary and St. Francis of Assisi as well as spirits associated with Native Americans such as Black Hawk. The spiritual leader would often exercise their gift as a medium and communicate information received from a deceased person with the congregation. The message from the dead during the séance would often relate to challenges a particular member is experiencing, such as marital or financial problems. Mediums avoided disclosing private details publicly. They invited members to join them for a one-to-one consultation to obtain more specifics.[35]

Although Black spiritual churches had a strong presence in Chicago during the Migration era, New Orleans became a central location of the spiritual movement during the 1920s. Mother Alethea Anderson, also called "Leafy," was central to the growth of spiritualism in the Crescent City. She embraced spiritualism while living in Chicago. After moving to New Orleans, she established the Eternal Life Christian Spiritualist Church. She referred to her church as a Christian Church to gain social acceptance among Black Christians. Like many Black Spiritual churches who came to prefer the signifier spiritual instead of spiritualist, Mother Anderson wanted people to see her church as Christian. A year after establishing her church, she attracted more than one hundred followers, consisting of Black and Italian Americans. Many of the persons she trained, especially women, eventually founded congregations in several cities throughout the United States, including Little Rock, Memphis, Houston, and Chicago. These churches remained connected to Mother Anderson's association.[36]

Besides failing to respect the growth of spiritual churches, especially in cities like New Orleans, some Black scholars overlooked ways spiritual churches have endeavored to advance social justice. Historian Joseph Washington spoke derisively of Black spiritual churches, referring to them as "a house of religious prostitution where religion is only the means for the end of commercialization" and as "a religion form without substance which seeks through fears of bad luck a profit in selling good luck."[37] Baer categorized their approach to social justice as a "thaumaturgical/manipulationist strategy." This means that spiritualist churches asserted that "magico-religious acts" and "positive thinking" could enable Blacks to experience upward mobility and to live the "American Dream."[38] Baer's categorization drew on the reductive accommodationist and protest dialectic, a binary taxonomy that does not account for the range of obscure expressions of Black religious activism.

Margarita Simon Guillory argues that spirituality and social justice are not mutually exclusive for Black spiritual churches. Mother Anderson and Mother Catherine are two spiritual church leaders who employed their religion to advance social justice in New Orleans and received significant discussion in Guillory's work. They both addressed social inequalities in New Orleans during the early twentieth century.[39]

Mother Anderson helped meet the needs of poor Black people in her church by helping them secure employment and teaching them entrepreneurship skills. Her spiritual church secured revenue by charging tuition for educational training programs, "private membership consultations," and "remittance fees for incorporation status."[40] She charged students interested in learning spiritual methods one dollar per day for fifty weeks. At times, she had as many as 75 students enrolled. Those who completed the program would often become teachers and medium themselves. Replicating Mother Anderson's model, many of her students founded spiritual churches, offered private consultations within Anderson's Eternal Life Christian Spiritual Association and charged clients for their services. Anderson showed her students how to profit within the American capitalist system.[41]

Mother Anderson invested some of revenue she received from private consultations, training programs, and church franchising into real estate. Yet, she was not purely profit-driven. Committed to helping poor people, she charged many of her clients on a sliding scale. At times, she offered her services free of charge to poor people. Further-more, she was philanthropic and stressed investing money back into the community. Her church organized a Social Aid Club to help the poor in "the sixth and lower seventh districts" receive basic necessities.[42] She also spearheaded "donation drives" to help Black Mississippians whose homes were severely damaged by a devastating flood.[43]

Mother Catherine Seal, who trained with Mother Anderson, is also a noteworthy social activist in the Black Spiritual tradition. She founded a spiritual church in New Orleans named House of Innocent Blood, also called the Manger. While suffering from partial paralysis, she conversed with a spirit who told her that she had the gift to heal. During a private meditation, the spirit also told her that Jesus was born in New Orleans instead of Bethlehem. Upon recovering from her paralysis, Mother Catherine explained that the spirit directed her to the precise location in the "lower ninth ward" where Jesus had been born. Subsequently, she established her church there, naming it the Manger. The church had an elaborately decorated chapel with a room signifying where the baby Jesus lay when he was born. It also had a large tent adjacent to the chapel where Mother Catherine took residence, held private consultations, and conducted healing services. There were several "long wooden cabins on the posterior side of the property" that served as temporary residences for people in need, such as young mothers, orphaned children, homeless people, and folks with infectious diseases like tubercu-losis.[44] The Manger was where ostracized and marginalized persons of all races could seek healing and comfort. Blacks and Whites, including Italian and German immigrants, lived in her residential cabins and joined her religious community.

Early-Twentieth-Century Black Muslims

As noted in Chapter 2, during the antebellum era, Black Muslims were not able to establish independent institutions. Sheik Daoud Ahmed Faisal (1892–1980), a Black Grenadian Muslim immigrant, founded one of the earliest Black Sunni religious institu-tions in America in 1924, the Islamic Mission of America. Established in Brooklyn, New York, Faisal's movement spread orthodox Sunni doctrines and practices among Blacks throughout the East Coast.[45] He taught that the Qur'an was the sacred message of Allah and led Black Americans in practicing the five pillars of Islam, consisting of:

1   a recitation of the basic confession that "There is no God but Allah, and Muhammad is his messenger";
2   prayer five times a day facing the holy city of Mecca;
3   fasting during the month of Ramadan;

4   almsgiving; and
5   the pilgrimage to the city of Mecca.[46]

Faisal did not promote violent jihad, defined as holy war in traditional Islam. Rather than striving to organize a revolutionary attack on white supremacy or leading members to engage in "politically subversive" activism, he focused on converting Black people to Islam and encouraging converts to follow the teaching of the prophet and to abide by the shari'a, the Muslim laws outlined in the Qur'an.[47] He held that the Qur'an includes "the complete Laws for the government and guidance of humanity" necessary for security and protection from evil, and he advised members to respect and follow the shari'a and the laws of the United States.[48] Some Black Muslims separated from Faisal's orthodox movement because they perceived it to be politically accommodationist and unconcerned with Black's oppressive situation.

Urban Black Americans' desire for freedom from white supremacy and self-determination likely influenced them to be receptive to Islamic movements considered unorthodox by traditional Muslims. Before scores of Black people joined the Moorish Science Temple of America and the Nation of Islam, the Ahmadiyya Movement attracted thousands of Black Americans. Founded in India in the Nineteenth Century by Mizra Ghulam Ahmad, a Punjab Muslim of Indian descent who believed himself to be "the Promised Messiah of Islam," the Ahmadiyya movement contested the orthodox Muslim teaching that prophecy ended with Muhammad.[49] The movement offered Black people "the first multi-racial model of American Islam" and an alternative to Christianity.[50] Mufti Muhammad Sadiq, an Indian Ahmadiyya missionary, helped expand the movement's reach in America by stressing to Black Americans that Islam was a racially inclusive faith and not inherently segregationist like White Protestant Christianity. Richard Turner posits that Sadiq's vision of Islam is idealistic and ignores the history of racial discrimination among Muslims around the globe. Still, the Ahmadiyya movement was effective at converting urban Blacks in cities such as Chicago, Detroit, Gary, and St. Louis who were disheartened with racist White churches. It was especially attractive to Black Garveyites who emphasized the need for Black people to join forces with other oppressed people around the globe. It sought to form an alliance between Punjab Indian Nationalists and Black Pan-Africanists who were standing in solidarity against colonialism and white supremacy. In an article in the *Muslim Sunrise*, the organization's periodical, Sadiq insisted that Garveyites could find "valuable [multi-racial] allies" among the Muslims in China, Arabia, Afghanistan, Turkey, Persia, and India.[51]

Moorish Science Temple of America

The Ahmadiyya movement likely inspired founders of Black Muslim movements to go against the grain of traditional Islam. Like Ahmad, Timothy Drew claimed to be a part of the prophetic lineage of Muhammad. Born in North Carolina on January 8, 1886, Drew founded the Moorish Science Temple of America (MSTA) in 1913. This was the first major independent Muslim institution founded by a Black person in the United States. Drew changed his name to Noble Drew Ali, and asserted that he was the reincarnation of Muhammad, the original founder of traditional Islam. He professed that Allah called him to become a prophet who revealed to Black people their nationality as Moors.[52] To "construct a new genealogy and ethnic identity for Black Americans," he adopted "ideas and symbols" from diverse traditions, including mainstream Islam,

Freemasonry, Theosophy, and Garveyism.[53] His religious text, the Holy Koran, exemplifies this eclecticism. It draws on multiple sources, including the Qur'an, the Bible, the *Aquarian Gospel of Jesus Christ*, a gnostic text written by Levi Dowling, and Sri Ramotherio's ancient Rosicrucian, Masonic text *Unto Thee I Grant*.[54] Besides appropriating Ramotherio's Masonic thought, some miscellaneous Freemasonry symbols he adopted included "the fez, turban, crescent and star, circle seven, all-seeing eye, clasped hands, Sphinx of Gaza, and the pyramids."[55] Ali utilized these esoteric symbols to support his claim that Black people had Moorish roots and noble ties to wise, ancient African civilizations.

In line with the Masonic tradition that stressed secrecy, Ali intended that the Holy Koran was to be accessible only to MSTA members. Ali's Koran was also a much shorter religious text than the original Qur'an of traditional Islam. One of his main arguments in the text is that Jesus's ancestral roots traced to the Moors of Africa instead of Europe. He insisted that Jesus' purpose was to redeem Black people from White oppression.[56] He also taught that global peace would occur when people of European and Asiatic ancestry follow their original religion. The MSTA excluded persons of European descent from becoming members and was open only to Asiatics, defined as non-Whites. According to Ali, Asiatics were the chosen of God. He taught that Allah would soon destroy European civilization and give power to the Moors.[57] Ali further spells out the teachings of the MSTA in a short doctrinal book entitled *Koran Questions for Moorish Americans*. He provided 101 questions with brief and straightforward answers.

The MSTA held worship services in temples. Ali established the first temple, named the Canaanite Temple, in 1913 in Newark, New Jersey. He also established temples in cities throughout the country, including (but not limited to) the northeast, the Midwest, and the South.[58] Worship services generally occurred on Fridays and Sundays during the evenings and typically lasted about three hours. Services often started with members "softly" and slightly singing "above a whisper" songs such as "Moslem's That Old Time Religion," a modification of "Give Me That Old Time Religion" and "Take My Hand, Precious Allah," a reworking of Dorsey's "Take My Hand, Precious Lord." MSTA members then recited a Muslim prayer while standing "facing east" and "holding up seven fingers."[59] They then read the MSTA Constitution and By-Laws and recited a select portion of the Holy Koran. Toward the end of the service, "a sheik" would speak to the worshippers about MSTA doctrines.[60]

The MSTA aimed to promote pride in African history and culture. Members of the MSTA added "el" or "bey" to their names to signify their Moorish background and nationality, which traces to the nation of Morocco, an ancient Islamic nation whose roots extend to the Egyptian empire.[61] The Moors held parades in which they wore MSTA apparel that reflected their beliefs to others. They hoped to attract Black people to see their religion's truth and become members.[62] Ali did not encourage followers to unite and return to Morocco as Garvey sought to galvanize diasporic Black people to return to the African motherland. Although some MSTA members were Garveyites and desired to leave America, many Moors viewed themselves as Americans and envisioned remaining in America for the foreseeable future. MSTA members established enclaves in Northern cities that focused on meeting members' needs. For example, some companies that MSTA members established in Chicago included "the Moorish Manufacturing Corporation, a grocery, a cafeteria, and a moving service."[63]

Ali admonished members not to speak against the flag and to be patriotic, loyal citizens. While some members refused to enlist in the army during World War II because

Figure 4.2. An image of the book cover of *Koran Questions for Moorish Americans* by Noble Drew Ali. The image displays Prophet Noble Drew Ali rescuing a lifeless child, representing fallen humanity. The image is consistent with the question and response in number 15 in the book: "For what purpose was the Moorish Science Temple of America Founded? For the uplifting of fallen humanity?" Published by Moorish Science Temple of America and Omar Ibn Said Collection, 1928.
Courtesy of the Library of Congress

they believed the Holy Koran promoted love and peace, many MSTA members proudly served in the military. Some MSTA members advocated for civil rights by lobbying government officials to support their freedom to pursue their religious mission. They were active in the movement to end segregation and supported civil rights legislation.[64]

After Ali died in 1929, some of his former followers claimed to be his successor, including (but not limited to) Sheik John Givens-El, who had served as Ali's chauffeur. Lifting himself as the reincarnation of Ali, he formed a splinter group named the Moorish Science Temple Divine and National Movement of North America. Although scholars debate the nature of Wallace Fard Muhammad's relationship with Ali, the Nation of Islam, the organization he founded in Detroit, Michigan, in 1930, promoted teachings similar to those of the MSTA.[65]

Nation of Islam

Rather than replicating MSTA doctrines, Fard started a new movement that built on and expanded Ali's teachings. Details about Fard's birth, upbringing, and death are obscure. Fard reported to members that he was born in Mecca in 1877 and that his ancestry traces to the prophet Muhammad. Yet, scholars have not found birth records or any evidence to substantiate his claim. Historical documents indicate that he lived in Detroit during the 1930s. While peddling silks and satin-like materials in Black communities that he claimed came directly from the African continent, he shared secret knowledge with people about Islam. He declared himself to be a prophet of Allah and started holding religious services for new converts. Members sang songs, prayed toward the east, and read the Qur'an, the original sacred text of orthodox Islam.[66] During sermons, Fard taught members doctrines from two books he authored, *The Secret Ritual of the Nation of Islam* and the *Teaching for the Lost-Found Nation of Islam in a Mathematical Way*. He promulgated the story of Yakub, a creation narrative that traced the origins of white supremacy to an evil Black scientist who created Whites from Blacks, the original people of the earth. He argued that Allah planned for Whites to rule for about 6,000 years. However, the period of White domination would end soon, and Black people would once again become dominant in society.[67]

Fard encouraged NOI members to adopt Muslim names that signaled and restored their original Muslim identity before enslavement. He taught Blacks that they should reject and replace their last names with an "X" to protest the forced adoption of White slaveholders' names.

Elijah Poole (1897–1975) was one of Fard's most devoted followers. Reared in poverty in Sandersville, Georgia, Poole's life was characteristic of many Black Southerners who migrated to the North seeking better opportunities. In 1923, he moved to Detroit and worked at a Chevrolet assembly line. He eventually lost this job because of the onset of the Great Depression in 1929. He remained unemployed for a few years. In 1930, he heard Fard preach. Upon hearing his message, Poole told Fard that he recognized his divinity as "Jesus," or God in the flesh. He became a loyal and respected minister in the NOI. Fard appointed him as leader of Temple No. 2 in Chicago in 1932.[68] He changed his last name to Muhammad.

Because of the organization's theology of inevitable divine judgment of White Americans, the FBI closely monitored the NOI. Local police attended some religious meetings and even arrested Fard multiple times during the 1930s. Following his release from custody for a third time in 1934, Fard left Chicago and was never seen again. Though other men claimed to be Fard's successor and competing factions developed in the organization, Muhammad emerged as the chief leader of the NOI after spending four years in a federal prison in Milan, Michigan, for draft evasion and sedition. His years of imprisonment boosted his reputation among Black Muslim factions. Upon his release, the NOI headquarters shifted to Chicago where Muhammad resided.[69]

During his tenure as leader of the NOI, Muhammad continued to advance Fard's teachings. He encouraged followers to follow traditional Muslim rituals and disciplines such as regular prayer and dietary restrictions. Pork was strictly forbidden. Muhammad also admonished Muslims to abstain from intoxicating liquors, cigarettes, and abusive drugs and to avoid adultery, criminal behavior, and addictive habits such as gambling. The NOI helped Black people who were drug addicts and ex-felons reform their lives. Muhammad continued the Fruit of Islam, which Fard had established, to empower Muslims in the NOI to protect themselves from racial violence and to provide brotherhood and a sense of pride and purpose to Black men amid the Great Depression. Muhammad also resumed Fard's Muslim Girls' Training Corp Class that taught Black Muslim women "to be proper wives and mothers."[70]

One of Muhammad's notable books was *The Supreme Wisdom: Solution to the So-Called Negroes' Problem* (1957), a two-volume text that contained a wide-ranging overview of the doctrines and teachings he learned from Fard. The book included topics such as "What Our Enemy is Doing," "No Integration," and "Heaven on Earth."[71] Muhammad taught that Allah would send a Mother Plane or Mothership to wreak havoc on White civilization. Containing "a small fleet of planes," this large ship could deploy "bombs with a destruction radius of 50 miles."[72] In line with this belief, members displayed the Nation of Islam flag in their homes, which was all red with a white crescent moon and a white star. Printed on the flag were the letters FJEI, which stand for freedom, justice, equality, and Islam. The NOI taught that God would destroy the American flag during the imminent day of judgment.[73]

The NOI perceived that the United States was too corrupt to be reformed. Hence, Muhammad viewed political activism as unnecessary. In line with Fard's message, he held the myth of Yakub provided a theological explanation for white supremacy. Yakub, the evil Black scientist, had influenced European countries to subjugate Black people, separating them from their original Muslim home of Mecca. Under Fard, the NOI taught that Muslims would be restored to Mecca. When Muhammed led the organization in the 1930s, he did not encourage members to leave America and return to Mecca. Muhammad believed that the NOI should build and establish separate communities for themselves in the United States replete with Black-owned schools and businesses.[74] Given this emphasis on racial separatism, the NOI has frequently been misconstrued as a Black Nationalist Movement. According to Stephen Finely, the NOI was a religious nationalist organization. The Black nationalist label "obscures the religious nature and meaning of its symbols and practices."[75]

International Peace Mission

Known originally as George Baker, Father Divine (1877–1865) was likely born in Savannah, Georgia, in 1877. Divine nor his followers disclosed many details about his upbringing. Before establishing the Peace Mission Movement in New York, he settled in Baltimore, Maryland, under the name Major Jealous Devine. In Baltimore, he started a mission that served impoverished people.[76] In 1919, he relocated to New York and continued to serve those in need by establishing a boarding house and job placement agency in Sayville, a hamlet in Long Island.[77] He offered housing and free food or significantly reduced meals to poor people. He officially referred to himself as Father Divine in 1930 during the Depression as his popularity increased. Numerous people visited his Peace Mission (PM) in Manhattan, New York, to share a meal at his table.

Rather than perceiving himself as a prophet of God like the MSTA and NOI founders, Baker asserted that he was God incarnate. Divine's followers, which consisted of people from different races and social classes, firmly believed in the divinity of its founder. An incident that occurred in 1932 reportedly supported his claim to divinity. On November 15, 1931, his neighbors called the police and reported that Divine and his followers were being a public nuisance. Police charged him and nearly eighty of his followers with disturbing the peace. After a jury found Divine guilty, Judge Lewis J. Smith sentenced him to a year in jail and fined him $500. Smith soon mysteriously suffered a cardiac arrest a few days later. Divine reportedly expressed, "I hated to do it."[78] He suggested that he punished the judge for being unmerciful. The court overturned his conviction, and the event bolstered many of his followers' faith that he, a short, brown-skinned, bald Black man, was God embodied in Black flesh. Divine insisted that he (God) elected to become a member of a racially oppressed group to "bring salvation to the lowly."[79]

Divine taught his followers that they could experience heaven on earth by accepting him. He viewed the traditional Christian otherworldly heaven as a figment of the imagination. He also held water baptism inconsequential and invited believers to be baptized with his Divine Spirit. The central component of PM worship services was the sharing of a meal. He welcomed followers to partake of sacred communion around a large banquet table filled with delicious food and nonalcoholic beverages instead of the traditional Christian elements.[80] PM members dined well amid the Great Depression when food was scarce, and people stood in long lines at soup kitchens. They sang congregational hymns as they ate. They listened to Divine deliver sermons, assuring them that they would experience heaven's richness on earth by adhering to his teachings. The authoritative text of the PM was the *New Day*, a weekly PM newspaper that started in 1934. Unlike the MSTA and NOI, the PM does not reference the Christian Bible or any figures therein. The *New Day* primarily centers on Divine and contains his sermons and summaries of his involvements and initiatives as PM leader.[81]

There were multiple branches of the PM in New York. The organization had thousands of members collectively. Divine welcomed members to disregard family, sex, and their ties to material things and to live communally. While some members who accepted Divine's teachings continued their routine jobs and civic duties, many of his closest followers quit their jobs, disconnected from family and friends, and dedicated their lives to Divine's will. They depended on the PM and Father Divine for support and resided in one of the organization's properties.[82] Followers combined resources to purchase "cooperative farms" in rural areas as well as "sex-segregated, celibate residences," also referred to as "extensions" or "heavens" in cities such as Newark, Bridgeport, and Los Angeles, and New York.[83] They called their communal properties collectively "The Promised Land." The Peace Mission was set up like a corporation. The organization owned various assets, including hotels and businesses in different states.[84]

PM extensions promoted peace and interracial solidarity. To encourage a "Universal Utopian Democracy" in which all could flourish regardless of race, Divine forbid followers from using racial categorizations.[85] The PM prohibited any form of racial

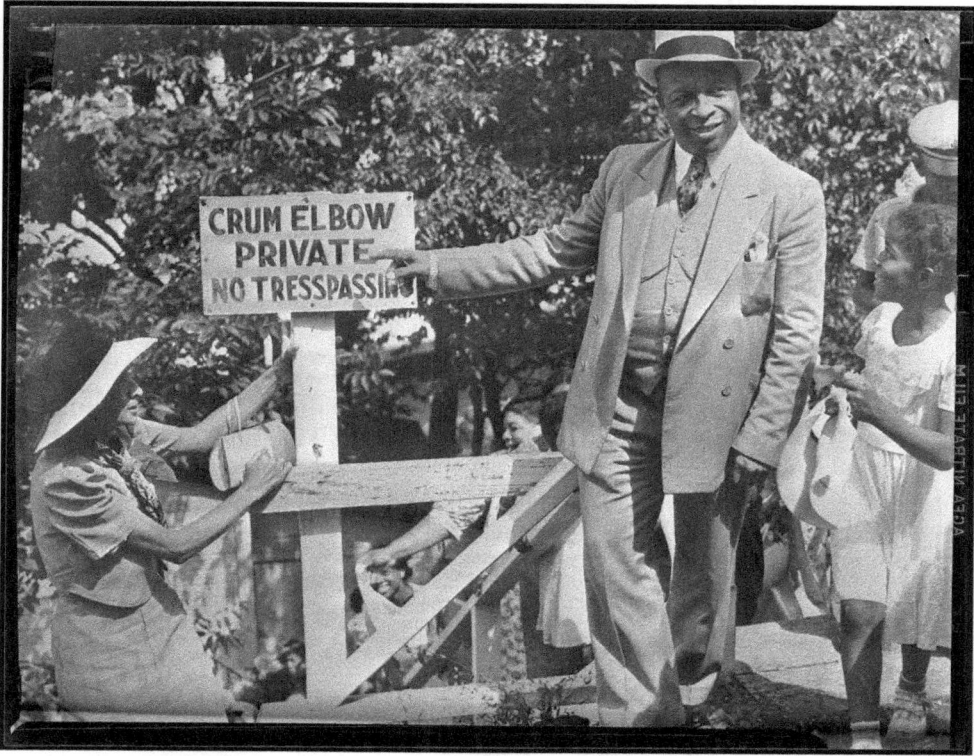

Figure 4.3. Howland Spencer made a gift of his share of Crum Elbow, a 500 acre estate, to Father Divine of Harlem and sold the rest for his relatives. The estate was opposite of that of President Roosevelt's mother. Father Divine points to a sign on the Crum Elbow estate. He is accompanied by a woman and a boy and a girl, perhaps his wife and children. Reported in "Roosevelt foe laude Divine," *Los Angeles Times*, July 30, 1938: 2, https://digital.library.ucla.edu/catalog/ark:/21198/zz002j8f13.
Courtesy Los Angeles Times Photographic Archive, UCLA Library Special Collections

discrimination within its ranks, spoke against segregation in society, and advocated for Congress "to pass federal antilynching legislation."[86] The PM also conducted voter registration drives and encouraged members to vote to elect political representatives who would advance Divine's social vision. The PM collaborated with groups such as the Communist Party and Harlem's All People's Party.[87] Deeply committed to advancing Divine's Kingdom of peace nationally and globally, the PM called for an end to all forms of violence. The religious organization protested capital punishment, admonished followers not to take up arms, and believed the world would be safer and better if weapons were destroyed or limited to being only owned by police agencies.[88] During a Convention in 1936, Divine presented the Righteous Government Platform and his plan for contesting racism and establishing a more inclusive and "righteous government." Nearly 6,000 persons from diverse races and walks of life attended the meeting and pledged to support Divine's proposal.

The Mt. Sinai Holiness Church and the Struggle for Gender Equality

During the Great Migration and Depression eras, women continued to strive for gender equality. Like Tate, discussed in the previous chapter, Ida Robinson (1891–1946) responded to gender oppression by establishing an independent holiness-Pentecostal denomination. Born to Robert and Annie Bell in Hazlehurst, Georgia, Robinson experienced salvation as a teenager. She joined the United Holy Church of America in 1908 and accepted the call to do outreach ministry, ministering to people in their homes in Pensacola, Florida. She relocated to Philadelphia in 1917 and became the pastor of Mount Olive Holy Church in 1919. Her energetic and engaging preaching style and melodic singing caused her fame to rise in the denomination. After a few years, Robinson supervised nearly sixty ministers and missionaries and became an influencer within the United Holy Church (UHC) of America. She formed a close relationship with denominational founders and was present at the first UHC convocation in Philadelphia in 1920.[89]

As an increasing number of holiness women admired Robinson and sought ordination, denominational leaders formally proclaimed that they would only ordain women privately and limited the opportunities for ordained women to serve as senior pastors. They relegated them to fulfilling roles as associate ministers, teachers, or missionaries. Disgruntled with this injustice toward women, Robinson sought God for direction and underwent an intense period of praying and fasting. After ten days, she envisioned God directing her to "come out on Mount Sinai and loose the women."[90] Based on that vision, she organized a convocation in September 1924 attended by seventeen churches, including some churches from the UHC. The church officially received a charter and chose the name Mount Sinai Holy Church of America, Inc. The church purchased a building from the Assemblies of God and established its headquarters in Philadelphia. The doctrine of Mount Sinai was similar to the United Holy Church of America.[91]

Robinson led the denomination for twenty-two years. She simultaneously pastored congregations in Philadelphia and New York, Mount Olive Holy Church, and Bethel Holy Church, respectively. She delivered sermons that reached a massive audience through the WNEW radio in New York and Virginia during the 1930s. Her ministry established an "accredited high school" as well as "missions in Cuba and Ghana."[92] Under her leadership, the denomination grew to 84 churches with congregations crossing the northeastern and southeastern United States. Robinson grew her church through cultivating and nurturing relationships with members and being invested in leadership development. She held services nearly every day of the week to allow emerging ministers and evangelists to share their gifts and develop self-confidence. She discipled groups of young ministers by having them accompany her when they traveled to minister to various churches. She especially groomed the three women bishops who succeeded her: Elmira Jeffries, Mary Jackson, and Amy Stevens. As the Senior bishop, she had the power to ordain women without restrictions and appoint them to churches. Of the one hundred and sixty-three ordained ministers in her denomination, one hundred and twenty-five were women. Women ministers constituted a sizable percentage of the elders and preachers of her denomination.[93]

In addition to advancing gender equality in the church, Robinson also addressed racial justice. In a sermon entitled "The Economic Persecution," delivered in 1935, she drew a parallel between the persecution early Christians experienced in the ancient Greco-Roman world and the oppressive circumstances Black people endured in the American South during the Jim Crow era. She explained that similar economic and political underpinnings that influenced Rome to persecute Christians drove the violent exploitation and disregard for Black life. She called out White "Christian" politicians in the South for twisting the actual teachings of Christ to support their political and economic interests. Prefiguring the anthem of the civil rights movement, "We Shall Overcome," Robinson admonished congregants to believe that victory against racial injustice would be possible during their lifetimes. She preached:

> So let us saints, pray that the Constantine of our day (if there be one) sends a letter to the modern pagans in the [polluted] southland in the form of "Anti-lynch" legislation that is now pending in Congress. We can overcome and we will overcome, and we will overcome, right here in this present world, the persecutions we [are] made to suffer, by our unjust brethren. It is written that "Ethiopians shall stretch their hands in righteousness to God" and by the help of God and the agencies He has so gloriously provided, we shall overcome.[94]

She inspired members to believe that God would indeed help them overcome racial injustice in this life. Martin Luther King Jr. was not a political figure like Constantine. However, he did send a letter from a Birmingham Jail directed to Southern White ministers who upheld the status quo. Robinson's sermon prefigured the civil rights movement and resounded its anthem, "We Shall Overcome."

Review and Discussion Questions

1   What types of changes and innovations did this era stimulate among urban Black Protestant churches in the North?
2   How did leaders of spiritual churches such as Mother Alethea Anderson and Mother Catherine Seal use their spiritual authority to help marginalized and oppressed communities?
3   Why did many urban Black people join esoteric organizations such as the Moorish Science Temple of America, the Nation of Islam, and the International Peace Mission during this period?
4   Why was Bishop Ida Robinson influential? How did she advocate for gender equality and for racial justice?

Notes

1 Father Divine, "The Realness of God, to you-wards ..." cited in Milton C. Sernett, ed., *African American Religious History: A Documentary Witness* (Durham, NC: Duke University Press, 1999), 185.
2 Benjamin Brawley, *Social History of the American Negro* (New York: Macmillan, 1921) 295; Gayraud S. Wilmore, *Black Religion and Black Radicalism: An Interpretation of the Religious history of Afro-American People* (Maryknoll, NY: Orbis Books, 1983, orig. 1973), 139; Nell Irvin Painter, *Creating Black Americans: African-American History and Its Meanings, 1619 to the Present* (New York: Oxford University Press, 2007), 364–365.
3 Milton C. Sernett, *Bound for the Promised Land: African American Religion and the Great Migration* (Durham, NC: Duke University Press, 1997), 3.
4 Darlene Clark Hine, William C. Hine, and Stanley Harrold, *African Americans: A Concise History, Combined Volume* (New York: Pearson, 2014), 441.
5 I do not concentrate much attention on Black Presbyterian, Episcopalian, and Roman Catholic denominations because they did not attract as many Black migrants from working-class

backgrounds as Black Protestant churches. Gayraud S. Wilmore, *Black Religion and Black Radicalism: An Interpretation of the Religious History of Afro-American People* (Maryknoll, NY: Orbis Books, 1983, orig. 1973), 144; Matthew J. Cressler, *Authentically Black and Truly Catholic: The Rise of Black Catholicism in the Great Migration* (New York: NYU Press, 2017).

6 Space restrictions do not permit an exhaustive survey of all the Black esoteric religions who expanded the boundaries of Black religion beyond Protestant Christianity during this time. For example, some additional urban religious movements that religious scholars have discussed at length include the Church of God or the Black Jews, the United House of Prayer for All People, Congregation Beth B'nai Abraham, and the Commandment Keepers Ethiopian Hebrew Congregations. Judith Weisenfeld, *New World a-Coming: Black Religion and Racial Identity during the Great Migration* (New York: NYU Press, 2017); Edward E. Curtis IV and Danielle Brune Sigler, ed., *The New Black Gods: Arthur Huff Fauset and the Study of African American Religions* (Bloomington, IN: Indiana University Press, 2009); Arthur Huff Fauset, *Black Gods of the Metropolis: Negro Religious Cults of the Urban North* (Philadelphia: PA, 2022, orig. 1944), 76; Stephen Finley, Margarita Guillory, and Hugh Page Jr., eds., *Esotericism in African American Religious Experience: There is a Mystery* (Boston, MA: Brill, 2015).

7 Gayraud S. Wilmore, *Black Religion and Black Radicalism: An Interpretation of the Religious history of Afro-American People* (Maryknoll, NY: Orbis Books, 1983, orig. 1973), 168–169.

8 Alexander Clark, "Socialism," *AME Review* (July 1886), 49–54, cited in Calvin S. Morris, "Reverdy Ransom, the Social Gospel and Race," *The Journal of Religious Thought* Vol. 35, No. 1 (1978): 10.

9 Joseph R. Washington, Jr., *Black Religion* (Boston: Beacon, 19640), 35, cited in Gayraud S. Wilmore, *Black Religion and Black Radicalism: An Interpretation of the Religious history of Afro-American People* (Maryknoll, NY: Orbis Books, 1983, orig. 1973), 144–145.

10 Gayraud S. Wilmore, *Black Religion and Black Radicalism: An Interpretation of the Religious history of Afro-American People* (Maryknoll, NY: Orbis Books, 1983, orig. 1973), 145.

11 Some other additional examples of "exceptional" Black pastors that Wilmore mentioned were Reverdy C. Ransom (1861–1959) and Alexander Walters of the AME Church (1858–1917). Gayraud S. Wilmore, *Black Religion and Black Radicalism: An Interpretation of the Religious history of Afro-American People* (Maryknoll, NY: Orbis Books, 1983, orig. 1973), 135, 161.

12 Douglas Jacobsen, *Thinking in the Spirit: Theologies of the Early Pentecostal Movement* (Bloomington, IN: Indiana University Press, 2003), 264; Lloyd Barba, "Jesus Would Be Jim Crowed: Bishop Robert Lawson on Race and Religion in the Harlem Renaissance," *Journal of Race, Ethnicity and Religion*, 6, no. 3 (August 2015), 21.

13 Lloyd Barba, "Jesus Would Be Jim Crowed: Bishop Robert Lawson on Race and Religion in the Harlem Renaissance," *Journal of Race, Ethnicity and Religion*, 6, no. 3 (August 2015), 26–27; Douglas Jacobsen, *Thinking in the Spirit: Theologies of the Early Pentecostal Movement* (Bloomington, IN: Indiana University Press, 2003), 264; Estrelda Y. Alexander, *Black Fire: One Hundred Years of African American Pentecostalism* (Downers Grove, IL: Intervarsity Press, 2011), 224.

14 Bettye Collier-Thomas, *Jesus, Jobs, and Justice Jesus, Jobs: African American Women and Religion* (New York: Alfred A. Knopf, 2010), 434–435.

15 Evelyn Brooks Higginbotham, *Righteous Discontent: The Women's Movement in the Black Baptist Church, 1880–1920* (Cambridge, MA: Harvard University Press, 1994).

16 Milton C. Sernett, *Bound for the Promised Land: African American Religion and the Great Migration* (Durham, NC: Duke University Press, 1997), 4.

17 Michael Harris, *The Rise of Gospel Blues: The Music of Thomas Andrew Dorsey in the Urban Church* (New York: Oxford University Press, 1994), 118; Wallace Best, *Passionately Human, No Less Divine: Religion and Culture in Black Chicago, 1915–1952* (Princeton, NJ: Princeton University Press, 2005), 11; Cosmopolitan Community Church, "A Rich History," retrieved from https://cosmocommchurch.org/a-rich-history.

18 Wallace Best, *Passionately Human, No Less Divine: Religion and Culture in Black Chicago, 1915–1952* (Princeton, NJ: Princeton University Press, 2005), 159.

19 Michael Harris, *The Rise of Gospel Blues: The Music of Thomas Andrew Dorsey in the Urban Church* (New York: Oxford University Press, 1994), 3.

20 Milton C. Sernett, *Bound for the Promised Land: African American Religion and the Great Migration* (Durham, NC: Duke University Press, 1997), 209.

21 Michael Harris, *The Rise of Gospel Blues: The Music of Thomas Andrew Dorsey in the Urban Church* (New York: Oxford University Press, 1994), xix.

22 Michael Harris, *The Rise of Gospel Blues: The Music of Thomas Andrew Dorsey in the Urban Church* (New York: Oxford University Press, 1994), 239.

23 Mahalia Jackson, "Singing of Good Tidings and Freedom," cited in Milton C. Sernett, ed., *African American Religious History: A Documentary Witness* (Durham, NC: Duke University Press, 1999), 539.

24 Wallace Best, *Passionately Human, No Less Divine: Religion and Culture in Black Chicago, 1915–1952* (Princeton, NJ: Princeton University Press, 2005), 10.

25 Wallace Best, *Passionately Human, No Less Divine: Religion and Culture in Black Chicago, 1915–1952* (Princeton, NJ: Princeton University Press, 2005), 96–99.

26 Hans A. Baer, *The Black Spiritual Movement: A Religious Response to Racism* (Knoxville, TN: University of Tennessee Press, 1984), 16.

27 Edward E. Curtis IV and Danielle Brune Sigler, ed., *The New Black Gods: Arthur Huff Fauset and the Study of African American Religions* (Bloomington, IN: Indiana University Press, 2009), 6.

28 Arthur Huff Fauset, *Black Gods of the Metropolis: Negro Religious Cults of the Urban North* (Philadelphia: PA, 2022, orig. 1944), 76; Edward E. Curtis IV and Danielle Brune Sigler, ed., *The New Black Gods: Arthur Huff Fauset and the Study of African American Religions* (Bloomington, IN: Indiana University Press, 2009), 7.

29 Richard Brent Turner, *Islam in the African-American Experience*, 2nd edition (Bloomington, IN: Indiana University Press, 2003), 82–83.

30 Stephen Finley, Margarita Guillory, and Hugh Page Jr., eds., *Esotericism in African American Religious Experience: There is a Mystery* (Boston, MA: Brill, 2015), xiii; Milton C. Sernett, ed., *African American Religious History: A Documentary Witness* (Durham, NC: Duke University Press, 1999), 453, 464; William H. Ferris, "Garvey and the Black Star Line," *Favorite Magazine*, July 1920; Roland Enicierico, "Black Star Line," *Encyclopedia of African American History, 1896 to the Present: From the Age of Segregation to the Twenty-first Century*, Paul Finkelman, ed. (New York: Oxford University Press, 2008); Colin Grant, *Negro with a Hat: The Rise and Fall of Marcus Garvey* (New York: Oxford University Press: 2008), 184–195.

31 Though Garvey has been described as a political Black nationalist, Mitch Horowitz presents him as an "esoteric prophet" who preached New Thought metaphysics and positive thinking to his followers. Mitch Horowitz, *Occult America: The Secret History of How Mysticism Shaped Our Nation* (New York: Bantam Books, 2009), 132–138.

32 Mary Ann Clark, "Spirit is Universal: Development of Black Spiritualist Churches," in *Esotericism in African American Religious Experience: There is a Mystery*, edited by Stephen Finley, Margarita Guillory, and Hugh Page Jr., eds. (Boston, MA: Brill, 2015), 95; Hans A. Baer, *The Black Spiritual Movement: A Religious Response to Racism* (Knoxville, TN: University of Tennessee Press, 1984), 4, 22–23.

33 Hans A. Baer, *The Black Spiritual Movement: A Religious Response to Racism* (Knoxville, TN: University of Tennessee Press, 1984), 9.

34 Mary Ann Clark, "Spirit is Universal: Development of Black Spiritualist Churches," in *Esotericism in African American Religious Experience: There is a Mystery*, edited by Stephen Finley, Margarita Guillory, and Hugh Page Jr., eds. (Boston, MA: Brill, 2015), 86, 99.

35 Mary Ann Clark, "Spirit is Universal: Development of Black Spiritualist Churches," in *Esotericism in African American Religious Experience: There is a Mystery*, edited by Stephen Finley, Margarita Guillory, and Hugh Page Jr., eds. (Boston, MA: Brill, 2015), 95–98; Hans A. Baer, *The Black Spiritual Movement: A Religious Response to Racism* (Knoxville, TN: University of Tennessee Press, 1984), 4–7.

36 Margarita Guillory, *Spiritual and Social Transformation in African American Spiritual Churches* (Boston, MA: Brill, 2015), 14–15; Mary Ann Clark, "Spirit is Universal: Development of Black Spiritualist Churches," in *Esotericism in African American Religious Experience: There is a Mystery*, edited by Stephen Finley, Margarita Guillory, and Hugh Page Jr., eds. (Boston, MA: Brill, 2015), 96.

37 Hans A. Baer, *The Black Spiritual Movement: A Religious Response to Racism* (Knoxville, TN: University of Tennessee Press, 1984), 10.

38 Hans A. Baer, *The Black Spiritual Movement: A Religious Response to Racism* (Knoxville, TN: University of Tennessee Press, 1984), 161.

39 Margarita Guillory, *Spiritual and Social Transformation in African American Spiritual Churches* (Boston, MA: Brill, 2015).

40 Margarita Guillory, *Spiritual and Social Transformation in African American 'Spiritual Churches* (Boston, MA: Brill, 2015), 17.

41 Margarita Guillory, *Spiritual and Social Transformation in African American Spiritual Churches* (Boston, MA: Brill, 2015), 18.

42 Margarita Guillory, *Spiritual and Social Transformation in African American Spiritual Churches* (Boston, MA: Brill, 2015), 21–23.

43 Margarita Guillory, *Spiritual and Social Transformation in African American Spiritual Churches* (Boston, MA: Brill, 2015), 24.

44 Margarita Guillory, *Spiritual and Social Transformation in African American Spiritual Churches* (Boston, MA: Brill, 2015), 44.

45 Richard Brent Turner, *Islam in the African-American Experience*, 2nd edition (Bloomington, IN: Indiana University Press, 2003), 120.

46 Richard Brent Turner, *Islam in the African-American Experience*, 2nd edition (Bloomington, IN: Indiana University Press, 2003), 111–112.

47 Edward E. Curtis IV, "Islamism and Its African American Muslim Critics: Black Muslims in the Era of the Arab Cold War" *American Quarterly*, 59, no. 3 (September 2007): 690.

48 Edward E. Curtis IV, "Islamism and Its African American Muslim Critics: Black Muslims in the Era of the Arab Cold War" *American Quarterly*, 59, no. 3 (September 2007): 690–691.

49 Richard Brent Turner, *Islam in the African-American Experience*, 2nd edition (Bloomington, IN: Indiana University Press, 2003), 112–113.

50 Richard Brent Turner, *Islam in the African-American Experience*, 2nd edition (Bloomington, IN: Indiana University Press, 2003), 109, 129.

51 Richard Brent Turner, *Islam in the African-American Experience*, 2nd edition (Bloomington, IN: Indiana University Press, 2003), 122–129.

52 Richard Brent Turner, *Islam in the African-American Experience*, 2nd edition (Bloomington, IN: Indiana University Press, 2003), 71–72; Arthur Huff Fauset, *Black Gods of the Metropolis: Negro Religious Cults of the Urban North* (Philadelphia: PA, 2022, orig. 1944), 48.

53 Richard Brent Turner, *Islam in the African-American Experience*, 2nd edition (Bloomington, IN: Indiana University Press, 2003), 72, 90.

54 Richard Brent Turner, *Islam in the African-American Experience*, 2nd edition (Bloomington, IN: Indiana University Press, 2003), 93.

55 Richard Brent Turner, *Islam in the African-American Experience*, 2nd edition (Bloomington, IN: Indiana University Press, 2003), 93–94.

56 Drew Al, Moorish Science Temple of America, and Omar Ibn Said Collection. *The Holy Koran of the Moorish Science Temple of America: circle 7* (United States: The Moorish Science Temple of America, 1927), manuscript/mixed material, retrieved from www.loc.gov/item/2018662631; Arthur Huff Fauset, *Black Gods of the Metropolis: Negro Religious Cults of the Urban North* (Philadelphia: PA, 2022, orig. 1944), 42; Edward E. Curtis IV and Danielle Brune Sigler, ed., *The New Black Gods: Arthur Huff Fauset and the Study of African American Religions* (Bloomington, IN: Indiana University Press, 2009), 73.

57 Edward E. Curtis IV and Danielle Brune Sigler, ed., *The New Black Gods: Arthur Huff Fauset and the Study of African American Religions* (Bloomington, IN: Indiana University Press, 2009), 48, 77; Arthur Huff Fauset, *Black Gods of the Metropolis: Negro Religious Cults of the Urban North* (Philadelphia: PA, 2022, orig. 1944), 42–44.

58 Arthur Huff Fauset, *Black Gods of the Metropolis: Negro Religious Cults of the Urban North* (Philadelphia: PA, 2022, orig. 1944), 42.

59 Richard Brent Turner, *Islam in the African-American Experience*, 2nd edition (Bloomington, IN: Indiana University Press, 2003), 92; Judith Weisenfeld, *New World a-Coming: Black Religion and Racial Identity during the Great Migration* (New York: NYU Press, 2017), 227–228; Arthur Huff Fauset, *Black Gods of the Metropolis: Negro Religious Cults of the Urban North* (Philadelphia: PA, 2022, orig. 1944), 48.

60 Judith Weisenfeld, *New World a-Coming: Black Religion and Racial Identity during the Great Migration* (New York: NYU Press, 2017), 228.

61 Arthur Huff Fauset, *Black Gods of the Metropolis: Negro Religious Cults of the Urban North* (Philadelphia: PA, 2022, orig. 1944), 41–44.

62 Judith Weisenfeld, *New World a-Coming: Black Religion and Racial Identity during the Great Migration* (New York: NYU Press, 2017), 222–228.

63 Judith Weisenfeld, *New World a-Coming: Black Religion and Racial Identity during the Great Migration* (New York: NYU Press, 2017), 222.

64 Judith Weisenfeld, *New World a-Coming: Black Religion and Racial Identity during the Great Migration* (New York: NYU Press, 2017), 220–221.

65 Joseph M. Murphy, and J. Gordon Melton, eds, *Encyclopedia of African American Religions* (New York: Garland Publishing, 1993), 506–507; Arthur Huff Fauset, *Black Gods of the Metropolis: Negro Religious Cults of the Urban North* (Philadelphia: PA, 2022, orig. 1944), 42; Martha F. Lee, *The Nation of Islam, An American Millenarian Movement* (Lewiston, NY: Edwin Mellen Press, 1988), 21–22.

66 Judith Weisenfeld, *New World a-Coming: Black Religion and Racial Identity during the Great Migration* (New York: NYU Press, 2017), 218.

67 Dennis A. Williams and Elaine Sciolino. "Rebirth of the Nation," *Newsweek* 87 (March 15, 1976): 33; Martha F. Lee, *The Nation of Islam, An American Millenarian Movement* (Lewiston, NY: Edwin Mellen Press, 1988), 22–25; C. Eric Lincoln, *The Black Muslims in America* (Boston, MA: Beacon Press, 1961), 10–15.

68 Martha F. Lee, *The Nation of Islam, An American Millenarian Movement* (Lewiston, NY: Edwin Mellen Press, 1988), 22–25. C. Eric Lincoln, *The Black Muslims in America* (Boston, MA: Beacon Press, 1961), 14–16.

69 Judith Weisenfeld, *New World a-Coming: Black Religion and Racial Identity during the Great Migration* (New York: NYU Press, 2017), 216; Martha F. Lee, *The Nation of Islam, An American Millenarian Movement* (Lewiston, NY: Edwin Mellen Press, 1988), 26–27.

70 Martha F. Lee, *The Nation of Islam, An American Millenarian Movement* (Lewiston, NY: Edwin Mellen Press, 1988), 22; Dennis A. Williams and Elaine Sciolino, "Rebirth of the Nation," *Newsweek*, March 15, 1976, 33.

71 C. Eric Lincoln, *The Black Muslims in America* (Boston, MA: Beacon Press, 1961), 132.

72 Judith Weisenfeld, *New World a-Coming: Black Religion and Racial Identity during the Great Migration* (New York: NYU Press, 2017), 215.

73 Judith Weisenfeld, *New World a-Coming: Black Religion and Racial Identity during the Great Migration* (New York: NYU Press, 2017), 215–217.

74 Judith Weisenfeld, *New World a-Coming: Black Religion and Racial Identity during the Great Migration* (New York: NYU Press, 2017), 214–218.

75 Stephen C. Finley, *In and Out of This World: Material and Extraterrestrial Bodies in the Nation of Islam* (Durham, NC: Duke University Press, 2022), 73, 158–159.

76 Arthur Huff Fauset, *Black Gods of the Metropolis: Negro Religious Cults of the Urban North* (Philadelphia: PA, 2022, orig. 1944), 55–56.

77 Arthur Huff Fauset, *Black Gods of the Metropolis: Negro Religious Cults of the Urban North* (Philadelphia: PA, 2022, orig. 1944), 56.

78 Robert Weisbrot, *Father Divine and the Struggle for Racial Equality* (Urbana, IL: University of Illinois Press, 1983), 49–53.

79 Arthur Huff Fauset, *Black Gods of the Metropolis: Negro Religious Cults of the Urban North* (Philadelphia: PA, 2022, orig. 1944), 63.

80 Judith Weisenfeld, *New World a-Coming: Black Religion and Racial Identity during the Great Migration* (New York: NYU Press, 2017), 231; Arthur Huff Fauset, *Black Gods of the Metropolis: Negro Religious Cults of the Urban North* (Philadelphia: PA, 2022, orig. 1944), 62–63.

81 Robert Weisbrot, *Father Divine and the Struggle for Racial Equality* (Urbana, IL: University of Illinois Press, 1983), 76; Arthur Huff Fauset, *Black Gods of the Metropolis: Negro Religious Cults of the Urban North* (Philadelphia: PA, 2022, orig. 1944), 60.

82 Arthur Huff Fauset, *Black Gods of the Metropolis: Negro Religious Cults of the Urban North* (Philadelphia: PA, 2022, orig. 1944), 56–60.

83 Judith Weisenfeld, *New World a-Coming: Black Religion and Racial Identity during the Great Migration* (New York: NYU Press, 2017), 234.

84 Robert Weisbrot, *Father Divine and the Struggle for Racial Equality* (Urbana, IL: University of Illinois Press, 1983), 125–130.

85 Arthur Huff Fauset, *Black Gods of the Metropolis: Negro Religious Cults of the Urban North* (Philadelphia: PA, 2022, orig. 1944), 55, 66; Judith Weisenfeld, *New World a-Coming: Black Religion and Racial Identity during the Great Migration* (New York: NYU Press, 2017), 231.

86 Judith Weisenfeld, *New World a-Coming: Black Religion and Racial Identity during the Great Migration* (New York: NYU Press, 2017), 228–229.

87 Judith Weisenfeld, *New World a-Coming: Black Religion and Racial Identity during the Great Migration* (New York: NYU Press, 2017), 229.

88 Though Divine was a pacifist, he encouraged PM members to support the United States and Allies during World War II through purchasing liberty bonds. Judith Weisenfeld, *New World a-Coming: Black Religion and Racial Identity during the Great Migration* (New York: NYU Press, 2017), 228–231; Robert Weisbrot, *Father Divine and the Struggle for Racial Equality* (Urbana, IL: University of Illinois Press, 1983), 152–157, 163–164.

89 Harold Dean Trulear, "Ida B. Robinson: The Mother as Symbolic Presence," in *Portraits of a Generation: Early Pentecostal Leaders*, edited by James R. Goff Jr. and Grant Wacker (Fayetteville, AR: University of Arkansas Press, 2002), 312–313; Harold Dean Trulear, "Reshaping Black Pastoral Theology: The Vision of Bishop Ida B. Robinson," *The Journal of Religious Thought*, 46, no. 1 (1989), 20; Estrelda Y. Alexander, *Black Fire: One Hundred Years of African American Pentecostalism* (Downers Grove, IL: Intervarsity Press, 2011), 166.

90 Estrelda Y. Alexander, *Black Fire: One Hundred Years of African American Pentecostalism* (Downers Grove, IL: Intervarsity Press, 2011), 166–167.

91 Estrelda Y. Alexander, *Black Fire: One Hundred Years of African American Pentecostalism* (Downers Grove, IL: Intervarsity Press, 2011), 167; Harold Dean Trulear, "Reshaping Black Pastoral Theology: The Vision of Bishop Ida B. Robinson," *The Journal of Religious Thought*, 46, no. 1 (1989), 20–22.

92 Harold Dean Trulear, "Reshaping Black Pastoral Theology: The Vision of Bishop Ida B. Robinson," *The Journal of Religious Thought*, 46, no. 1 (1989), 23–24.

93 Hans A. Baer and Merrill Singer, *African American Religion in the Twentieth Century: Varieties of Protest and Accommodation* (Knoxville, TN: University of Tennessee Press, 1992), 165–166; Harold Dean Trulear, "Reshaping Black Pastoral Theology: The Vision of Bishop Ida B. Robinson," *The Journal of Religious Thought*, 46, no. 1 (1989), 23–24.

94 Bettye Collier-Thomas, *Daughters of Thunder: Black Women Preachers and Their Sermons, 1850–1979* (San Francisco, CA: Jossey-Bass Publishers), 204.

Further Readings

Best, Wallace. *Passionately Human, No Less Divine: Religion and Culture in Black Chicago, 1915–1952*. Princeton, NJ: Princeton University Press, 2005.

Curtis, Edward E.IV, and Danielle Brune Sigler, eds. *The New Black Gods: Arthur Huff Fauset and the Study of African American Religions*. Bloomington, IN: Indiana University Press, 2009.

Fauset, Arthur Huff. *Black Gods of the Metropolis: Negro Religious Cults of the Urban North*. Philadelphia, PA: University of Pennsylvania Press, 2022. Originally published in 1944.

Guillory, Margarita. *Spiritual and Social Transformation in African American Spiritual Churches*. Boston, MA: Brill, 2015.

Jacobs, Claude F. and Andrew J. Kaslow. *The Spiritual Churches of New Orleans: Origins, Beliefs, and Rituals of an African-American Religion*. Knoxville, TN: University of Tennessee Press, 1991.

Muhammad, Elijah. *Message to the Black Man in America*. Chicago, IL: Secretarius MEMPS Publications, 2009.

Owens, Rosalie S. *Bishop Ida Bell Robinson: The Authoritarian Servant Leader*. North Charleston, SC: CreateSpace Independent Publishing Platform, 2018.

Sernett, Milton C. *Bound for the Promised Land: African American Religion and the Great Migration*. Durham, NC: Duke University Press, 1997.

Turner, Richard Brent. *Islam in the African-American Experience*. 2nd ed. Bloomington, IN: Indiana University Press, 2003.

Weisbrot, Robert. *Father Divine and the Struggle for Racial Equality*. Urbana, IL: University of Illinois Press, 1983.

Weisenfeld, Judith. *New World a-Coming: Black Religion and Racial Identity during the Great Migration*. New York: NYU Press, 2017. doi:10.18574/9781479853687.

5 "We Shall Overcome"

Spiritual Strivings during the Civil Rights Era

We shall overcome, we shall overcome
We shall overcome someday
Oh, deep in my heart, I do believe,
We shall overcome someday.
We are not alone, we are not alone
We are not alone today
Oh, deep in my heart, I do believe,
We are not alone today.
　　　　　　　"We Shall Overcome"
　　　　　　　(traditional gospel song)

Peter Seeger, Guy Carawan, and Candie Carawan drew on the Black musical tradition when developing "We Shall Overcome" into a civil rights song during workshops at the Highlander Folk School.[1] It became the anthem of the Movement and was one of many freedom songs activists sang during mass meetings and nonviolent demonstrations. The spiritual and cultural resources of Black Christians undergirded the civil rights movement. According to sociologist Aldon Morris, churches also provided a wealth of material resources, including an organized mass base and leadership of clergypersons largely economically independent of the larger White society, an institutionalized financial base through which protests were financed, and meeting places where the masses planned tactics and strategies and collectively committed themselves to the struggle.[2] Movement participants met in the basements and meeting halls of Baptist, Methodist, and Pentecostal churches. Recognizing the significance of churches, white supremacists attempted to undermine movement efforts by bombing ninety-three churches between 1962 and 1965.[3] Bayard Rustin, a central pioneer of nonviolent philosophy who helped to orchestrate several civil rights organizations and mass movements such as the March on Washington, acknowledged that pastors helped to inspire "enthusiasm" and courage among movement participants who risked their livelihood and lives.[4] Religious songs and ministers' sermons fueled activists to face nearly impossible odds. Christian activists used sermons, gospel hymns, and prayer to reinforce the message of nonviolent resistance.

While Black churches helped propel the Movement forward, their influence must not be overstated. Numerous Black Christians did not participate in the Movement. Youth and college students throughout the country affiliated with organizations such as the Student Nonviolent Coordinating Committee and the Congress of Racial Equality boldly spearheaded freedom rides, sit-ins, voter education projects, and student walkouts of

DOI: 10.4324/9781003359197-6

schools. Still, it was a Black Baptist minister, Reverend Dr. Martin Luther King Jr., who emerged as the symbolic and central figure during the mid-twentieth-century movement. The organization he founded, the Southern Christian Leadership Conference (SCLC), strategically employed nonviolent resistance to attract the media's attention so as to influence Congress to pass critical civil rights legislation. Though SCLC activists, especially King, received extensive news coverage, multiple Black religious activists, including but not limited to Joseph H. Jackson, Septima Clark and Ella Baker, and Malcolm X, critiqued King and proposed alternate religious responses to white supremacy. This chapter comparatively examines the spiritual strivings of influential Black religious leaders during the civil rights era.

Reverend Dr. Martin Luther King Jr.'s Emergence as the Symbol of Nonviolent Direct Action

More than any civil rights activist, King emerged as an iconic figure of the civil rights struggle. His leadership of the Montgomery Bus Boycott contributed to his rise as the most renowned and prominent civil rights activist during the 1950s and 1960s, the defining decades of the modern civil rights movement when civil rights organizations mobilized masses of people to exert pressure on the federal government to defend Blacks' civil rights. Following the boycott, King founded and became the first president of the Southern Christian Leadership Conference (SCLC) in 1957. Drawing on Scripture and Christian principles and the teachings of Mahatma Gandhi, the organization orchestrated nonviolent protest demonstrations throughout the United States, especially the South, for more than a decade. The organization provided support to organized and functioning grassroots campaigns. Because of his popularity and celebrity within the movement, local affiliates frequently invited King and other SCLC leaders to join their campaigns and galvanize the masses. Whether in Montgomery, Birmingham, Albany, or Memphis, King helped draw an audience to hear him preach. He inspired folks to put their bodies on the line and support the struggle financially. Thousands of people attended mass meetings, voter registration drives, and marches when they heard King and SCLC would be present. His unwavering commitment to his Christian faith, which stressed agape love and justice, inspired Black Christians to believe that God was on their side and that the divine would help them be victorious in their moral struggle against white supremacy.

Because of King's popularity, civil rights scholars such as historians Taylor Branch, Adam Fairclough, and David J. Garrow studied King and the SCLC extensively. Historians have identified how King's influence overshadowed the contributions of numerous rank-and-file grassroots activists who organized and advanced local movements for justice throughout America.[5] Similarly, the overconcentration on King caused historians to overlook women's contributions to the Montgomery Bus Boycott and other local movements. Jo Ann Gibson Robinson, a professor at Alabama State College and leader in the Montgomery Bus Boycott, emphasized in her memoir the essential contributions a variety of Montgomery women made to the struggle. For example, the Women's Political Council, founded by Mary Fair Burks in 1946, spearheaded voter registration efforts in churches and colleges in Montgomery. Women met with city leaders regarding equal access to public parks and accommodations before the start of the Montgomery bus boycott. Robinson wrote a letter to the mayor of Montgomery seeking to persuade him and local leaders to respond to insulting practices on the buses. Claudette Colvin and Mary Louis Smith were young women who protested segregation on Montgomery buses before Rosa Parks. The police arrested them on different occasions for defying bus segregation laws.[6] Both young women were teenagers and were from the working-class community. Upon discovering that Colvin was pregnant, some Montgomery NAACP and WPC officials decided that she was an unsuitable "candidate for a test case."[7]

As noted previously, SCLC intentionally planned for King to be in the media lime-light, especially the national news media. While Black newspapers routinely covered King and contributed to the mobilization of Black people throughout the civil rights era, Black newspapers primarily circulated among Black communities. They did not reach the masses of Americans. Many Southern White newspapers covered news in the White community and targeted a White readership. White-owned newspapers typically devoted minimal attention to Black Americans except for those who committed a criminal offense or acquired fame. Many Southern White newspapers, by and large, identified with the dominant establishment and provided biased coverage of the Movement, if they covered it at all.[8]

King and SCLC leaders aimed to use dramatic nonviolent demonstrations to attract the attention of national news media. A few years after the Montgomery Bus Boycott, SCLC collaborated with SNCC to desegregate Albany, GA, between November 1961 and the summer of 1962. The city of Albany was not in compliance with the ruling of the Interstate Commerce Commission, which mandated the desegregation of all trans-portation facilities. SNCC leaders invited King to help energize the local Movement. However, compared to later movements that King would lead, such as the Birmingham and Selma campaigns, the Albany Movement did not produce significant results and was anticlimactic. The local police chief, Laurie Pritchett, avoided negative media publicity by not responding to the nonviolent demonstrations with violence. He instructed his officers not to antagonize demonstrators engaging in civil disobedience. They peacefully arrested protesters and loaded them in paddy wagons. Consequently, the media did not report violent incidents.

On the other hand, Reverend Fred Shuttleworth informed King that Birmingham police officials could not exercise a similar restraint as Pritchett. He anticipated that they would respond with violence toward "peaceful" demonstrators.[9] He and other SCLC officials believed that any racist attacks would be newsworthy. Under the direction of police Safety Commissioner Eugene "Bull" Connor, the Birmingham police behaved as SCLC officials anticipated that they would. Unlike Pritchett's Albany officers, who merely arrested nonviolent demonstrators, the Birmingham Police harassed nonviolent protestors, including women and children. They sprayed them with high-pressure water hoses, released German shepherd dogs to attack them, and beat them with batons. The national news media recorded and photographed the violent attacks. Furthermore, the press interviewed King. Andrew Young advised King to prepare short messages for "television news broadcasts."[10] SCLC strategically planned demonstrations early in the day to align with the schedules of television news programs. In contrast to con-temporary news stations, which perpetually have live broadcasts throughout the day, and social media outlets such as Instagram and Facebook Live, during the 1960s, the evening news only appeared at specific times, and the stories were prerecorded. King and SCLC officials understood that news camera persons and reporters needed to record demonstrations before 2 p.m. for the footage to air on the evening broadcast.[11]

Learning from the Albany and Birmingham campaigns, King and SCLC developed the following strategy, which was published in the *Saturday Review of Literature*:

1   Nonviolent demonstrators go into the streets to exercise their constitutional rights.
2   Racists resist by unleashing violence against them.
3   Americans of conscience, in the name of decency, demand federal intervention and legislation.
4   The Administration, under mass pressure, initiates measures of immediate intervention and remedial legislation.[12]

Nonviolent direct action aimed to coerce the federal government, the chief executive, and Congress to use its power and authority to address racial injustice promptly and directly. Parts two and three of the plan, however, were contingent on public disdain and outcry, with nonviolent demonstrators being immoral victims of violent racists. For this to happen, the press needed to be present at civil rights demonstrations to capture and expose racial injustice precipitated by law enforcement officials. Interested in expanding their audience, national news organizations assigned reporters and photographers to cover civil rights drama as it was unfolding.[13] Journalists from nationally syndicated papers like the *New York Times* and *Los Angeles Times* courageously traveled South to report on the movement.[14] When Claude Sitton became national editor of the *New York Times* in 1964, he instructed reporters to provide coverage for all Southern demonstrations involving King. He expected *Times* reporters and camerapersons to be on call and be prepared to capture the drama. He understood the grave danger King faced in the South and perceived that a racist White person might try to assassinate him for challenging the racial status quo. According to Roberts and Klibanoff, "Whatever happened to King, for better or worse, Sitton wanted the *Times* to be there."[15]

The *New York Times* was, by no means, the only national news outlet interested in covering King during the civil rights movement. Richard Lentz examines how three national news magazines, *Time, Newsweek, and U.S. News and World Report,* covered King from the period of the Montgomery Bus Boycott to the Poor People's Campaign.[16] *Times* and *Newsweek* wrote favorable articles about King, praising his promotion of nonviolence and condemning violent Southern police officials who assaulted nonviolent protestors. King appeared on the cover of *Time* on February 18, 1957. The magazine acknowledged his leadership of the Montgomery Bus Boycott. *Time* magazine honored him as the 1963 "Man of the Year" in January 1964. Among other things, King delivered his iconic "I Have a Dream" message during the March on Washington and wrote his "Letter from a Birmingham Jail" during the Birmingham campaign. *Times* and *Newsweek* routinely supported King as a moderate civil rights leader and viewed him as a better alternative to Malcolm X and the more militant Stokely Carmichael. They uplifted King's nonviolent message when condemning urban rebellions in Watts and other localities.

Many journalists who lauded King's leadership of the civil rights struggle in the South turned against him when he began to protest racial and economic injustice throughout America and the globe and when he spoke out against the War in Vietnam. Prominent national news magazines opined that he should stay in the lane of civil rights. Following King's assassination, national news outlets discarded King's radical statements and "resurrected [him] as a gentle prophet," exalting his message of faith and optimism in American ideals and his commitment to nonviolence.[17] After King was assassinated in 1968, singer and longtime civil rights supporter Harry Belafonte grew angry at a *New York Times* reporter standing next to him at the funeral: "I could not help but tell him that this grievous moment was in part the result of a climate of hate and distortion that

Figure 5.1 A photograph of Dr. King and other civil rights leaders talking with reporters after meeting with President John F. Kennedy after the March on Washington, DC. Photograph by W.K. Leffler (1963).
Courtesy of the Library of Congress

the *New York Times* and other papers had helped create … Just coming to grieve the loss was no cleansing of guilt."[18] Belafonte held that the *New York Times* did not truly understand King's prophetic message and helped influence the public to turn against him before his assassination.

Besides misconstruing King, the media often did not fully understand the Movement. According to Charles Payne, the press frequently downplayed the roles of local activists and grassroots community organizers who participated in the Southern civil rights movement and tended to hone in on the national civil rights leaders. For example, he notes that when King came to Birmingham, the press wanted to hear from King instead of Fred Shuttlesworth, a local activist leading the Birmingham movement. Looking to King and SCLC leaders as figures they could consult to obtain "the movement perspective," the press devoted little attention to Shuttlesworth and "missed an opportunity to learn something about the historical depth of the struggle and the variety of leadership styles that sustained it."[19] All things considered, in their preoccupation with King, historians, and civil rights scholars have overlooked, neglected, and misunderstood many religious activists who had alternative approaches to pursuing racial justice

Joseph H. Jackson, a Constitutional and Ecumenical Approach to Social Justice

Joseph H. Jackson (1900–1990) is one example of a Black religious figure whose vision for social justice has been overlooked and misinterpreted. He was a Black Baptist minister who disagreed with King. Ordained to the Baptist ministry in 1922, Jackson ascended to the highest ranks within the National Baptist Convention of the USA, Inc. (NBCUSA), the most prominent Black denomination. Jackson led congregations in rural Mississippi, Nebraska, and Pennsylvania. In 1941, he became senior pastor of the distinguished Olivet Baptist Church in Chicago, Illinois. He served for nineteen years as executive secretary of the Foreign Mission Board of the NBC. He became president of the NBCUSA in 1953 and remained in the position for twenty-nine years.[20]

King was a devoted member of the NBCUSA. He and his family had a close relationship with Jackson. However, the relationship soured during the 1950s, primarily over civil rights. As leader of the SCLC, King desired for the Black Baptist Churches in his denomination to support the civil rights struggle. He wanted the NBCUSA to collaborate with the SCLC and become a center for the civil rights struggle. However, he held that nonviolent direct action conflicted with American democracy and advised NBC members not to participate in boycotts, protest marches, and even the historic March on Washington in 1963.[21]

In addition to civil rights, the leaders disagreed about the length of tenure of the NBCUSA president. Once Jackson became president in 1953, he fought to remain in power and opposed a tenure amendment, which restricted the time the president would serve in office to a few years. King came to view Jackson "as an autocratic leader with a thirst for control."[22] He aspired to galvanize Baptist leaders to remove Jackson as president and replace him with his friend, Gardner C. Taylor, who was more in line with his civil rights vision.[23] After being unsuccessful, King and Taylor separated from the NBCUSA. They rallied nearly 500,000 Black Baptists to follow them and form a separate denomination, the Progressive National Baptist Convention (PNBC). The first meeting was held on September 11, 1961, and Taylor became the inaugural president. Under his leadership, the PNBC fully supported SCLC's nonviolent direct-action agenda.

Though Jackson disagreed with King and the men had a sour relationship following King's effort to replace him with Taylor, Jackson remained popular among Black Baptists within the NBCUSA. Furthermore, Jackson was not altogether opposed to the civil rights struggle. According to historian Wallace Best, scholars have frequently portrayed Jackson as a mere accommodationist who accepted the status quo and as the older apolitical contrast to the younger, more radical King. Both ministers agreed about the problems of racial discrimination and injustice and the need for civil rights. Shortly after passing *Brown vs. Board of Education,* Jackson called for Congress to declare May 17 "Anti-Segregation Day."[24] He made public statements endorsing immediate voting rights for disenfranchised Blacks in the Jim Crow South.[25] He helped to spearhead the "Urge Congress Movement," which encouraged Black Christians, Black professionals, labor organizations, fraternities, and sororities to write letters to congressional representatives urging them to support the Civil Rights Bill of 1957. Under Jackson's leadership, the NBCUSA established a Civil Rights Commission. He believed that Black Churches should continue to pursue social justice through working through the courts and legislative channels. He encouraged Black people to know and uphold their constitutional rights as American citizens. Black pastors in urban centers could mobilize Blacks to support candidates they believed might help advance the plight of African Americans.[26] Similar to Booker T. Washington, Jackson proposed a self-help agenda, suggesting that Blacks invest their resources in establishing Black educational institutions, cleaning up their neighborhoods, and creating employment programs. Mary O. Ross, the Women's Convention president from 1961 to 1995 and successor to Nannie Burroughs, stood with

Jackson. She admonished fellow women in the NBCUSA not to support King's non-violent direct-action program but to pursue social advancement by establishing Black schools and businesses.[27]

Jackson fundamentally perceived King's protest politics as a threat to the national unity needed for America to rise victorious against communism. As Americans dealt with the threat of Communism, Jackson deemed that all Americans should stand united along all lines of difference, including race.[28] Besides civil rights, Jackson disagreed with King about the church's function and purpose in society. He formed the Commission on Ecumenical Christianity because he desired for the denomination to collaborate with Christians around the globe to advance the work of Christ through establishing missions, educational programs, and various social ministries. As a Black Protestant denominational leader, Jackson went out of his way to schedule a meeting with the Pope of the Roman Catholic Church because he believed that the global church should work collectively to respond to social problems, including Blacks' struggles with injustice in America. After meeting with Jackson, the Pope invited him to the Second Vatican Council in 1962. Jackson was the only Black Protestant leader the Pope had asked to attend this historic meeting. Best explains, "Jackson's ecumenical work represented an unprecedented emphasis on the world religious scene, an emphasis that eluded nearly every prominent African American minister at the time."[29] To put it another way, Jackson was working with the World Council of Churches to consider how the global church could use its agency, resources, and collective power to fulfill the social justice mission of Christ and alleviate racism and other injustices.

Septima Clark and Ella Baker, a Community Organizing Approach to Social Justice

Given the patriarchal arrangement of society, men occupied the highest ranks of all major civil rights organizations. By focusing mainly on the male figureheads of the movement, the press rendered women activists invisible. Women made significant contributions to civil rights organizations and campaigns. For example, women such as Dorothy Height and Anna Arnold Hedgeman helped organize the historic March on Washington in 1963. Hedgeman served alongside Bayard Rustin and A. Philip Randolph on the executive committee. At the local level, Black women such as Annie May King housed and fed college students in 1964 during Freedom Summer. Numerous unnamed grassroots Black women advanced the movement through their work in churches, women's clubs, associations, and sororities. Women of diverse races and faiths contributed, including women such as Sandra Cason, who served as a staff member for the SCLC. Seeing the parallel between the oppression of Jews during the Holocaust and Black people in America, Jewish women such as Dottie Miller Zellner and Elaine DeLott Baker were drawn to the Southern movement. Of all the diverse women who contributed to the struggle, Black women have been the pillars of the movement and helped propel its successes at the grassroots level.[30] It is important to consider that Black women often constituted the majority of Black churches and coordinated the programming of various local and national civil rights organizations.

Among Black women activists during the mid-twentieth century, Septima Poinsette Clark (1898–1987) and Ella Josephine Baker (1903–1986) promoted "community organizing" as a method for pursuing civil rights. Community organizing stressed the "long-term development of leadership in ordinary men and women."[31] It contrasted with the community mobilizing strategy that "focused on large scale, relatively short public events," which King and SCLC adopted in various cities nationwide.[32]

Baker and Clark ostensibly came to embrace community organizing through their affiliation with the Highlander Folk School. Founded by Don West and Myles Horton in 1932, Highlander was a social activist training school for many activists during the 1950s, including but not limited to figures such as Rosa Parks, Martin Luther King, Andrew Young, and Diane Nash. Per its statement of purpose, the school aimed to expand "the scope of democracy to include everyone" and to deepen the concept's meaning "to include every relationship."[33] Highlander stressed that people experiencing poverty should be included in democracy and that oppressed people should be at the forefront of freedom struggles. The organization endeavored to esteem the cultures from which participants came. Workshop leaders encouraged Black American activists to draw on spirituals, church hymns, and various forms of music from their culture for inspiration.[34]

Clark first visited Highlander in 1954. She embraced its philosophy and principles. Born in Charleston, South Carolina, in 1898, Clark became a civil rights activist during her middle-aged years.[35] She often worked behind the scenes as an educator and active participant in the NAACP. After serving about four decades as a public school teacher, Clark lost her job due to her membership in the NAACP. Following the *Brown* ruling, many Southern White citizenship councils, which consisted of White business owners and others in positions of power, used their authority to fire Black people who were members of the NAACP. Clark accepted a job offer from Highlander to become the director of workshops. In this new role, she spearheaded the development of citizenship schools in South Carolina. The schools taught Black people how to improve their communities through voting, civic engagement, and lobbying local government officials to provide more enhanced municipal services in their areas.[36] In 1961, SCLC accepted Highlander's invitation to supervise the administration of citizenship schools beyond South Carolina. SCLC brought Clark on board as a member of its executive committee. She helped SCLC expand the citizenship schools in other Southern states.

Critical of the classism within SCLC, Clark critiqued many SCLC leaders for being elitist. She noted that Ralph Abernathy would intentionally arrive late to church services "to flaunt his mastery over the common people."[37] She desired civil rights leaders to treat all participants as equals, embody and practice inclusive politics, and strive to develop solid relationships and connections among movement participants. She held that leadership development among local leaders was critical to community advancement and civil rights.

Clark also disagreed with SCLC's authoritarian and charismatic leadership style, which resembled the patriarchal leadership arrangement in many Black churches. She wrote King a letter, asking him to consider empowering local leaders to lead instead of always being at the forefront of civil rights demonstrations. Clark said King read her letter to the executive committee and chuckled at her suggestion. It bothered her that no one in the room defended her or dared say anything to challenge King or any male leaders because they feared losing their position in the organization. She asserted, "You can't go over that bossman; you have to listen. You have to sit and listen and not speak. That was true in every organization I've been in."[38] It also troubled Clark that Abernathy kept repeatedly asking other male members in her presence why she was permitted to serve on the SCLC executive board. She explained, "I think we live in a man-made world, and because of that, as a man, he didn't feel as if women had enough intelligence to do a thing like I was doing."[39] King justified her inclusion on the board by accentuating her instrumental role in advancing citizenship schools. Still, Clark felt that her male counterparts ignored her during board meetings. She recalled having to wait until the end of the meeting to interject her viewpoints on issues being discussed. She said, "We [the women] never were able to put ourselves on the agenda to speak to the group."[40]

Similar to Clark, Baker reported experiencing blatant sexism within the SCLC. Baker was a prominent member of several civil rights organizations, including the NAACP, SCLC, and SNCC. Born in Norfolk, Virginia, to Blake and Georgiana Ross Baker, Ella Baker grew up in the church and was baptized when she was nine.[41] Her mother's involvement in the church and community inspired her civic and civil rights activism.[42] Her family upheld the dignity and sacredness of human life and stressed that Christians had a responsibility to serve others. They also emphasized that establishing strong human relationships is more important than acquiring wealth and material possessions.[43]

Baker became "an assistant field secretary" for the NAACP in 1941. She later rose to the ranks of national director of NAACP branches and established youth councils throughout the country. She resigned as national director of branches because she felt the organization was underutilizing its staff. She deemed that the NAACP did not embody the true spirit of democracy and egalitarianism reflected at the Highlander Fok School. Though she stepped down from her national leadership position, she continued to serve the NAACP at the local level, including serving as president of the New York City Branch. She critiqued the organization for not empowering its regional branches and having too much authority concentrated at the national office.[44]

Bayard Rustin and Stanley Levison recruited Baker to help the newly established SCLC get a firmer footing after the boycott. Baker traveled South in 1957 and became the new executive director of the SCLC.[45] As an experienced community organizer, she managed the organization's day-to-day operations, finances, and strategic planning. She drew on the vast social connections she had established while working in the NAACP to organize SCLC's "voter registration and citizenship training drives."[46] She aspired to persuade the organization to recruit more women to participate and serve within it ranks.

Like Clark, Baker voiced criticism of SCLC's charismatic, hierarchical structure. She believed that charismatic leaders could become infatuated with recognition, lose sight of the purpose of the struggle, and adopt the oppressors' values.[47] She expressed:

> I have always felt it was a handicap for oppressed people to depend so largely on a leader, because unfortunately in our culture, the charismatic leader usually becomes a leader because he has found a spot in the public limelight. It usually means that the media made him, and the media may undo him. There is also the danger in our culture that, because a person is called upon to give public statements and is acclaimed by the establishment, such a person gets to the point of believing that he *is* the movement.[48]

Baker's critique likely had King in mind. She confided to Clark that an SCLC brochure should not include "sixteen pictures of Dr. King."[49] The extensive media coverage King received troubled Baker. Baker agreed with Clark that King played the role of a hero too often and stifled and suppressed the leadership potential of local influencers. Baker held that leaders need not aspire to be or become saviors—the figure followers look to for salvation. Instead, leaders should teach others to recognize their agency to lead and to derive solutions for problems.

Baker suspected that nonviolent demonstrations would not be a potent force continually. She stressed the need for "the development of stable, ongoing organizations at the local level."[50] In his last book, *Where Do We Go From Here: Chaos or Community?*, King seemingly acknowledged her critique. He noted that folks who participated in demonstrations became energized following a crisis but became accustomed to "inaction from day to day."[51] He explained, "We unconsciously patterned a crisis policy and program and summoned support not for daily commitment but for explosive events alone."[52] King eventually agreed with Baker that real change could not follow without sustained effort and organization.

Though King seemed to grasp Baker's criticism, he and many SCLC leaders rejected her ideas when she was a member of the SCLC leadership team. In 1959, Baker wrote a memo to SCLC outlining a proposal for a "Crusade for Citizenship."[53] In a nutshell, her proposal consisted of the following four points:

1 SCLC should coordinate leadership conferences and workshops for local leaders throughout the South.
2 SCLC should enlist and mobilize a thousand ministers to canvas local neighborhoods and register citizens to vote.[54]
3 SCLC should facilitate "a campaign to reduce illiteracy" and invite women's groups, church groups, and sororities to participate.
4 SCLC should organize training teams to teach nonviolent resistance to local community leaders.[55]

SCLC did not adopt Baker's proposal. The organization primarily remained committed to community mobilizing, and King stayed at the forefront. Baker criticized many Black ministers for being unwilling to join youth and women activists in doing *spadework*, which is defined as the humble work necessary to produce change. Churchwomen have often performed such work, including but not limited to canvassing neighborhoods, visiting barbershops and grocery stores, and helping members resolve conflict. This work did not yield rewards or recognition.

Baker resigned from the SCLC in the summer of 1960. She shared her wisdom and genius with student leaders spearheading the newly forming Student Nonviolent Coordinating Committee. She helped organize the sit-in activists conference at Shaw University, mentored and advised several activists, and strove to ensure they were not usurped by established civil rights organizations. Baker ostensibly influenced Robert (Bob) Moses, the director of SNCC's project in McCombs, Mississippi. In line with her community organizing model, he stressed working with local Black leaders to advance voting rights for African Americans. In 1964, he recruited White, upper-class students from Northern universities to volunteer to spend the summer helping register African Americans to vote and teach at freedom schools. Besides Moses, Stokely Carmichael was a student leader with SNCC. Though he initially embraced nonviolent resistance and collaborated with King, Carmichael often called King "da Lord," critiquing his charismatic leadership style just as Baker did.

Malcolm X's Black Nationalist and Black Unity Agenda

In addition to Baker, Carmichael also derived inspiration from Minister Malcolm X. Along with Willie Ricks, Carmichael introduced the slogan "Black Power" into the civil rights movement during the James Meredith March Against Fear in 1966. Black Power drew on Malcolm X's rhetoric and perspective and incorporated his critiques of King and the civil rights movement and his Black nationalist philosophy.

Malcolm X's experiences with racism and poverty, and his rearing in a Black nationalist household, informed his pessimistic perception of America. Born in Omaha, Nebraska, in 1925 to Earl and Louise Little, Malcolm X's birthname was Malcolm Little. His mother was an immigrant from Grenada, and his father was a Baptist minister from Georgia. His parents were active members of a local chapter of Garvey's UNIA. They encouraged him and his six siblings to embrace their Blackness. Harassed by white supremacist organizations, Earl was coerced to relocate from Nebraska to Milwaukee, Wisconsin, and ultimately to Lansing, Michigan. He died when Malcolm was six years of age as a result of a streetcar accident. Malcolm's mother held that the real culprit for her husband's death was a white supremacist group, the Black Legion. In his autobiography, Malcolm agreed with his mother. He faulted white supremacy for the death of his father and the subsequent nightmare that he experienced during his youth and young adult life. After his father's death, Malcolm's mother had a severe mental health crisis. A social service agency separated Malcolm and his siblings and placed them in foster homes. Malcolm's life gradually spiraled downward. He dropped out of school in the eighth grade and became a hustler. He sold and abused drugs and burglarized homes. After being convicted of robbery, the state of Massachusetts sentenced him to 10 years in prison. He served eight years at Charlestown State Prison and the Norfolk Prison Colony.[56]

Before going to prison, Malcolm had rejected his father's Baptist faith and was disconnected from the church. In prison, he received the nickname "Satan" because of his hostile posture toward religion.[57] Malcolm's brother, Reginald, who had recently converted to the NOI, wrote him a letter saying, "Malcolm, don't eat any pork, and don't smoke any more cigarettes. I'll show you how to get out of prison."[58] Reginald whetted Malcolm's interest in religion. A fellow inmate, John Elton Bembry, whom Malcolm called "Bimbi," reawakened in Malcolm a drive to learn about religion and other subjects. He especially moved him to become receptive to the teachings of the NOI and ultimately convert in 1948 while incarcerated.[59]

After his release from prison, Elijah Muhammad, the head of the Nation of Islam, convinced Malcolm to drop the name of his parents, Little, and replace his surname with an X. Malcolm X's wits, charisma, and rhetorical abilities enabled him to surge within the NOI leadership ranks. Within years of his release from prison, he became a national Muslim minister and a renowned spokesperson for the NOI. He spearheaded the establishment of a newspaper for the NOI entitled *Muhammad Speaks*. He opened and led multiple temples in urban centers and helped boost the growth of the NOI from a few hundred members to thousands. Malcolm X preached Muhammad's teachings and became the public face of the NOI during the 1950s. He promulgated the myth of Yakub and argued that White people are irredeemable devils (see Chapter 4). He insisted that White civilization would end soon. He opposed King's dream of integration and full inclusion in American society. He held that it was foolish for Black people to integrate into a country destined for divine judgment. He also held that integration was based on a premise of Black inferiority instead of equality. Many Blacks who desired to integrate perceived Whiteness as superior and accepted the myth that Black people were culturally, intellectually, and morally inferior. Besides condemning Whites, Malcolm endeavored to esteem Black people. He called for Blacks to prioritize self-love over against the

Christian notion of "loving one's enemies." He spoke against the nonviolent tactics of the civil rights movement because he perceived nonviolence to be in opposition to self-love and the defense of Black life from racial violence.

Although Malcolm X was popular among Blacks in the urban North, many White Americans became familiar with him in 1959 following his appearance in a documentary entitled "The Hate That Hate Produced" on *The Mike Wallace Show*. The documentary portrayed the NOI as a hateful organization that despised White people. The liberal media was disturbed by Minister Malcolm's provocative interrogation of systemic racism and his castigation of the nonviolent civil rights movement. He criticized SCLC for allowing children and youth to be subjected to violence during the Birmingham movement. He derided the March on Washington as the "Farce on Washington," a "Chump's March," and a "circus."[60] He asserted that the liberal establishment had coopted the march. He explained that demonstrators could not bring their original signs to the march and that the revolutionary spirit of the march had been quieted down. He expressed:

> Who ever heard of angry revolutionists harmonizing "We Shall Overcome ... Some Day ..." while tripping and swaying arm-in-arm with the people they were supposed to be angrily revolting against? Who ever heard of angry revolutionists swinging their bare feet together with their oppressor in lily-pad park pools, with gospels and guitars and "I Have a Dream" speeches?[61]

Simply put, the integrationist nature of the march troubled Malcolm, who deemed King's dream for an integrated America as being disconnected from the lived experiences of Blacks in urban ghettoes in the North. He held that King and many moderate civil rights leaders were naïve regarding White liberals. Deeming that the march ultimately did not accomplish its goals, he explained to an *Amsterdam News* reporter that the "black masses" remain largely unemployed and impoverished.[62] According to Malcolm, the death of four young girls—Addie Mae Collins, Cynthia Wesley, Carole Robertson, and Denise McNair—as a result of the bombing of the Sixteenth Street Baptist Church was an example of the pernicious violence against Black bodies that persisted despite the march.

While Malcolm discussed race in many of his speeches and illuminated the pervasive nature of American racism, as an NOI leader, he did not organize a robust initiative to struggle for racial justice. Instead of striving for full political rights for Blacks in America, Muhammad encouraged NOI followers to separate from Whites (see Chapter 4). He taught that God would judge White America. For these reasons, the organization was not at the forefront of the movement to demolish Jim Crow. Though the organization did not encourage members to participate in the civil rights struggle, the NOI embraced political activism regarding Black Muslims. For example, during the 1960s, the NOI fought for incarcerated converts to be able to purchase Qur'ans, for NOI ministers with criminal records to be permitted to return to prisons to share the teachings of the NOI, and for correctional institutions to respect the dietary restrictions of Black Muslims, especially prohibitions against eating pork.[63]

As a Muslim minister, Malcolm X desired to broadly advance civil rights for Black people. NOI leaders accused Malcolm of straying from Muhammad's teachings and becoming too political. The NOI forbade adherents from becoming directly involved in the civil rights movement. Though Malcolm preached Muhammad's apocalyptic message that God would judge the racist White establishment; he believed Black Muslims should not simply wait on divine action but should directly contribute to the civil rights struggle. Malcolm's speech, "Message to the Grassroots," delivered on December 10, 1963, reflected his emerging political philosophy. He encouraged Blacks in attendance to work across differences to confront their common oppressor. He contrasted the "black revolution" and the "negro revolution," positing that the former consisted of bloody struggles for liberation such as those taking place with oppressed groups in Africa and Asia. He equated the latter with the nonviolent civil rights movement and explained that it was not an authentic revolution because it aimed to integrate Blacks with their White oppressors. He argued that true revolutions are "bloody" and subversive.[64] He also drew on the "field negro" versus "house negro" metaphor to distinguish his approach to social justice from mainstream civil rights leaders. According to Malcolm, during slavery, the house negroes were treated well by their masters. They ate the master's food, lived in his house, and were programmed to be responsive to his needs. The field negroes were "the majority of slaves" who were brutally mistreated by enslavers. They toiled for long hours in the agricultural fields, were poorly fed and clothed, and lived uncomfortably in the slave cabins. Most of all, they despised their masters and pressed to escape slavery by any means. The field negroes supported the Black revolution.[65]

Minister Malcolm spoke derisively of King and criticized him and other civil rights leaders who allied with White liberals as house negroes. However, his perspective of King and the movement changed following his separation from the NOI after Muhammad silenced him for making a sarcastic comment about President John F. Kennedy's assassination on November 22, 1963. During a Q&A session after he delivered his speech "On God's Judgment of White America" on December 4, 1963, Malcolm told a reporter that he interpreted Kennedy's assassination as an example of "America's chickens coming home to roost." He said, "Being an old farm boy myself, chickens coming home to roost never did make me sad; they've always made me glad."[66] Malcolm learned from Muhammad's son, Wallace, that top leaders within the NOI were jealous of his popularity and were seeking a reason to strip him of his position within the organization. His views regarding race also shifted after his hajj, the pilgrimage to Mecca that Muslims are expected to make during their lifetime. While in Mecca in 1964, Malcolm bonded with Muslims with a White complexion. He came to reject the broad generalization of Whites he learned and preached in the NOI as being wrong. During his pilgrimage, he embraced Sunni Islam, the traditionalist and mainstream branch of Islam. He received a new name, El-Hajj Malik El-Shabazz. Upon returning to the United States on June 28, 1964, he formed the Organization of Afro-American Unity (OAAU). During his opening address for the new organization, he welcomed and encouraged Blacks to work across their lines of difference to pursue freedom and justice. The two primary aims of the OAAU were for "self-determination" and "national unity." The program consisted of "five strategic points":

1   **Restoration**—Restore severed lines of communications with Africa via "independent national and international" modes of media.
2   **Reorientation**—Develop a global perspective and consciousness.
3   **Education**—Develop original pedagogical methods to liberate the minds of Black youth.
4   **Economic Security**—Blacks must creatively overcome economic enslavement affecting Black people throughout the diaspora.
5   **Self-Defense**—Blacks have the right to defend themselves by any means necessary.[67]

He encouraged Blacks to redefine and internationalize the struggle by seeking to appeal to the United Nations to hold the United States accountable for crimes against Black people. He called for broadening the freedom struggle beyond civil rights to human rights. He believed that Blacks in America should join forces with Blacks throughout the world, resisting colonial oppression.[68] Malcolm's sister, Ella Collins, collaborated with Malcolm X in developing the "AIMS and Objectives of the OAAU," which were as follows:

1 Free Black Americans from Economic Oppression.
2 Create Business Opportunities and Jobs
3 Establish an Environment of Security, Stability, Dignity, and Initiative for Our Youth.
4 Demand Justice Whenever It Becomes Evident that the Laws as Composed and Enforced are Contrary To the Welfare and Well-Being of Our People, by Any Means Necessary.
5 Pledge Unity and Strive for Understanding Among Black Americans.
6 Restore Communication and Trade with Africa.
7 Devise Original Educational Methods.
8 Stimulate International Economic and Political Awareness.
9 Act an Overseas "Voice" for Afro-Americans.
10 To Provide A Means to Defend Ourselves by Any Means Necessary from Racist Oppression where the Government Proves It Is Unwilling an/or Unable To Do So.[69]

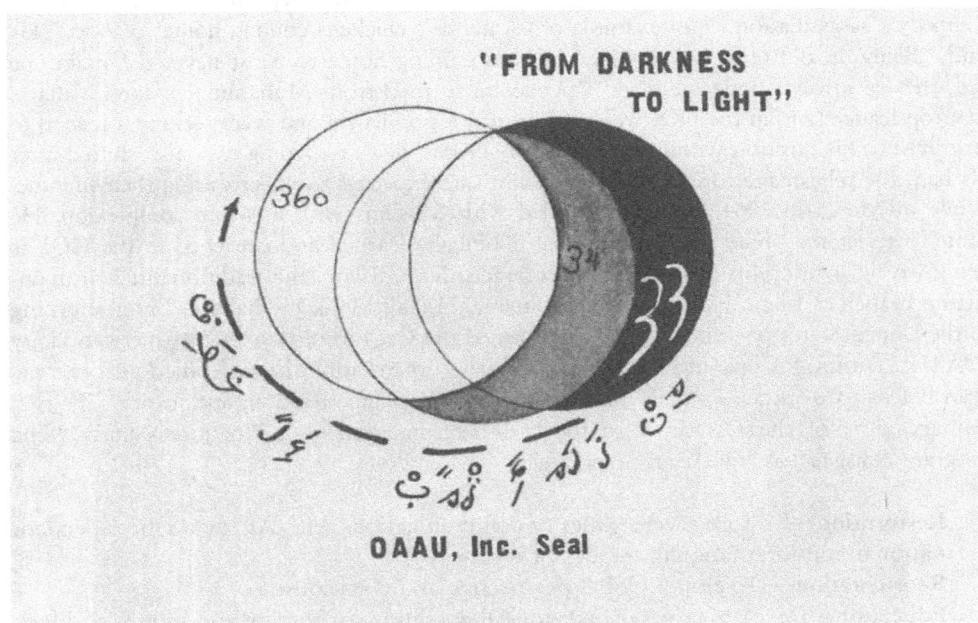

Figure 5.2 An image of the seal of the OAAU, consisting of a graphic of four overlapping circles with the numbers 360 and 34, and Arabic text underneath. Black text on the page reads "FROM DARKNESS / TO LIGHT."
OAAU, Inc.

A few days after founding the OAAU, Malcolm telegraphed King, expressing his desire to collaborate.[70] Malcolm took the initiative to travel to Selma to visit with King during the Selma Campaign. When he could not meet with King, who had been arrested during a demonstration, he met with King's wife, Coretta. He told her, "I want Dr. King to know that I didn't come to Selma to make his job difficult. I really did come thinking I could make it easier. If the white people realize what the alternative is, perhaps they will be more willing to hear Dr. King."[71] Malcolm came to see that he and King were fighting for the same goal.

Though Malcolm expressed a willingness to work with mainstream civil rights activists to advance liberation for Blacks, he continued to critique nonviolent resistance. He was adamant that Black people must be free to choose whatever strategy they deemed necessary to obtain freedom and justice. He argued that limiting the Black freedom struggle to nonviolent means was unfair. He called on Black Americans to recognize and affirm their right to bear arms to protect and defend themselves against violence. He reasoned that they should not try to appease the moral sensibilities of their oppressors:

> We don't believe we can win in a battle where the ground rules are laid down by those who exploit us. We don't believe that we can carry on our struggle trying to win the affection of those who, for so long, have oppressed and exploited us ... we believe that we're within our rights to fight those criminals by any means necessary.[72]

He also criticized King's redemptive suffering theology, which contended that Black Christian civil rights activists could help save America through their noble and peaceful suffering as Christ's suffering on the cross redeemed humankind from sin. While Malcolm no longer hated and despised all Whites, he did not believe that nonviolent resistance would redeem or alter America's soul. He suspected that racism would persist in America. Before his death, he predicted that the civil rights and voting rights bill that Congress passed into law were symbolic victories and would only produce token gains. He projected that these measures would not radically alter the suffering of the Black masses or cure America of racism.

Summing up Malcolm's civil rights legacy, historian Peniel Joseph referred to Malcolm X as "America's prosecuting attorney." This descriptor signified his unwavering commitment to speaking truthfully about the depth of the problem of institutional racism, including its endemic nature in American society. Malcolm also vigorously defended the dignity and beauty of Black people and inspired Black people to be proud of their skin, culture, and heritage. He laid the foundation for the Black consciousness and Black power movements of the late 1960s and 1970s.[73]

Black religious leaders did not agree regarding the most effective strategy to overcome social injustice during the mid-twentieth century. King, Jackson, Septima Clark, Ella Baker, and Malcolm X proposed distinct methods, drawing on their religious, social, and political convictions. It is plausible that many Black religious leaders agreed that the civil rights movement remains unfinished, despite key civil rights victories such as the Civil Rights Act of 1964 and the Voting Rights Act of 1965. Furthermore, the "dominant narrative" of civil rights, which acknowledges activism that occurred between 1954 and 1965, dates that mark the Supreme Court's landmark ruling in *Brown vs. Board of Education* and the signing of the Voting Rights Act, respectively, does not give due consideration to the activism that occurred outside of this historical timeframe.[74] The civil rights movement was only beginning to gain momentum in 1965 rather than conclude. Ella Baker disagreed with an assertion made by a civil rights leader that the movement was in its last stages. During her speech at the Hattiesburg Freedom Day Rally on January 21, 1964, she asserted, "We are just beginning the freedom struggle."[75] The South only started implementing changes and becoming more integrated after 1965. Rather than culminating, Baker held that the movement was merely entering a new phase. King and Malcolm X remained active in the struggle for social justice until their assassinations.

Review and Discussion Questions

1   Did King and SCLC effectively employ nonviolent resistance to manipulate the media? Or did the media distort King's influence on the civil rights movement? How might the media's portrayal of King have possibly helped and hindered the broader goals of the movement?
2   How did Jackson's civil rights and social justice approach differ from Martin Luther King Jr.'s strategy? What might numerous Black Baptists in the NBCUSA have found attractive about Jackson's approach?
3   How might Septima Clark and Ella Baker's experiences as women leaders in a male-dominated civil rights movement reflect broader gender issues within the movement? Would the movement have been more impactful if King and SCLC leaders had accepted Baker and Clark's critiques and proposals?
4   How did Malcolm X's involvement with the Nation of Islam (NOI) shape his critiques of the civil rights movement? How did his views and strategy for social justice evolve after his hajj?

Notes

1   Charles Payne, *I've Got the Light of Freedom: The Organizing Tradition and the Mississippi Freedom Struggle* (Berkeley, CA: University of California Press, 2007), 71.
2   Aldon Morris, *The Origins of the Civil Rights Movement* (New York: Free Press, 1984), 4.
3   C. Eric Lincoln and Lawrence H. Mamiya, *The Black Church in the African American Experience* (Durham, NC: Duke University Press, 1990), 212.
4   David L. Chappell, *A Stone of Hope: Prophetic Religion and the Death of Jim Crow* (Chapel Hill, NC: University of North Carolina Press, 2004), 62–63.
5   My first book, *Saints in the Struggle: Church of God in Christ Activists in the Memphis Civil Rights Movement, 1954–1968*, traces Black Pentecostals' unnoticed contributions to the Memphis Sanitation Strike and the struggle in Memphis. Mason Temple, the denomination's headquarters of the Church of God in Christ, was not merely a venue where King delivered his final sermon. Black Pentecostals such as J.O. Patterson Sr. and Gilbert E. Patterson were quite involved and invested in advocating for poor sanitation workers and even participated in meetings with the Community on the Move for Equality.
6   Bettye Collier-Thomas, *Jesus, Jobs, and Justice Jesus, Jobs: African American Women and Religion* (New York: Alfred A. Knopf, 2010), 426–428.
7   Bettye Collier-Thomas, *Jesus, Jobs, and Justice Jesus, Jobs: African American Women and Religion* (New York: Alfred A. Knopf, 2010), 428.
8   Patrick S. Washburn, *The African American Newspaper: Voice of Freedom* (Evanston, IL: Northwestern University Press, 2006), 5, 83.; Jack Nelson, "The Civil Rights Movement: A Press Perspective," *The Washington Journalism Review*, April 1991, 5–6; Charles Payne, *I've Got the Light of Freedom: The Organizing Tradition and the Mississippi Freedom Struggle* (Los Angeles, CA: University of California Press, 2007), 392, 400–401.
9   Gene Roberts and Hank Klibanoff, *The Race Beat: The Press, The Civil Rights Struggle and the Awakening of a Nation* (New York: Vintage, 2007), 305.

10 Gene Roberts and Hank Klibanoff, *The Race Beat: The Press, The Civil Rights Struggle and the Awakening of a Nation* (New York: Vintage, 2007), 305.

11 Gene Roberts and Hank Klibanoff, *The Race Beat: The Press, The Civil Rights Struggle and the Awakening of a Nation* (New York: Vintage, 2007), 311.

12 Gene Roberts and Hank Klibanoff, *The Race Beat: The Press, The Civil Rights Struggle and the Awakening of a Nation* (New York: Vintage, 2007), 376.

13 Gene Roberts and Hank Klibanoff, *The Race Beat: The Press, The Civil Rights Struggle and the Awakening of a Nation* (New York: Vintage, 2007), 376–377.

14 The media's influence should not be overstated. Congressman John Lewis may have unconsciously given the media too much credit when expressing that without the media "the civil rights movement would have been like a bird without wings, a choir without a song." In an oral history interview, he lauded reporters and photographers for capturing the Movement as it unfolded. The media recorded the police brutality that he and other demonstrators experienced when they marched across the Edmund Pettis Bridge in Selma, Alabama. Jeanne Theoharis, *A More Beautiful and Terrible History: The Uses and Misuses of Civil Rights History* (Boston, MA: Beacon Press, 2018), 102.; Gene Roberts and Hank Klibanoff, *The Race Beat: The Press, The Civil Rights Struggle and the Awakening of a Nation* (New York: Vintage, 2007), 250, 407.

15 Gene Roberts and Hank Klibanoff, *The Race Beat: The Press, The Civil Rights Struggle and the Awakening of a Nation* (New York: Vintage, 2007), 378.

16 Richard Lentz, *Symbols, the News Magazine and Martin Luther King* (Baton Rouge, LA: Louisiana State University Press, 1999), 2.

17 Richard Lentz, *Symbols, the News Magazine and Martin Luther King* (Baton Rouge, LA: Louisiana State University Press, 1999), 307.

18 Jeanne Theoharis, *A More Beautiful and Terrible History: The Uses and Misuses of Civil Rights History* (Boston, MA: Beacon Press, 2018), 116.

19 Charles Payne, *I've Got the Light of Freedom: The Organizing Tradition and the Mississippi Freedom Struggle* (Los Angeles, CA: University of California Press, 2007), 392, 400–401; Richard Lentz, *Symbols, the News Magazine and Martin Luther King* (Baton Rouge, LA: Louisiana State University Press, 1999), 2.

20 Larry G. Murphy, J. Gordon Melton, and Gary L. Ward, eds., *Encyclopedia of African American Religions* (New York: Garland Publishing, 1993), 387.

21 Vaughn Booker, "Civil Rights Religion?: Rethinking 1950s and 1960s Political Activism for African American Religious History" *Journal of Africana Religions*, 2, no. 2 (2014): 216, retrieved from www.jstor.org/stable/10.5325/jafrireli.2.2.0211.

22 Wallace Best, "'The Right Achieved and the Wrong Way Conquered': J. H. Jackson, Martin Luther King, Jr., and the Conflict Over Civil Rights" *Religion and American Culture*, 16, no. 2 (Summer 2006), 198, www.jstor.org/stable/10.1525/rac.2006.16.2.195.

23 Wallace Best, "'The Right Achieved and the Wrong Way Conquered': J. H. Jackson, Martin Luther King, Jr., and the Conflict Over Civil Rights" *Religion and American Culture*, 16, no. 2 (Summer 2006), 203.

24 Wallace Best, "'The Right Achieved and the Wrong Way Conquered': J. H. Jackson, Martin Luther King, Jr., and the Conflict Over Civil Rights" *Religion and American Culture*, 16, no. 2 (Summer 2006), 196, 209.

25 Wallace Best, "'The Right Achieved and the Wrong Way Conquered': J. H. Jackson, Martin Luther King, Jr., and the Conflict Over Civil Rights" *Religion and American Culture*, 16, no. 2 (Summer 2006), 210.

26 Louis H. Ford, a pastor in the Church of God in Christ in Chicago, also disagreed with King's nonviolent direct-action approach. Ford held that Blacks were better off pursuing social justice through working with political leaders. Robert Michael Franklin, *Another Day's Journey: Black Churches Confronting the American Crisis* (Minneapolis, MN: Fortress Press, 1997), 51.; Vaughn Booker, "Civil Rights Religion?: Rethinking 1950s and 1960s Political Activism for African American Religious History" *Journal of Africana Religions*, 2, no. 2 (2014): 215–216.

27 Wallace Best, "'The Right Achieved and the Wrong Way Conquered': J. H. Jackson, Martin Luther King, Jr., and the Conflict Over Civil Rights" *Religion and American Culture*, 16, no. 2 (Summer 2006), 205.; Bettye Collier-Thomas, *Jesus, Jobs, and Justice Jesus, Jobs: African American Women and Religion* (New York: Alfred A. Knopf, 2010), 436.

28 Wallace Best, "'The Right Achieved and the Wrong Way Conquered': J. H. Jackson, Martin Luther King, Jr., and the Conflict Over Civil Rights" *Religion and American Culture*, 16, no. 2 (Summer 2006), 203–209.

29 Wallace Best, "'The Right Achieved and the Wrong Way Conquered': J. H. Jackson, Martin Luther King, Jr., and the Conflict Over Civil Rights" *Religion and American Culture*, 16, no. 2 (Summer 2006), 214–215.

30 Several women civil rights activists have written autobiographies and memoirs such as Anne Moody's *Coming of Age in Mississippi* (1968), Jo Ann Robinson's *Montgomery Bus Boycott and the Women Who Started It* (1987), Dorothy Cotton's *If Your Back's Not Bent: The Role of the Citizenship Education Program in the Civil Rights Movement* (2012), and Angela Davis's *An Autobiography* (1974); Bettye Collier-Thomas, *Jesus, Jobs, and Justice Jesus, Jobs: African American Women and Religion* (New York: Alfred A. Knopf, 2010), 424–425.; Steven F. Lawson, *Rights Crossroads: Nation, Community, and the Black Freedom Struggle* (Lexington, KY: University Press of Kentucky, 2003), 274–277.

31 Charles Payne, *I've Got the Light of Freedom: The Organizing Tradition and the Mississippi Freedom Struggle* (Los Angeles, CA: University of California Press, 2007), 3.

32 Charles Payne, *I've Got the Light of Freedom: The Organizing Tradition and the Mississippi Freedom Struggle* (Los Angeles, CA: University of California Press, 2007), 3.

33 Charles Payne, *I've Got the Light of Freedom: The Organizing Tradition and the Mississippi Freedom Struggle* (Los Angeles, CA: University of California Press, 2007), 68.

34 Steven F. Lawson, *Rights Crossroads: Nation, Community, and the Black Freedom Struggle* (Lexington, KY: University Press of Kentucky, 2003), 271.

35 Charles Payne, *I've Got the Light of Freedom: The Organizing Tradition and the Mississippi Freedom Struggle* (Los Angeles, CA: University of California Press, 2007), 71.; Jacqueln Dowd Hall, "'I train the people to do their own talking': Septima Clark and the Women in the Civil Rights Movement" *Southern Cultures*, 12, no. 2 (May 20, 2010), 32.

36 Jacqueln Dowd Hall, "'I train the people to do their own talking': Septima Clark and the Women in the Civil Rights Movement" *Southern Cultures*, 12, no. 2 (May 20, 2010), 33.; Charles Payne, *I've Got the Light of Freedom: The Organizing Tradition and the Mississippi Freedom Struggle* (Los Angeles, CA: University of California Press, 2007), 72.

37 Charles Payne, *I've Got the Light of Freedom: The Organizing Tradition and the Mississippi Freedom Struggle* (Los Angeles, CA: University of California Press, 2007), 76.

38 Charles Payne, *I've Got the Light of Freedom: The Organizing Tradition and the Mississippi Freedom Struggle* (Los Angeles, CA: University of California Press, 2007), 76.; Jacqueln Dowd Hall, "'I train the people to do their own talking': Septima Clark and the Women in the Civil Rights Movement" *Southern Cultures*, 12, no. 2 (May 20, 2010), 48.

39 Jacqueln Dowd Hall, "'I train the people to do their own talking': Septima Clark and the Women in the Civil Rights Movement" *Southern Cultures*, 12, no. 2 (May 20, 2010), 48.

40 Jacqueln Dowd Hall, "'I train the people to do their own talking': Septima Clark and the Women in the Civil Rights Movement" *Southern Cultures*, 12, no. 2 (May 20, 2010), 48.; Charles Payne, *I've Got the Light of Freedom: The Organizing Tradition and the Mississippi Freedom Struggle* (Los Angeles, CA: University of California Press, 2007), 77.

41 Todd J. Moye, *Ella Baker: Community Organizer of the Civil Rights Movement* (Blue Ridge Summit, PA: Blue Ridge Summit, 2013), 19.

42 Charles Payne, *I've Got the Light of Freedom: The Organizing Tradition and the Mississippi Freedom Struggle* (Los Angeles, CA: University of California Press, 2007), 80.

43 Charles Payne, *I've Got the Light of Freedom: The Organizing Tradition and the Mississippi Freedom Struggle* (Los Angeles, CA: University of California Press, 2007), 81.

44 Steven F. Lawson, *Rights Crossroads: Nation, Community, and the Black Freedom Struggle* (Lexington, KY: University Press of Kentucky, 2003), 273.; Charles Payne, *I've Got the Light of Freedom: The Organizing Tradition and the Mississippi Freedom Struggle* (Los Angeles, CA: University of California Press, 2007), 90–92.

45 Todd J. Moye, *Ella Baker: Community Organizer of the Civil Rights Movement* (Blue Ridge Summit, PA: Blue Ridge Summit, 2013), 90–93.

46 Todd J. Moye, *Ella Baker: Community Organizer of the Civil Rights Movement* (Blue Ridge Summit, PA: Blue Ridge Summit, 2013), 92.

47 Charles Payne, *I've Got the Light of Freedom: The Organizing Tradition and the Mississippi Freedom Struggle* (Los Angeles, CA: University of California Press, 2007), 83.

48 Charles Payne, *I've Got the Light of Freedom: The Organizing Tradition and the Mississippi Freedom Struggle* (Los Angeles, CA: University of California Press, 2007), 93.

49 Jacqueln Dowd Hall, "'I train the people to do their own talking': Septima Clark and the Women in the Civil Rights Movement" *Southern Cultures*, 12, no. 2 (May 20, 2010), 48.

50 Charles Payne, *I've Got the Light of Freedom: The Organizing Tradition and the Mississippi Freedom Struggle* (Los Angeles, CA: University of California Press, 2007), 94–95.

51 Martin Luther King Jr., *Where Do We Go From Here: Chaos or Community?* (Boston, MA: Beacon Press, 1994, orig. 1968), 167.

52 Martin Luther King Jr., *Where Do We Go From Here: Chaos or Community?* (Boston, MA: Beacon Press, 1994, orig. 1968), 167–168.

53 Charles Payne, *I've Got the Light of Freedom: The Organizing Tradition and the Mississippi Freedom Struggle* (Los Angeles, CA: University of California Press, 2007), 94–95.

54 Charles Payne, *I've Got the Light of Freedom: The Organizing Tradition and the Mississippi Freedom Struggle* (Los Angeles, CA: University of California Press, 2007), 94–95.

55 Charles Payne, *I've Got the Light of Freedom: The Organizing Tradition and the Mississippi Freedom Struggle* (Los Angeles, CA: University of California Press, 2007), 94–95.

56 Malcolm X, *The Autobiography of Malcolm X, With the Assistance of Alex Haley* (New York: Ballantine Books, 2015, orig. 1964), 38–39.

57 Malcolm X, *The Autobiography of Malcolm X, With the Assistance of Alex Haley* (New York: Ballantine Books, 2015, orig. 1964), 153–154.

58 Malcolm X, *The Autobiography of Malcolm X, With the Assistance of Alex Haley* (New York: Ballantine Books, 2015, orig. 1964), 155–156.

59 Malcolm X, *The Autobiography of Malcolm X, With the Assistance of Alex Haley* (New York: Ballantine Books, 2015, orig. 1964), 153–154.

60 *Miami Herald*, September 19, 1963; *Amsterdam News* (New York), September 7, 1963, p. 6; *Amsterdam News* (New York), October 19, 1963, p. 7, cited in James H. Cone, *Martin & Malcolm & America: A Dream or a Nightmare* (Maryknoll, NY: Orbis Books, 1991), 113.

61 Malcolm X, "Message to the Grassroots," retrieved from https://teachingamericanhistory.org/document/message-to-grassroots.

62 *Amsterdam News* (New York), September 7, 1963, p. 6; *Amsterdam News* (New York), October 19, 1963, p. 7; cited in James H. Cone, *Martin & Malcolm & America: A Dream or a Nightmare* (Maryknoll, NY: Orbis Books, 1991), 113.

63 Vaughn Booker, "Civil Rights Religion?: Rethinking 1950s and 1960s Political Activism for African American Religious History" *Journal of Africana Religions*, 2, no. 2 (2014): 228–229.

64 Malcolm X, "Message to the Grassroots," in George Breitman, ed., *Malcolm X Speaks* (New York: Grove Press, 1966), 4–17.

65 Malcolm X, "Message to the Grassroots," in George Breitman, ed., *Malcolm X Speaks* (New York: Grove Press, 1966), 4–17.

66 Malcolm X, *Malcolm X Speaks*, ed. George Breitman (New York: Grove Press, 1965), 18.

67 Malcolm X, *February 1965: The Final Speeches,* edited by Steve Clark (New York: Pathfinder Press, 1992), 257–266.

68 Peniel E. Joseph, *The Sword and the Shield: The Revolutionary Lives of Malcolm X and Martin Luther King Jr.* (New York: Basic Books, 2020), 196.

69 Organization of Afro-American Unity Inc. leaflet., "Aims & Objectives," 1964, Collection of the Smithsonian National Museum of African American History and Culture, retrieved from https://nmaahc.si.edu/object/nmaahc_2013.46.20.

70 Peniel E. Joseph, *The Sword and the Shield: The Revolutionary Lives of Malcolm X and Martin Luther King Jr.* (New York: Basic Books, 2020), 197.

71 Coretta Scott King, *My Life with Martin Luther King, Jr.* (New York: Holt, Rinehart and Winston, 1969), 256, cited in James H. Cone, *Martin & Malcolm & America: A Dream or a Nightmare* (Maryknoll, NY: Orbis Books, 1991), 210.

72 Bruce Perry, ed., *Malcolm X: The Last Speeches* (New York: Pathfinder Press, 1989), 111–181; Cited in James H. Cone, *Martin & Malcolm & America: A Dream or a Nightmare* (Maryknoll, NY: Orbis Books, 1991), 211.

73 Peniel E. Joseph, *The Sword and the Shield: The Revolutionary Lives of Malcolm X and Martin Luther King Jr.* (New York: Basic Books, 2020), 290.

74 Timothy J. Minchin, "Beyond the Dominant Narrative: The Ongoing Struggle for Civil Rights in the US South, 1968–1980," *Australian Journal of American Studies*, 25, no. 1 (July 2006), 66.
75 Ella Baker, "Address at the Hattiesburg Freedom Day Rally," January 21, 1964, retrieved from https://voicesofdemocracy.umd.edu/ella-baker-freedom-day-rally-speech-text.

Further Readings

Chappell, David L. *A Stone of Hope: Prophetic Religion and the Death of Jim Crow.* Chapel Hill, NC: University of North Carolina Press, 2004.

Cleage, Albert. *Black Christian Nationalism: New Direction for the Black Church.* Detroit, MI: Luxor Publishing of the Pan-African, 1987.

Collier-Thomas, Bettye. *Jesus, Jobs, and Justice: African American Women and Religion.* New York: Alfred A. Knopf, 2010.

Cone, James H. *Martin & Malcolm & America: A Dream or a Nightmare.* Maryknoll, NY: Orbis Books, 1991.

Joseph, Peniel E. *The Sword and the Shield: The Revolutionary Lives of Malcolm X and Martin Luther King Jr.* New York: Basic Books, 2020.

King, Martin Luther, Jr. *Where Do We Go From Here: Chaos or Community?*Boston, MA: Beacon Press, 1994. Originally published 1968.

Marable, Manning. *Malcolm X: A Life of Reinvention.* New York: Penguin Books, 2011.

Moye, Todd J. *Ella Baker: Community Organizer of the Civil Rights Movement.* Blue Ridge Summit, PA: Blue Ridge Summit, 2013.

Payne, Charles M. *I've Got the Light of Freedom: The Organizing Tradition and the Mississippi Freedom Struggle.* Berkeley, CA: University of California Press, 2007.

Ross, Rosetta. *Witnessing and Testifying: Black Women, Religion, and Civil Rights.* Minneapolis, MN: Fortress Press, 2003.

6 "Keep Hope Alive"

Spiritual Strivings during the Post-Civil Rights Era

Though the civil rights movement influenced a rise in the number of Black elected officials at all levels of government and significant growth in the Black middle class, many Black people felt that liberal integrationism merely resulted in token gains. As early as the late 1960s, Black Americans reared in urban ghettoes lost hope in civil rights activists' promise that "we shall overcome." Some expressed their social discontent in riots in various cities. Many Black Americans also felt churches had become apathetic to the various social crises of the post-civil rights era—the rise in gang violence, the proliferation of crack cocaine in Black communities, and the AIDS epidemic. To strive for social justice in the post-civil rights context, many Black religious innovators nostalgically refreshed and remixed the teachings and practices of past religious figures.[1] For example, Reverend Jesse Jackson's popular catchphrase "Keep hope alive" reverberated King's optimistic "I Have a Dream" speech delivered in 1963. Just as King encouraged Americans to envision a brighter and more racially harmonious America, during his 1988 Democratic National Convention, Jackson admonished listeners to not yield to despair, stating, "You must not surrender! You may or may not get there but just know that you're qualified! And you hold on, and hold out! We must never surrender! America will get better and better. Keep hope alive. Keep hope alive! Keep hope alive!"[2] Besides examining how Jackson and other religious leaders continued King's tradition of civil rights activism, this chapter also considers ways post-civil rights Black religious leaders extended the legacies of religious leaders from preceding eras. It explores the rekindling of New Thought Metaphysics, the revival of the Nation of Islam, the development of Black Liberation Theology, and the reemployment of cooperationist activism.

Rekindling New Thought Metaphysics: Reverend Ike and the Prosperity Gospel

The prosperity message, which holds that Christians can live a prosperous, fulfilled life through faith in Christ and applying the scriptures, is part of the religious innovation thread running across Black history.[3] Its lineage traces to New Thought teachings—a blend of Christian teachings with nineteenth-century metaphysics that holds that the source of reality is the perfect mind of God. In *Name It and Claim It? Prosperity Preaching in the Black Church*, Stephanie Mitchem explores why numerous Black Christians found prosperity theology attractive. She argues that the prosperity gospel responds to Black people's "spirituality of longing" for acceptance and inclusion in America.[4]

While several Black religious innovators, such as Father Divine and Charles Manuel Grace, also known as "Sweet Daddy," taught the prosperity message during the Great

DOI: 10.4324/9781003359197-7

Migration, Frederick Eikerenkoetter II, known as Reverend Ike, helped make new thought metaphysics popular among Blacks during the 1960s and 1970s. He challenged mainstream evangelical Christians' views about wealth and money. In 1965, he founded the Miracle Temple and preached the New Thought teachings of White ministers such as Norman Vincent Peale and the famous motivational speaker Dale Carnegie. Contending that some Christians wrongly interpreted Paul's words in 1 Timothy 6:10, Reverend Ike told his followers, "The lack of money [not the love of money] is the root of all evil."[5] Rather than following the lead of many evangelical ministers and encouraging poor Black people to strive for eternal life in heaven, Reverend Ike told his followers, "Don't wait for your pie in the sky by and by; have it now with ice cream and a cherry on top."[6] He encouraged his listeners not to pray to some external God but to look for God within themselves and to work to solve their problems. Reverend Ike also criticized the Poor People's Campaign and Black Power:

> That's why you'll never catch me riding around with a bunch of rabble rousers chanting black power. Black power without green power is no power. And when you get enough green power, people won't care what color your face or anything else is![7]

His sermons, broadcast via radio and television networks, offered Black people a theology that insisted that by tapping into God within them they could have anything they desired, including health, wealth, and prosperity.[8]

Traditional clergy and civil rights activists certainly disagreed with Reverend Ike. Nonetheless, numerous Black people found his message appealing. He established a congregation of nearly 5,000 persons. At the high point of his popularity during the 1970s, he had an audience of roughly 2.5 million. His sermons were broadcast on about 1,770 radio stations and several television networks. Reverend Ike sold several books, tapes, and videos. He spearheaded a magazine named *Action!* and acquired a television program, *Joy of Living*, in 1973. He used his radio and television platform to promote and sell his products, "extolling his 'Blessing Plan,' as well as products promising to heal or enrich the purchaser—if the person had faith and contributed to his church."[9] He reaped millions of dollars from sales and donations from supporters. He unashamedly spent money on flamboyant clothing and luxury cars.

Alongside other Black religious leaders such as Father Divine, Sweet Daddy Grace, and Johnnie Colemon, Reverend Ike helped influence the Word of Faith Movement, an amalgam of evangelical and Pentecostal theology. White Pentecostal figures such as A.A. Allen and Oral Roberts were integral to developing the Word of Faith Movement. In line with their Pentecostal beliefs in the power of prayer and divine healing, they stressed that God could perform miracles and work wonders in every aspect of believers' lives—physical, mental, financial, etc.[10] Kenneth Hagin, a White televangelist who contributed to the growth of the Word of Faith Movement during the 1970s, iterated Scriptures like Proverbs 18:21, which states, "Life and death are in the power of the tongue." Based on his interpretation of this verse, he encouraged believers to practice "positive confession," which means using affirmative language to speak the desires of the heart into existence.[11]

Standing in the self-help tradition, Word of Faith ministers admonished impoverished Black people that they could experience financial blessings by applying the teachings of Scripture and through "sowing seeds" or investing money in their church.[12] To experience God's blessing believers simply needed to be in right standing with God and ask

God to fulfill the desires of their hearts. The righteous only need "name it and claim it" and wait for God to fulfill Divine promises outlined in Scripture. Numerous people of diverse races found the prosperity message accessible and appealing. Megachurches, defined as "churches that have memberships of at least two thousand" and "are housed in spectacular buildings on large campuses," started to blossom as pastors preached the prosperity gospel.[13] Some notable megachurches established by Black ministers affiliated with the Word of Faith Movement include the Crenshaw Christian Center and World Changers Church. These churches used radio, television, and the newly developing World Wide Web to expand and grow their ministries. Within a decade of starting his ministry, Frederick K.C. Price, the founder of Crenshaw Christian Center, ministered to millions via his *Ever Increasing Faith* broadcast. Creflo Dollar's World Changers Church, based in College Park, Georgia, grew swiftly in the 1980s. In 2004, Dollar expanded his ministry from Georgia to New York and held worship services on Saturdays in the Madison Square Garden, the coliseum where the New York Knicks play basketball games. Thousands of people attended the religious services.[14]

The prosperity gospel upholds American capitalism and the Horatio Alger myth that posits hard work and effort are the keys to success. Pastors taught poor people that they could overcome poverty and access the American Dream by applying the teachings of Scripture and New Thought metaphysics. In a sermon entitled "Made after His Kind," Dollar encouraged members that the Scriptures teach that humans, who are made in the image of God, possess supernatural power.[15] In line with New Thought metaphysics, Dollar stressed that people could influence or alter the world around them by developing a God consciousness or becoming conscious of God's presence within them.[16] The prosperity gospel assures believers, regardless of their racial or socio-economic background, that they can experience success and thrive materially within our American capitalistic system. Poor Black Christians can rise from rags to riches by exercising their faith.[17]

Some critics of the prosperity gospel contend that it does not offer an adequate response to longstanding disparities in hiring, underemployment, or unemployment between Blacks and Whites. In line with the American self-help tradition, it admonishes impoverished people to take personal responsibility and become better stewards of their time and money. The appeal of the prosperity message among Black people in the post-civil rights era is undeniable. Television broadcasts such as Juanita Bynum's "No More Sheets" and T.D. Jakes's "Woman Thou Art Loosed" were quite popular during the 1990s and 2000s. The membership of many Black megachurches flourished as traditional historical Black churches experienced a decline. As Mitchem contended, the prosperity message satisfied many African Americans' "spirituality of longing" for personal inclusion in the American Dream. Prosperity ministers unashamedly reflected their ascendancy into the elite class by wearing designer suits and purchasing million-dollar mansions, luxurious cars, and even private jets. However, Black scholars and theologians like James Cone have been critical of the prosperity message, holding it to be antithetical to the authentic liberating and revolutionary gospel of Jesus Christ.

James Cone and Black Liberation Theology: Synthesizing Martin Luther King Jr. and Malcolm X

Though Malcolm X was a Muslim minister, his message and speeches, especially "Message to the Grassroots" (1963) and "The Ballot or the Bullet" address (1964), revolutionized the thinking of African American Christians disillusioned by liberal integrationism and King's nonviolent approach to civil rights.[18] Some Black Christians felt King's approach merely resulted in token gains for Black people and failed to advance justice for the masses. Albert Cleage, the founder of the Black Christian Nationalist Movement and the Shrine of the Black Madonna, invited Malcolm to address his congregation in 1963. Inspired by Malcolm, in 1968, Cleage wrote *The Black Messiah* and affirmed Jesus as a revolutionary Black man. Besides Cleage, Black Christians affiliated with the National Committee of Negro Churchmen (NCBC), the National Council of Churches, and with Black caucuses within the predominantly White denominations such as the Black Methodists for Church Renewal, grappled with the meaning of Christian faith considering the ongoing systemic injustice Black people were facing in the 1960s, notwithstanding crucial victories of the civil rights era. Many of the Black leaders in these organizations affirmed Black Power, which was being vilified in the media and even questioned and critiqued by Dr. King. About forty-eight ministers affiliated with NCBC submitted an article in the *New York Times* in 1966, endorsing Black power. Their defense of Black power helped lay the foundation for Black theology.[19] James Cone coined "black theology" in *Black Power and Black Theology* (1969), written during the summer following King's assassination.[20] Cone joined the faculty at Union Theological Seminary in 1969 and became Charles A. Briggs Professor of Systematic Theology in 1977. He was the first African American theologian to construct a systematic theology centering on liberation. In *A Black Theology of Liberation,* he systematically reinterpreted the meaning and purpose of the Christian faith from the Black experience. He argued that liberation is the heart and essential content of the gospel and Christian theology.

Cone credited King's activism and Malcolm X's bold critique of white supremacy for inspiring him to interpret Christianity through the prism of the Black experience.[21] He aimed to demonstrate that Black Power was in line with Christianity and was an authentic expression of the gospel of Christ because it was good news for poor and oppressed people.[22] He argued that many of the White theologians he studied in graduate school, such as Paul Tillich, Karl Barth, Rudolph Bultmann, Gordon Kaufmann, Dietrich Bonhoeffer, and Reinhold Niebuhr, did not correctly understand Christianity because they failed to attend to the predicament of oppressed Black people. He explained, "No white theologian has ever taken the oppression of blacks as a point of departure for analyzing God's activity in contemporary America."[23] Cone systematically reinterpreted the central hallmarks of the Christian faith, for example, the doctrines of God, humanity, the Church, the world, and the end times in the light of the theological norm of liberation, and he concluded that Jesus is Black because he was an advocate for the downtrodden. Rather than claiming that Jesus was of African ancestry or racially Black, Cone contended that Jesus was ontologically Black because he identified with oppressed Black people and supported their liberation.

Black liberation theology was subject to much constructive criticism by Black theologians as the new field emerged.[24] In *Liberation and Reconciliation* (1971), J. Deotis Roberts argued that Black theologians must not lose sight of the ultimate post-revolutionary goal of reconciliation in pursuing liberation. In essence, liberation is not in and of itself the end goal. Roberts asserted that "the liberating Christ is also the redeeming Christ."[25] He upheld King and SCLC leaders' emphasis on agape love as central to "redeeming the soul of America" and forming a beloved community. Yet, he stressed that liberation from structural evil and justice must occur before authentic reconciliation occurs.

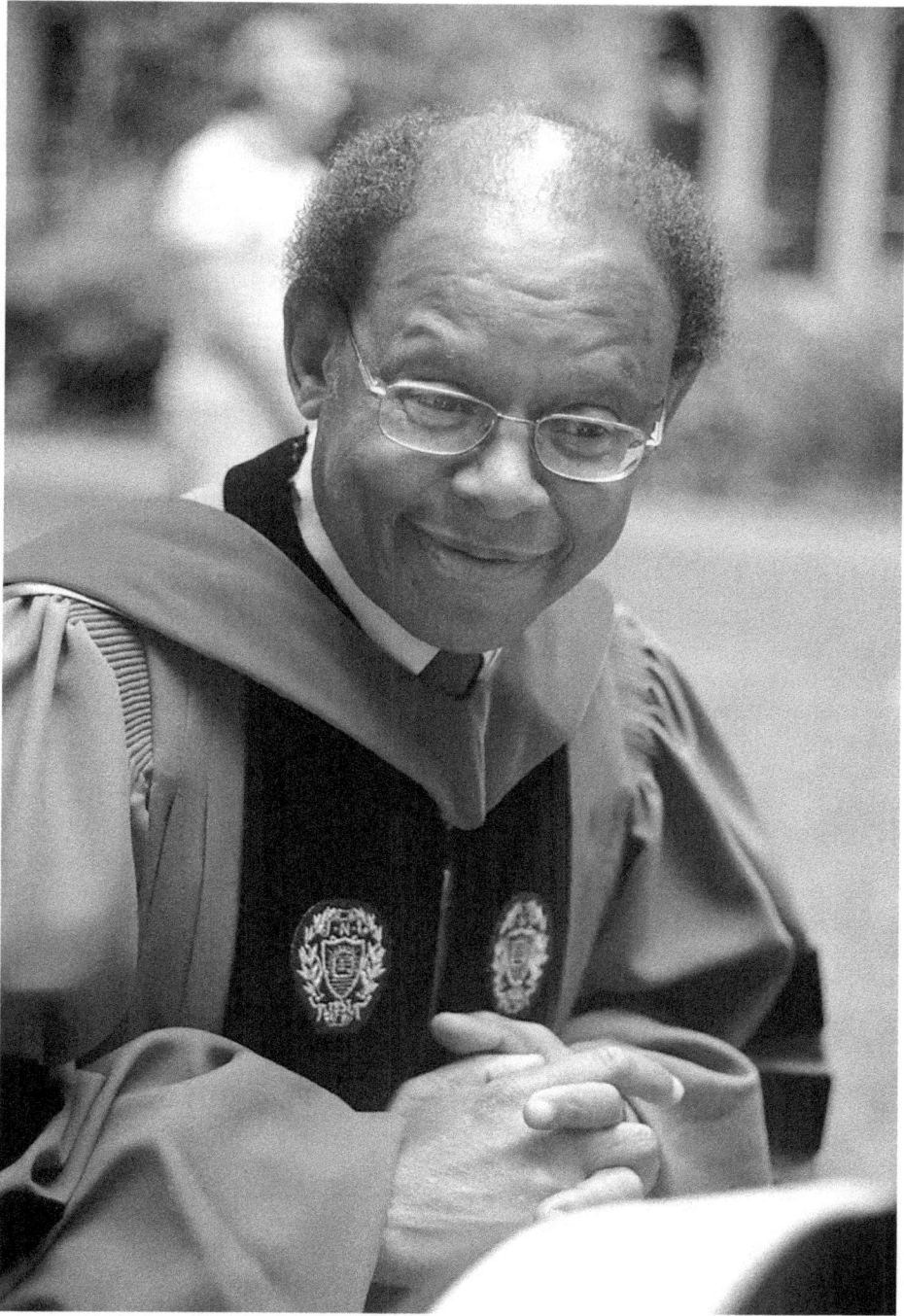

Figure 6.1. A portrait of Dr. James Cone (1936–2018) at the 174th Convocation of Union Theological Seminary in the City of New York, September 9, 2009.
Courtesy of Steve McFarland, Flickr

Several pastoral theologians (pastors who have received advanced degrees in theology) also criticized Black liberation theology for not having strong ties to Black churches or other religious institutions.[26] James Harris, a theologian and senior pastor at Second Baptist Church in Richmond, Virginia, notes that Black theology is primarily restricted to academic institutions and that "only academics are discussing it and writing about it."[27] He suggests that evangelical theology is more widely known and accepted among Black churches and that Black theology is essentially "foreign to the black community." Raphael Warnock, a current senator and pastor of the historic Ebenezer Baptist Church in Atlanta, Georgia, agrees and contends that "black theology's most consistent conversation partner has not been the black church or the black mosque but the white academy."[28] Denis Wiley, a pastor of Covenant Baptist Church in Washington, DC, who studied with Cone and received his PhD in systematic theology from Union Theological Seminary, argues that most Black churches have not been receptive to Black liberation theology.[29] Although there are some exceptions, he states, "Black theology within the Black Church has been largely intuitive, unreflective, and unself-critical."[30] This means that Black liberation theologians have not held Black pastors and churches to task for examining their effectiveness at striving for liberation in Black communities.

Indeed, some Black Christian leaders such as Freddy Haynes, Jacqueline Lewis, Yvette Flunder, and Jeremiah Wright have incorporated Black liberation theology in their preaching and ministries. Furthermore, these ministers led churches that exuded a praxis of Black theology by developing ministry programs that aimed to serve the poor and vulnerable members of society, including but not limited to prisoners and ex-felons, people suffering from alcohol and drug addictions, underserved youth, men and women who contracted AIDS, and people with developmental and intellectual disabilities.[31] According to Wiley, such Black pastors and their churches are exceptions and do not reflect the chasm that has long existed between Black liberation theology and Black churches.

The reality is that Black theological discourse has been confined to erudite academic circles and spaces where Black theologians spend most of their time. Dwight Hopkins, a second-generation Black liberation theologian, called on Black theologians who often became interested in religion because of their experience in churches to maintain their connections to local churches and resist the temptation to devote the entirety of their time to research, teaching, and service to the academy. Ultimately, many Black liberation pastoral theologians believe that Black churches can become agents of liberation for Black communities when Black liberation theology becomes a part of the praxis of Black churches.[32]

Womanist Theology

Womanist theology is a vital offshoot and critique of Black liberation theology. Womanist scholars derive the term "womanist" from the novelist Alice Walker's book, *In Search of Our Mothers Gardens: Womanist Prose*. They deemed that Walker's definition of "womanish" accurately described the unique experience of Black women who have historically struggled with the triple oppressions of racism, sexism, and classism. Distinct from White feminism and Black liberation theology, womanism endeavors to free Black women from racist and sexist normative gazes and to tell the stories of marginalized and silenced Black women.[33]

A wide range of womanist scholars such as Katie Cannon, Rosetta Ross, Yvonne Chireau, Joan M. Martin, Emilie Townes, Daphne C. Wiggins, and Stacey Floyd-Thomas accentuated Black women's voices in slave narratives, autobiographies, and literature. The wealth of primary sources produced by Black women provides an ethically rich motherlode that womanists have endeavored to mine to counteract negative caricatures of Black women and Black culture and to uplift the transformative ways Black women have striven to fashion a more equitable social world. Although this book does not have space to focus on all seminal womanist scholars, Katie G. Cannon, Jacquelyn Grant, and Delores Williams were early leading womanist scholars who developed the field. All three women studied at Union Theological Seminary.[34] Womanist scholars have consistently advocated for marginalized Black people who experience oppression from without and within Black religious communities and families.[35]

Cannon, a trailblazer in the field of womanist ethics, was the first African American woman scholar to utilize Walker's "womanist" description of Black women's experiences to name the work of Black "womanist" scholars of religion. She introduced womanist theology when presenting an academic paper at the American Academy of Religion entitled "The Emergence of Black Feminist Consciousness" in 1985. In *Black Womanist Ethics* (1988), Cannon contends that the lessons Black women have learned from struggling to survive the triple oppressions of racism, sexism, and classism provide the basis for constructing a womanist ethics distinct from ethics produced by Black and White men.[36] She found Black women's literature to be a primary source for deriving Black women's ethics. She devoted particular attention to Zora Neale Hurston's life and works to describe the ethical wisdom produced by Black women who have struggled to survive triple oppressions with limited life options.[37]

Besides Cannon, Delores Williams was another womanist pioneer. She discussed the parallels between Hagar and African American women in her classic work, *Sisters in the Wilderness* (1993). Hagar is a biblical figure who was an abused and exploited enslaved African Sarai coerced to be a surrogate mother when she could not conceive. After she miraculously became pregnant during her elderly years and gave birth to Isaac, Sarai forced Hagar and her son Ishmael into exile.[38] Williams identified Hagar's surrogacy and her wilderness experience as a mode of resistance, a place of divine encounter, and a site of survival. She argued that Hagar's experience of survival in the wilderness is a more accurate description of the Black experience in the United States than the Exodus narrative of the children of Israel discussed in preceding chapters. Like Hagar, throughout American history, Black people have had to learn to survive various forms of oppression. Williams challenged the orthodox Christian doctrine of redemptive suffering upheld by Black liberation theologians. Interpreting the theology through the lens of Hagar and Black women's experiences, she argued that redemptive suffering theology is oppressive because it makes Jesus into a surrogate, a scapegoat who bears human sin through dying on the cross. In replace of redemptive suffering theology, which focuses on Jesus' sacrificial death, she proposed that Christians focus instead on Jesus' life and ministry, which upheld service to social outcasts and community wholeness. Womanist scholarship has advanced beyond its earliest trailblazers. Womanist scholars have held fast to the pioneers' "original orientation: a concern for the Black church and community, the privileging of Black women's experiences, an intersectional perspective that sees oppression as multidimensional, and a blunt interrogation of doctrine and prior theological claims."[39]

Black Humanist Theology

For the most part, Black and womanist theologians maintained fundamental belief in liberation and radical transformation of the social, political, and economic order through Divine power. Most Black liberation theologians upheld faith in God and Christianity. William R. Jones's provocative *Is God a White Racist? A Preamble to Black Theology* (1973) challenges Cone's fundamental assumption that the Christian God is benevolent and liberating. He argued that Black liberation theology failed to grapple with Blacks' suffering in history and to justify that God has indeed been a liberator for Black people. He asked Cone and other Black theologians to consider the possibility that the Divine could be "a White racist" who prefers to uphold the interests of the prevailing racial hierarchy rather than people living in poverty.[40] In light of persisting suffering, he advances *humanocentric theism*. This orientation accentuates the importance of human agency and resistance against oppressive forces instead of ongoing appeals to divine strength and power.[41] Jones laid the foundation for Black humanist or nontheistic theology. He introduced to Black Theology "the possibility of nontheistic theologizing as organic to African American [socio-political] praxis."[42]

Building on Jones's work, Anthony Pinn challenges the theistic straitjacket of academic Black theological discourse. Although a surface-level understanding of theology centers on God (Theo), the term is more than a reference to a divine being; within religion, the concept functions as a "centering trope" for that which has historically provided people with "more expansive meaning and purpose."[43] Pinn argues that the traditional god category does not capture the variety of nontheistic ways Black people are religious. Rather than studying exclusively divine revelation, Pinn "takes a full range of human experience and cultural creations as the proper material for the development of theology."[44] He traces humanism in Black religious history, including in the secular work songs, Black folktales, blues music, and in the literature of writers such as Richard Wright, Loraine Hansberry, Alain Locke, and James Weldon Johnson.[45] Black Humanist fellowships were less pervasive in Black communities than traditional religious institutions such as Black churches. Still, Pinn discusses the history of Black humanist organizations such as the American Humanist Association, the Ethical Cultural Society Movement, African Americans for Humanism, and the Unitarian Universalist Association (UUA). All of these organizations met Black humanists' religious longing for community and connection.[46]

Black humanists also worked with a wide range of social justice organizations throughout the long civil rights struggle, including but not limited to the Communist Party, SNCC, the NAACP, and the Black Panther Party. Lewis McGee, an African American leader in the UAA who contributed to the civil rights struggle, summed up UAA beliefs:

> We believe in the human capacity to solve individual and social problems and thus to make progress. We believe in a continuing search for truth and life is an adventurous quest. We believe in the scientific method as valid in ascertaining factual knowledge. We believe in democratic process in our human relations. We believe in ethical conduct. We believe in a dynamic universe, the evolution of life, the oneness of human family and the unity of life with the material universe ... We believe in the creative imagination as a power in promoting the good life.[47]

Humanism accentuates human agency, ingenuity, "education at all levels," "self-help," and "self-reliance."[48] It stresses that Black people should strive to maximize their human potential to be change agents instead of seeking liberation via an external metaphysical power.[49]

Reviving the Nation of Islam

The original NOI disbanded under the leadership of Warith Deen Mohammed (formerly known as Wallace Muhammad), the son and successor of Elijah Muhammad. He rejected his father's teaching that Whites were devils. He dissolved the Fruit of Islam. He integrated the NOI into the World Muslim Mission and with mainstream Sunni Islam. Louis Farrakhan disagreed with Mohammed's dissolution of the NOI and held that the new leader had abandoned the founder's Black religious nationalist message and beliefs that gave hope to numerous Black people. Born as Louis Eugene Walcott in 1933 in New York, Louis Farrakhan joined the NOI in 1955 after hearing Elijah Muhammad speak during a Savior's Day Convention and listening to Muslim ministers such as Minister Malcolm X unpack NOI beliefs and teachings during religious services. After converting, he accepted the name Louis 2X. He gave up his profession as a calypso performer, devoted himself to the NOI, accepted the call to become a minister, and spread the message throughout the globe. He worked closely with Minister Malcolm X at Temple No. 7. He rose swiftly within the organization's ranks, eventually replacing Malcolm X as leader of Temple No. 7 and as national Muslim minister.[50] He in time adopted the name Abdul Haleem Farrakhan and became popularly known as Louis Farrakhan.

Farrakhan reorganized the NOI as the Lost-Found Nation of Islam in 1977. He established the *Final Call* newspaper in 1979, drawing on the NOI's earlier *Muhammad Speaks* newspaper. He promoted establishing Black-owned businesses such as restaurants, grocery stores, and farmers' markets to promote Black economic independence and reduce Black people's reliance on White-controlled institutions. He adopted and extended the myth of Yakub and the apocalyptic beliefs of Muhammad, which held that White domination would end with the dramatic arrival of an advanced Mother Plane. Though many Americans have criticized Farrakhan as a racist and antisemitic fanatic, he revived the NOI and helped influence thousands of Black people to join the organization. New NOI chapters were established throughout the country and overseas in Ghana, London, and the Caribbean islands.[51]

In 1985, Farrakhan had a vision and out-of-body experience of being taken into a Mother Wheel, an unidentified flying object (UFO), in Tepotzotlán, México. This vision impacted his leadership of the NOI. He recalled:

> [O]n the night of September 17, 1985, I was carried up on that mountain, in a vision, with a few friends of mine. As we reached the top of the mountain, a Wheel, or what you call an unidentified flying object, appeared at the side of the mountain and called to me to come up into the Wheel. Three metal legs appeared from the Wheel, giving me the impression that it was going to land, but it never came over the mountain.[52]

Farrakhan's description of the Mother Wheel was similar to the tripod Martian UFOs that invaded London in H.G. Wells's novel *The War of the Worlds* (1898). The Mother Wheel does not merely bear the resemblance of an UFO. It is one. He further recalled that the Mother Wheel transported him into a room where he heard the voice of Elijah Muhammad, who died in 1975, speak to him. He told him, "President Reagan has met with the Joint Chiefs of Staff to plan a war. I want you to hold a press conference in Washington, D.C. to announce their plan and say to the world that you got the information from me on the Wheel."[53] It took Farrakhan nearly four years to decipher

Muhammad's cryptic words as a prophetic warning of the impact that the "War Against Drugs" would have on Black Americans. Indeed, the Get Tough on Crime politics and the criminalization of Blacks for nonviolent drug-related offenses accelerated what legal scholar Michelle Alexander termed mass incarceration and negatively impacted Black communities and families during the 1990s and 2000s during Republican and Democratic presidential administrations. Farrakhan warned America that God would return to execute divine judgment and would send "UFOs" to vindicate Blacks, whom he viewed as God's chosen people.[54]

The Mother Wheel signifies the superior knowledge of extraterrestrial civilizations in which Black people are connected. Finley says, "Farrakhan proclaims that black bodies are distinct and mysterious and that they have an intimate relationship with the Wheel—a symbolic and esoteric relationship that no other people share."[55] Abandoning Muhammad's belief that Fard was solely God in the flesh, Farrakhan argued that Fard reflected the "consciousness, power, and creativity that all African Americans can possess" when they receive esoteric knowledge and "divine ideals."[56]

Farrakhan's vision of the Mothership undergirded his leadership of the Million Man March on October 16, 1995. The hundreds of thousands of Black men who assembled during the march gave Farrakhan a platform to proclaim the message he received aboard the Mother Wheel to the nation and the world. In his keynote address entitled, "Toward a More Perfect Union," he discussed social injustices that plagued Black people and urged Black men to return to their homes and "join some church, synagogue, temple, or mosque

Figure 6.2. Minister Louis Farrakhan speaks and waves to the crowd while a member of the Nation of Islam stands guard at the Million Man March on October 16, 1995, in Washington, DC. The march aimed to galvanize men to respect themselves and others spiritually, morally, mentally, socially, politically, and economically.
Photo by Porter Gifford/Liaison.

that is teaching spiritual and moral uplift."[57] He expressed his hope that the Million Man March would foster unity among diasporic Black people and connect the NOI to global Islam.[58] Farrakhan perceived his orchestration of the march in Washington, DC as a fulfillment of Muhammad's commandment to him aboard the Mother Wheel in 1975.

On the fifth anniversary of the Million Man March, Farrakhan spearheaded a Million Family March that included women and was open to people of diverse races. The march addressed a variety of issues related to families, such as equitable access to healthcare, education, welfare, and substance abuse prevention and treatment programs. The Million Man March also provided inspiration for the Million Woman March, organized in Philadelphia, PA, on October 25, 1997. Though it was not directly tied to the NOI, the Million Woman March attracted nearly 500,000 people and addressed the plight of Black women in America.[59]

Albeit Farrakhan credits his vision aboard the Mother Wheel as inspiring his leadership of the Million Man March, his relationship with Malcolm X likely also influenced his political activism. Farrakhan's message and speaking style certainly resembled his former mentor. He emerged as the outspoken and public voice of the NOI after Malcolm X's fissure with the organization and has remained the face of the NOI for decades after he reorganized it in 1977.

Carrying the Mantle of Dr. King: Reverends Jesse Jackson and Al Sharpton

Historians have grappled with who in the Black Christian tradition emerged as the successor to Reverend Dr. King. Reverend Ralph Abernathy, King's right arm during the civil rights movement, succeeded him as SCLC president. However, he lacked the charisma to fill King's shoes. He was unable to maintain unity in the organization. The number of SCLC staff members waned from 150 in the 1960s to about sixty-one in 1972.[60] The SCLC also experienced a decline in its finances.

SNCC, CORE, the NAACP, and other notable civil rights groups had a decline in membership and finances similar to that of SCLC during the 1970s. Rising inflation influenced wealthy donors and foundations to lessen the money provided to national civil rights groups.[61]

In light of these challenges and for other reasons, many civil rights organizations shifted their focus from protest to electoral politics, investing limited resources in mobilizing Black people to pursue social change through voting. Black churches contributed to the election of Black clergy in the United States Congress and various state and local government positions. Former civil rights activists, such as SNCC's John Lewis and SCLC's Andrew Young, were among the six Black clergy members elected to Congress since 1971. Others included Walter Fauntroy, William Gray III, Floyd Flake, and J.C. Watt.[62]

Notwithstanding the decline of national civil rights organizations and the shift toward electoral activism, some small protest demonstrations occurred in various cities. For example, nearly 500 Black people participated in a protest march in Augusta, Georgia, in May 1970 following the death of Charles Oatman, a Black youth detained at the Richmond County Jail. Although police claimed he died from falling from his top cell bunk, an autopsy revealed he had been tortured, burned with cigarettes, and murdered. In response, some protestors torched the Georgia state flag, inciting a riot. Police retaliated with violence and killed six Black people. SCLC leaders responded to the violence by organizing a march from Perry to Atlanta, attended by nearly 10,000 people.

Another notable example of protest during the early 1970s is a boycott orchestrated by the Wilmington Ten. In 1971, Reverend Ben Chavis, a leader for the United Church of Christ's Commission for Racial Justice, traveled to Wilmington, North Carolina, to help advance a boycott organized by local Black high school students to protest educational inequality. Working with the students, he galvanized about 500 youths to participate. A riot developed when several Black protesters defended themselves and other Black residents from the attacks of White vigilantes and Ku Klux Klan members. The governor deployed the National Guard to restore order. Two people died during the heated racial conflict. The police arrested Chavis and nine others meeting at the Gregory Congregational Church, accusing them of arson and intentionally setting ablaze Mike's Grocery store on February 6, 1971. Firefighters also reported that a sniper was shooting at them from the top of Gregory Congregational Church, where Chavis and the students were meeting. Convicted based on the conflicting testimony of two Black residents who were allegedly bribed to fabricate their story, the nine Black individuals who met at the church received sentences of nearly three decades. The lone White woman, Ann Shepherd, who supported the protest, received a fifteen-year sentence.[63] Demonstrators led a mass march from Charlotte to Raleigh to prompt Governor Jim Hunt to issue a pardon. The National Wilmington Ten Defense Committee attempted to persuade the Carter administration to intervene. He influenced the U.S. Justice Department to convince Governor Jim Hunt to reduce the outrageous sentences in 1978. It wasn't until 1980 that Amnesty International was able to convince the Fourth Circuit of Appeals to "overturn the convictions" and release the prisoners.[64]

As new civil rights leaders such as Reverend Davis were emerging during the 1970s, many veteran civil rights leaders such as Floyd McKissick, Bayard Rustin, John Lewis, Fannie Lou Hamer, Julian Bond, Andrew Young, and Coretta Scott King (Martin Luther King's widow) did not simply vanish from the scene. They continued to pursue social justice through various means. During the 1980s and 1990s, Reverend Jesse Jackson and Reverend Al Sharpton were two figures who arguably picked up the protest mantle of King.

Reverend Jesse Jackson

According to Michael Eric Dyson, Jackson "best captured" the spirit of King and "extended his work."[65] Born on October 8, 1941, in Greenville, North Carolina, to Helen Burns and Noah Louis Robinson, Jackson participated in sit-in demonstrations in downtown Greensboro while enrolled in the Agricultural Technical College. After obtaining his bachelor's degree in 1964, he served on the staff of Governor Terry Sanford and helped organize the Young Democratic Club in North Carolina.[66] He enrolled in Chicago Theological Seminary in 1965. Jackson volunteered during the Selma campaign and developed a rapport with King and the SCLC's inner circle members.[67] He officially joined the organization when he was twenty-four years of age, and King appointed him as the leader of Operation Breadbasket in Chicago in 1965. The initiative boycotted businesses that sold goods to Black consumers but refused to hire Black workers or do business with Black contractors.[68] Jackson emerged as the national leader of Operation Breadbasket in 1967. He became an ordained Baptist minister in 1968 and co-pastor of the Fellowship Missionary Baptist Church. Jackson believed that the fourth phase of the freedom struggle was the movement for economic justice, which King spearheaded before his death.[69] Jackson called on Americans in post-civil rights America to advance King's "unfinished movement."[70]

Though Jackson remained affiliated with Operation Breadbasket, internal conflicts with Reverend Abernathy influenced him to part ways with the SCLC in 1971 and establish People United to Save Humanity (PUSH). In less than a decade, the organization grew to have more than seventy chapters throughout the United States.[71] In line with Operation Breadbasket, PUSH had an economic agenda, and the organization protested and boycotted businesses that discriminated against people of color. The organization persuaded famous corporations such as Coca-Cola, Burger King, and General Motors to work with "minority vendors."[72] In 1968, Jackson also stood in solidarity with Cesar Chavez and the United Farm Workers of America when the organization led a hunger strike to boycott the low pay and horrible working conditions of farmers harvesting grapes in California.

Jackson also led several protest demonstrations. Twenty years after the historic march on Washington, in 1983 he co-led a March on Washington attended by nearly 250,000 people.[73] When speaking at the march, he emphasized the importance of continuing to protest and strive for civil rights. He expressed, "From the outhouse to the statehouse to the courthouse to the White House, we will march on. March on!"[74]

During the 1980s, Reverend Jackson emerged as the most towering Black religious figure in politics.[75] His effective leadership of Operation Breadbasket and PUSH, and his ties to Black churches, boosted his popularity and laid the foundation for his presidential campaigns in 1984 and 1988. During his bid for the Democratic nomination, Jackson founded the National Rainbow Coalition, which expanded King's prophetic vision for a multiracial movement into politics. He believed that a broad, diverse coalition of poor and marginalized people could redeem America. He contended that America needed "new values and new vision" to be saved from peril under the Reagan administration, which cut programs for people with low incomes and had ties to apartheid South Africa.[76] Jackson came in third place in the primaries in 1984, winning several primaries and caucuses and securing 18.2 percent of the vote or about 3.5 million votes. He received far more delegates than the one vote Douglass and the fourteen votes Shirley Chisholm received in their respective Republican and Democratic primaries in 1888 and 1972. Before this point, Douglass and Chisholm had been the only Black people to receive delegate votes during presidential primaries. Ultimately, during the 1988 presidential election, Jackson received more than 7 million votes, won several states, and came in second to Michael Dukakis in the Democratic primary. Though he did not win the Democratic nomination for president, Jackson's status as a celebrity increased, and he continued to use his stardom to promote social justice.

Reverend Al Sharpton

Reverend Al Sharpton is another Black religious figure who arguably continued the legacy of King. He emulated the public leadership of both King and Jackson, becoming a household name. Born in 1954 in New York City to Ada and Alfred Charles Sharpton Sr., Sharpton was reared amid the civil rights movement. He grew up in the Church of God in Christ and started preaching at age four. Formally called the "Wonderboy," he was ordained at ten years of age by Bishop Frederick Douglas Washington, the pastor of Washington Temple Church of God in Christ. Sharpton met King when attending programming led by Operation Breadbasket in Brooklyn.[77] He became a youth director of Operation Breadbasket in 1968 and formed a relationship with Jesse Jackson, the national program director. Upon completing high school, he enrolled in Brooklyn

College. However, he dropped out after two years. He dedicated his life to activism, establishing the National Youth Movement with the support of legendary civil rights activist Bayard Rustin. When raising funds for his new organization, the young Sharpton developed a close relationship with James Brown, a renowned soul artist. At the request of the legendary singer, Sharpton permed his hair like Brown. To honor his friend and mentor, he went against the grain of adorning a fade or a jerry curl, popular hairstyles Black American men wore during the 1980s and 1990s.[78]

Though many of Sharpton's critics questioned his hairstyle and perceived him to be a "racial ambulance chaser" and "anti-Semitic racist," Sharpton gained respect among Black people for organizing scores of marches and rallies in Brooklyn, New York.[79] Utilizing "a politics of manhood," he presented himself as a bold and proud Black man who would not bear racial disrespect from the establishment.[80] In 1986, he led a demonstration to protest the racially motivated attack on three Black men in the Howard Beach neighborhood of Queens, New York. One of the men, Michael Griffith, was killed after a group of White youths chased him onto a highway. He led marches and demanded justice for Griffith, bringing national media attention to his death. Sharpton represented Tawana Brawley, a fifteen-year-old Black girl who alleged that six White males, of whom at least one was a cop, assaulted and raped her in Wappingers Falls, New York, on November 28, 1987. After a careful analysis of "police and medical records," a grand jury concluded Brawley had lied. This incident negatively damaged Sharpton's reputation.[81] Nonetheless, the Brawley incident did not prevent Sharpton from continuing to stand in solidarity with Black victims of racial injustice. Through his National Action Network, founded in 1991, Sharpton has remained involved in movements protesting the deaths of African American men and women such as Amadou Diallo, Trayvon Martin, Eric Garner, Brianna Taylor, George Floyd, and numerous others. Sharpton exemplified the protest tradition of King through his charisma, organizational acumen, and ability to attract news coverage to social injustice. Like Jackson, he sought to pursue change through accessing political power. He ran for multiple political offices, including for US Senate in 1992 and 1994, the mayor of New York in 1997, and president of the United States in 2004.

Upholding the Legacy of Mary McLeod Bethune: Black Churches and Post-Civil Rights Cooperationist Activism

Besides continuing to pursue social justice through protest and electoral politics, Black religious figures have also collaborated with politicians and government entities to pursue social change. This form of activism is referred to as cooperationist activism. Mary McLeod Bethune (1875–1955), a prominent educator and founder of the Daytona Normal and Industrial School for Negro Girls (Bethune Cookman College), was a cooperationist activist during the 1930s and 1940s. A devout Black Presbyterian and graduate of the Moody Bible Institute, Bethune's faith inspired her civic activism. She founded the National Council of Negro Women (NCNW), an organization devoted to pursuing equal educational and employment opportunities, federal legislation to end lynching, voter disenfranchisement, and restrictive covenants.[82] The organization, at one point, represented nearly 900,000 Black women. Her close friendship with Eleanor Roosevelt, the wife of President Franklin Delano Roosevelt, paved the way for her to organize and lead FDR's unofficial Black Cabinet and to work with his administration to advocate for civil rights and opportunities for Black people.

Cooperationist activism upholds the importance of bureaucratic enfranchisement, defined as "a process by which the interests of a constituency are formally represented in government agencies to influence how electorally defined agency missions or program objectives are implemented."[83] Distinct from mere enfranchisement or casting a ballot, bureaucratic enfranchisement stresses that churches and other groups should take the next step and become directly involved in "planning and implementing public programs."[84]

Cooperationist activism was strongly adopted among Black churches during the Clinton and Bush administrations' Charitable Choice initiatives in the 1990s and 2000s.[85] Charitable Choice refers to provisions in U.S. federal law that allow faith-based organizations to compete with other nonprofits for government funding to establish job training, childcare, substance abuse treatment, and homelessness prevention programs. Charitable Choice enables the government to transfer Temporary Assistance for Needy Families Program (TANF), Welfare to Work, and Community Service Block grant funds to religious institutions engaged in non-sectarian charitable community endeavors.[86]

During the 1990s, churches affiliated with various historic Black church denominations applied for and received government contracts in different cities throughout the country, including but not limited to Chicago, New York, Milwaukee, Louisville, Los Angeles, Oakland, and Philadelphia. Many Black churches found Charitable Choice attractive because they believed it would enable them to access the funding needed to fulfill their church missions and social outreach visions. Black pastors were most represented among diverse religious leaders who met with President Bush in 2001 to discuss faith-based initiatives. They came to the table because they wanted to receive government funding to provide affordable housing, employment, and other social services to residents in underserved communities.[87]

The Boston Ten Point Coalition, a faith-based organization formed in the early 1990s by a group of clergy and lay leaders in Boston to address youth violence, gang activity, and urban decay in their communities, was an exemplar of cooperationist activism.[88] The coalition consisted of several interdenominational Black churches in Boston, including but not limited to the Bethel AME Church, Twelfth Baptist Church, the Charles Street AME Church, and the Azusa Christian Community Church. Members of the coalition were open to working with public officials to obtain resources to provide counseling, mentoring, and employment programs for disadvantaged Black youth. The coalition cooperated with the judicial system in arbitrating cases and with police officials in identifying threats and criminals in the community. They addressed complaints regarding police brutality and sought to enhance relations between the police and residents in Black communities.[89]

Leaders within the NAACP and Congressional Black Caucus opposed Welfare reform and Charitable Choice because they held it reduced public assistance funding directed to urban poor people. It inappropriately placed the onus of meeting the needs of poor people on underequipped and overstretched faith communities. Some viewed Charitable Choice as a smokescreen that enabled conservative politicians to justify reducing the size of the federal government and a slick maneuver for the government to evade its responsibility to impoverished people. Though the government might attest it was working with Black churches, the reality was that only a tiny percentage (8%) of Black churches obtained competitive government funding for their social programs. The results of a National Congregations Study survey conducted by Lincoln and Mamiya of 1531 urban Black churches revealed that most Black churches did not receive government contracts to fund their social outreach initiatives.[90]

Black church leaders committed to protest politics have been reluctant to endorse collaborations with the state because they deemed government grants could compromise the prophetic voice of Black churches. Speaking out against injustice in New York resulted in one Harlem pastor jeopardizing a significant funding opportunity that could have enabled him and his church to improve their community. The Harlem pastor explained, "As many units of housing my church has completed in partnership with the city government ... we've lost out due to my politics and big mouth."[91] The New York Housing Department chose a Muslim Mosque as "the community sponsor" for the Alliance for Neighborhood Commerce, Homeownership, and Revitalization (ANCHOR) program in central Harlem. The church lost the opportunity to acquire land to construct "778 mixed-income housing units" and to create retail space to establish businesses that would supply more than a hundred jobs to local residents.[92] The point of the matter, simply put, is that churches that receive government grants can compromise their freedom to challenge the establishment.

Arguably, the zenith of post-civil rights activism occurred with the 2008 election of Barack Obama, the first Black or biracial president in the history of the United States. Black people who embraced many social justice orientations reviewed in this chapter, including the self-help tradition, Black liberation theologies, protest politics, and cooperationist politics, were proud of Obama's historic election. He inspired people of various hues to believe that America could become a genuinely democratic nation where freedom and justice reigned. Yet, before his election, he was subject to racial attacks by the "birther" movement, which advanced conspiracies that he was born in Hawaii and was not an American citizen. The media attempted to derail his campaign by taking the sermons of his former pastor, Reverend Jeremiah Wright Jr., out of context. For example, the press inappropriately circulated a clip of Wright shouting, "God Damn America." They portrayed Wright as unpatriotic and eventually Obama severed ties with him. Obama was ultimately victorious in the Democratic Primaries and became the first Black president in 2008. By the end of his two terms in office, he was able to use executive authority and influence to advance progressive legislation such as the Affordable Care Act and to protect the rights of gays, lesbians, transgender, and non-conforming Americans from hate crimes and discrimination. Still, many Black people were disillusioned that he did not or perhaps could not use his authority to rid America of systemic racism. The ascendancy of Black Lives Matter during his first term signaled that the country was not as close to the horizon of justice and equality for all as Obama imagined.

Review and Discussion Questions

1   How did the prosperity message relate to past movements that preceded it? Why did people from marginalized and underserved communities find the prosperity message appealing during the 1970s and 1980s?

2   How did Black liberation theology echo the thought of Martin Luther King and Malcolm X? What are some limitations of Black theology according to Black pastors, womanists, and humanists?

3   What are the similarities between King and Reverends Jesse Jackson and Al Sharpton? How did Jackson and Sharpton seek to confront social injustice in novel ways during the 1980s and 1990s?

4   Why did Black churches and religious institutions embrace cooperationist activism during the 1990s and 2000s? What compromises might arise when religious institutions cooperate with the political establishment? Do the potential benefits outweigh the compromises?

Notes

1 Some Black Americans turned to Eastern philosophies such as Zen Buddhism and aspired to adjust to persisting racial inequities by learning the art of being awake and following Buddhist principles such as the "Four Simple Truths." Angel Kyodo Williams, *Being Black: Zen and the Art of Living with Fearlessness and Grace* (New York: Penguin Books, 2002).

2 Jesse Jackson, "Common Ground and Common Sense," address delivered July 19, 1988. In *Let Nobody Turn Us Around: Voices of Resistance, Reform, and Renewal; An African American Anthology*, edited by Manning Marable and Leith Mullings, (New York: Bowman & Littlefield Publishers, Inc., 2000), 575–577.

3 Stephanie Y. Michem, *Name It and Claim It? Prosperity Preaching in the Black Church* (Cleveland: The Pilgrim Press, 2007), 121–122.

4 Stephanie Y. Michem, *Name It and Claim It? Prosperity Preaching in the Black Church* (Cleveland: The Pilgrim Press, 2007), 121–122.

5 Scott Billingsley, *It's a New Day: Race and Gender in the Modern Charismatic Movement* (Tuscaloosa, AL: University of Alabama Press, 2008), 142.

6 Kate Bowler, "The Prosperity Gospel in America," *Oxford Research Encyclopedia of Religion*, February 26, 2018, retrieved October 4, 2024, from https://oxfordre.com/religion/view/10.1093/acrefore/9780199340378.001.0001/acrefore-9780199340378-e-429.

7 Cited in Jonathan L. Walton, "The Greening of the Gospel (and Black Body): Rev. Ike's Gospel of Wealth and Post-Blackness Theology," *Pneuma*, 33 (2011): 198.

8 Christopher Lehmann-Haupt, "Reverend Ike, Who Preached Riches, Dies at 74," *New York Times*, July 29, 2009.

9 Henry Louis Gates and Evelyn Brooks Higginbotham, eds., *African American Lives*, s.v. "Reverend Ike" (New York: Oxford University Press, 2004), 711–712; Leo Standora, "Luxury-Loving Rev. Ike is Dead," *New York Times*, 30 July 2009.

10 Katherine Attanasi and Amos Young, ed., *Pentecostalism and Prosperity: The Socio-Economics of the Global Charismatic Movement* (New York: Palgrave Macmillan, 2012), 3–5; Milmon F. Harrison, *Righteous Riches: The Word of Faith Movement in Contemporary African American Religion* (New York: Oxford University Press, 2005), 134–135.

11 Milmon F. Harrison, *Righteous Riches: The Word of Faith Movement in Contemporary African American Religion* (New York: Oxford University Press, 2005), 8–12, 70–74; Katherine Attanasi and Amos Young, ed., *Pentecostalism and Prosperity: The Socio-Economics of the Global Charismatic Movement* (New York: Palgrave Macmillan, 2012), 111–112; CERCL Writing Collective, *Breaking Bread, Breaking Beats* (Minneapolis, MN: Fortress Press, 2014), 84–85.

12 CERCL Writing Collective, *Breaking Bread, Breaking Beats* (Minneapolis, MN: Fortress Press, 2014), 86.

13 Milmon F. Harrison, *Righteous Riches: The Word of Faith Movement in Contemporary African American Religion* (New York: Oxford University Press, 2005), 143; Jonathan L. Walton, *Watch This! The Ethics and Aesthetics of Black Televangelism,* (New York: New York University Press, 2009), 2; CERCL Writing Collective, *Breaking Bread, Breaking Beats* (Minneapolis, MN: Fortress Press, 2014), 86.

14 Katherine Attanasi and Amos Young, ed., *Pentecostalism and Prosperity: The Socio-Economics of the Global Charismatic Movement* (New York: Palgrave Macmillan, 2012), 112; Jonathan L. Walton, *Watch This! The Ethics and Aesthetics of Black Televangelism,* (New York: New York University Press, 2009), 146–149.

15 Jonathan L. Walton, *Watch This! The Ethics and Aesthetics of Black Televangelism,* (New York: New York University Press, 2009), 150; CERCL Writing Collective, *Breaking Bread, Breaking Beats* (Minneapolis, MN: Fortress Press, 2014), 86–89.

16 Jonathan L. Walton, *Watch This! The Ethics and Aesthetics of Black Televangelism,* (New York: New York University Press, 2009), 152; CERCL Writing Collective, *Breaking Bread, Breaking Beats* (Minneapolis, MN: Fortress Press, 2014), 86–89.

17 Milmon F. Harrison, *Righteous Riches: The Word of Faith Movement in Contemporary African American Religion* (New York: Oxford University Press, 2005), 148–152.

18 Rosetta E. Ross, "Black Theology and the History of U.S. Black Religions: Post Civil Rights Approaches to the Study of African American Religions," *Religion Compass* 6/4 (2012): 252–253.

19 Gayraud S. Wilmore and James H. Cone, eds, *Black Theology: A Documentary History, Volume One: 1966–1979* (Maryknoll, NY: Orbis Books, 1979), 23.

20 Cone's books, *Black Theology and Black Power* (1969), *A Black Theology of Liberation* (1970), and *God of the Oppressed* (1975), "formed the founding corpus of what became black theology in the United States academy." Ross, "Black Theology and the History of U.S. Black Religions," 253.

21 Raphael G Warnock, *The Divided Mind of the Black Church: Theology, Piety, and Public Witness* (New York: New York University Press, 2014), 73.

22 James H. Cone, *Black Theology and Black Power* (Maryknoll, NY: Orbis Books, 1970), 25–26, 37–38.

23 James H. Cone, *A Black Theology of Liberation* (Maryknoll, NY: 1990, orig. 1970), 9.

24 There are numerous interlocutors I do mention in this section due to space limitations. My intention here is to provide an overview of scholarship produced by scholars of Black religion that speak to Black religious scholars' debates regarding theology and social justice.

25 J. Deotis Roberts, *Liberation and Reconciliation: A Black Theology* (Louisville, KY: John Knox Press, 2005), 18–21.

26 Cone was reared and ordained in the AME Church. Katie Cannon also served as a minister in the United Presbyterian USA. Ordained in 1974, she was the first Black woman ordained in the denomination. Ordained in the AME Church in 1974, Grant has served as an assistant minister at multiple churches and has presented several papers on women in the AME church.

27 Raphael G Warnock, *The Divided Mind of the Black Church: Theology, Piety, and Public Witness* (New York: New York University Press, 2014), 111–112.

28 Raphael G Warnock, *The Divided Mind of the Black Church: Theology, Piety, and Public Witness* (New York: New York University Press, 2014), 111–112.

29 Gayraud S. Wilmore and James H. Cone, eds, *Black Theology: A Documentary History, Volume Two: 1980–1992* (Maryknoll, NY: Orbis Books, 1993), 132.

30 Gayraud S. Wilmore and James H. Cone, eds, *Black Theology: A Documentary History, Volume Two: 1980–1992* (Maryknoll, NY: Orbis Books, 1993), 132.

31 This list is by no means exhaustive.

32 Raphael G Warnock, *The Divided Mind of the Black Church: Theology, Piety, and Public Witness* (New York: New York University Press, 2014), 111–112.

33 Stacey M. Floyd-Thomas, *Mining the Motherlode: Methods in Womanist Ethics* (Cleveland, OH: Pilgrim Press, 2006).

34 Cone served as a mentor for Grant and Williams. Beverly Wildung Harrison advised Cannon. Ebony Marshall Turman, "Black Women's Faith, Black Women's Flourishing," *The Christian Century*, March 13, 2019, retrieved from www.christiancentury.org/article/critical-essay/black-women-s-faith-black-women-s-flourishing.

35 Frederick L. Ware, "Methodologies in African American Theology," cited in Katie G. Cannon and Anthony B. Pinn, eds., *The Oxford Handbook of African American Theology* (New York: Oxford University Press, 2014), 132.

36 Katie G. Cannon, *Black Womanist Ethics* (Atlanta, GA: Scholars Press, 1988), 90; M. Shawn Copeland, "African American Religious Experience," cited in Katie G. Cannon and Anthony B. Pinn, eds., *The Oxford Handbook of African American Theology* (New York: Oxford University Press, 2014), 56.

37 Cannon, *Black Womanists Ethics*, 17.

38 Delores S. Williams, *Sisters in the Wilderness: The Challenge of Womanist God-Talk* (Maryknoll, NY: Orbis Books, 1993); M. Shawn Copeland, "African American Religious Experience," Cited in Katie G. Cannon and Anthony B. Pinn, eds., *The Oxford Handbook of African American Theology* (New York: Oxford University Press, 2014), 57.

39 Marshall Turman, "Black Women's Faith, Black Women's Flourishing," *The Christian Century*, March 13, 2019, retrieved from www.christiancentury.org/article/critical-essay/black-women-s-faith-black-women-s-flourishing.

40 William R. Jones, *Is God a White Racist?: A Preamble to Black Theology* (Garden City, NY: Anchor Press, 1998, orig. 1973).

41 William R. Jones, *Is God a White Racist?: A Preamble to Black Theology* (Garden City, NY: Anchor Press, 1998, orig. 1973), 202. Cone responded to Jones's critique by appealing to metaphysics and Christian religious experience. James Cone, *God of the Oppressed* (New York: Harper & Row, Publishers, 1975), 191–192.

42 Anthony B. Pinn, "Humanism in African American Theology," in *The Oxford Handbook of African American Theology*, edited by Katie G. Cannon, and Anthony B. Pinn (New York: Oxford University Press, 2014), 282.

43 Anthony B. Pinn, "Humanism in African American Theology," in *The Oxford Handbook of African American Theology*, edited by Katie G. Cannon, and Anthony B. Pinn (New York: Oxford University Press, 2014), 288.

44 Anthony B. Pinn, "Humanism in African American Theology," in *The Oxford Handbook of African American Theology*, edited by Katie G. Cannon, and Anthony B. Pinn (New York: Oxford University Press, 2014), 288.

45 Anthony B. Pinn, *Introducing African American Religion* (New York: Routledge, 2013), 66–67.

46 Anthony B. Pinn, *Introducing African American Religion* (New York: Routledge, 2013), 242–245; Anthony B. Pinn, *The African American Religious Experience in America* (Westport, CT: Greenwood Press, 2006), 66–72.

47 Mark D. Morrison-Reed, *Black Pioneers in a White Denomination*, 3rd ed. (Boston: Skinner House Books, 1994), 92, cited in Anthony B. Pinn, *The African American Religious Experience in America* (Westport, CT: Greenwood Press, 2006), 72.

48 Anthony B. Pinn, *Introducing African American Religion* (New York: Routledge, 2013), 243.

49 Anthony B. Pinn, *The African American Religious Experience in America* (Westport, CT: Greenwood Press, 2006), 74.

50 Stephen C. Finley, *In and Out of This World: Material and Extraterrestrial Bodies in the Nation of Islam* (Durham, NC: Duke University Press, 2022), 133–134.

51 Stephen C. Finley, *In and Out of This World: Material and Extraterrestrial Bodies in the Nation of Islam* (Durham, NC: Duke University Press, 2022), 132–143; Lawrence A. Mamiya, "Louis Farrakhan," *Encyclopedia Britannica*, September 12, 2024, retrieved from www.britannica.com/biography/Louis-Farrakhan, accessed September 19, 2024.

52 Stephen C. Finley, *In and Out of This World: Material and Extraterrestrial Bodies in the Nation of Islam* (Durham, NC: Duke University Press, 2022), 137.

53 Stephen C. Finley, *In and Out of This World: Material and Extraterrestrial Bodies in the Nation of Islam* (Durham, NC: Duke University Press, 2022), 138.

54 Stephen C. Finley, *In and Out of This World: Material and Extraterrestrial Bodies in the Nation of Islam* (Durham, NC: Duke University Press, 2022), 146.

55 Stephen C. Finley, *In and Out of This World: Material and Extraterrestrial Bodies in the Nation of Islam* (Durham, NC: Duke University Press, 2022), 150.

56 Stephen C. Finley, *In and Out of This World: Material and Extraterrestrial Bodies in the Nation of Islam* (Durham, NC: Duke University Press, 2022), 149–150.

57 *New York Times*, October 17, 1995, retrieved from www.nytimes.com/1995/10/17/us/march-washington-excerpts-farrakhan-talk-still-2-americas-one-black-one-white.html.

58 Stephen C. Finley, *In and Out of This World: Material and Extraterrestrial Bodies in the Nation of Islam* (Durham, NC: Duke University Press, 2022), 154–155.

59 "Million Family March," *NPR*, October 16, 2000; Michael Fletcher and DeNeer Brown, "Anticipation, Hopes Build for Million Woman March," *The Washington Post*. October 24, 1997; Pamela Oliver, "Organizing the Million Woman March" *Race, Politics, Justice*. January 28, 2023.

60 Timothy J. Minchin, "Beyond the Dominant Narrative: The Ongoing Struggle for Civil Rights in the US South, 1968–1980" *Australian Journal of American Studies*, 25, no. 1 (July 2006), 69.

61 Timothy J. Minchin, "Beyond the Dominant Narrative: The Ongoing Struggle for Civil Rights in the US South, 1968–1980" *Australian Journal of American Studies*, 25, no. 1 (July 2006), 69.

62 R. Drew Smith, ed., *From Every Mountainside: Black Churches and the Broad Terrain of Civil Rights* (Albany, NY: State University of New York, 2013), 3–4, 59–60; David Masciotra, *I Am Somebody: Why Jesse Jackson Matters* (New York: Bloomsbury Publishing, 2020), 182.

63 Timothy J. Minchin, "Beyond the Dominant Narrative: The Ongoing Struggle for Civil Rights in the US South, 1968–1980" *Australian Journal of American Studies*, 25, no. 1 (July 2006), 73.

64 Timothy J. Minchin, "Beyond the Dominant Narrative: The Ongoing Struggle for Civil Rights in the US South, 1968–1980" *Australian Journal of American Studies*, 25, no. 1 (July 2006), 74.

65 Michael Eric Dyson, *April 4, 1968: Martin Luther King, Jr.'s Death and How It Changed America*. (New York: Basic Books, 2009), 170.

66 Larry G. Murphy, J. Gordon Melton, and Gary L. Ward, eds., *Encyclopedia of African American Religions* (New York: Garland Publishing, 1993), 385.

67 Michael Eric Dyson, *April 4, 1968: Martin Luther King, Jr.'s Death and How It Changed America*. (New York: Basic Books, 2009), 176; Clarence Taylor, *Black Religious Intellectuals: The Fight for Equality from Jim Crow to the 21st Century* (New York: Taylor and Francis Group, 2002), 131.

68 Michael Eric Dyson, *April 4, 1968: Martin Luther King, Jr.'s Death and How It Changed America*. (New York: Basic Books, 2009), 177.

69 R. Drew Smith, ed., *New Day Begun: African American Churches and Civic Culture in Post-Civil Rights America* (Durham, NC: Duke University Press, 2003), 98.

70 R. Drew Smith, ed., *New Day Begun: African American Churches and Civic Culture in Post-Civil Rights America* (Durham, NC: Duke University Press, 2003), 98.

71 Timothy J. Minchin, "Beyond the Dominant Narrative: The Ongoing Struggle for Civil Rights in the US South, 1968–1980" *Australian Journal of American Studies*, 25, no. 1 (July 2006), 77.

72 Timothy J. Minchin, "Beyond the Dominant Narrative: The Ongoing Struggle for Civil Rights in the US South, 1968–1980" *Australian Journal of American Studies*, 25, no. 1 (July 2006), 77.

73 Robert Wuthnow, *Faith Communities and the Fight for Racial Justice: What Has Worked, What Hasn't, and Lessons We Can Learn* (Princeton, NJ: Princeton University Press, 2023), 104.

74 Robert Wuthnow, *Faith Communities and the Fight for Racial Justice: What Has Worked, What Hasn't, and Lessons We Can Learn* (Princeton, NJ: Princeton University Press, 2023), 105.

75 Michael Eric Dyson, *April 4, 1968: Martin Luther King, Jr.'s Death and How It Changed America*. (New York: Basic Books, 2009), 195; Timothy J. Minchin, "Beyond the Dominant Narrative: The Ongoing Struggle for Civil Rights in the US South, 1968–1980" *Australian Journal of American Studies*, 25, no. 1 (July 2006), 79.

76 R. Drew Smith, ed., *New Day Begun: African American Churches and Civic Culture in Post-Civil Rights America* (Durham, NC: Duke University Press, 2003), 96; George E. Curry, "Jesse Jackson Honored for Anti-Apartheid Work," *Washington Informer*, May 1, 2013, retrieved from www.washingtoninformer.com/jesse-jackson-honored-for-anti-apartheid-work.

77 Michael Eric Dyson, *April 4, 1968: Martin Luther King, Jr.'s Death and How It Changed America*. (New York: Basic Books, 2009), 202–203.

78 Clarence Taylor, *Black Religious Intellectuals: The Fight for Equality from Jim Crow to the 21st Century* (New York: Taylor and Francis Group, 2002), 129.

79 Clarence Taylor, *Black Religious Intellectuals: The Fight for Equality from Jim Crow to the 21st Century* (New York: Taylor and Francis Group, 2002), 118–120.

80 Clarence Taylor, *Black Religious Intellectuals: The Fight for Equality from Jim Crow to the 21st Century* (New York: Taylor and Francis Group, 2002), 124.

81 Clarence Taylor, *Black Religious Intellectuals: The Fight for Equality from Jim Crow to the 21st Century* (New York: Taylor and Francis Group, 2002), 207.

82 Anthea Butler, *Women in the Church of God in Christ: Making a Sanctified World* (Chapel Hill, NC: The University of North Carolina Press, 2007), 99–100; "NCNW Launches Fight for Civil Rights," *New York Amsterdam News*, February 12, 1949.

83 Michael Leo Owens, *God and Government in the Ghetto: The Politics of Church-State Collaboration in Black America* (Chicago, IL: University of Chicago Press, 2007), 52.

84 Michael Leo Owens, *God and Government in the Ghetto: The Politics of Church-State Collaboration in Black America* (Chicago, IL: University of Chicago Press, 2007), 51.

85 R. Drew Smith, ed., *New Day Begun: African American Churches and Civic Culture in Post-Civil Rights America* (Durham, NC: Duke University Press, 2003), 7.

86 Michael Leo Owens, *God and Government in the Ghetto: The Politics of Church-State Collaboration in Black America* (Chicago, IL: University of Chicago Press, 2007), 3; R. Drew Smith, ed., *New Day Begun: African American Churches and Civic Culture in Post-Civil Rights America* (Durham, NC: Duke University Press, 2003), 235.

87 Michael Leo Owens, *God and Government in the Ghetto: The Politics of Church-State Collaboration in Black America* (Chicago, IL: University of Chicago Press, 2007), 2; R. Drew Smith, ed., *New Day Begun: African American Churches and Civic Culture in Post-Civil Rights America* (Durham, NC: Duke University Press, 2003), 6.

88 Glad Tidings Church of God in Christ received funding for its Institute of Success Program, which offers job training and computer courses to TANF recipients. Michael Leo Owens, *God and Government in the Ghetto: The Politics of Church-State Collaboration in Black America* (Chicago, IL: University of Chicago Press, 2007), 2–3.

89 Michael Leo Owens, *God and Government in the Ghetto: The Politics of Church-State Collaboration in Black America* (Chicago, IL: University of Chicago Press, 2007), 1.
90 R. Drew Smith, ed., *New Day Begun: African American Churches and Civic Culture in Post-Civil Rights America* (Durham, NC: Duke University Press, 2003), 254–256.
91 R. Drew Smith, ed., *New Day Begun: African American Churches and Civic Culture in Post-Civil Rights America* (Durham, NC: Duke University Press, 2003), 239.
92 R. Drew Smith, ed., *New Day Begun: African American Churches and Civic Culture in Post-Civil Rights America* (Durham, NC: Duke University Press, 2003), 239.

Further Readings

Cone, James H. *A Black Theology of Liberation*. Maryknoll, NY: Orbis Books, 1990. Originally published 1970.
Cannon, Katie G. *Black Womanist Ethics*. Atlanta, GA: Scholars Press, 1988.
Farrakhan, Louis. *A Torchlight for America*. Chicago, IL: FCN Publishing Co., 1993.
Finley, Stephen C. *In and Out of This World: Material and Extraterrestrial Bodies in the Nation of Islam*. Durham, NC: Duke University Press, 2022.
Gardell, Mattias. *In the Name of Elijah Muhammad: Louis Farrakhan and the Nation of Islam*. Durham, NC: Duke University Press, 2005.
Owens, Michael Leo. *God and Government in the Ghetto: The Politics of Church-State Collaboration in Black America*. Chicago, IL: University of Chicago Press, 2007.
Pinn, Anthony B. *The End of God-Talk*. New York: Oxford University Press, 2011.
Smith, R. Drew, ed. *From Every Mountainside: Black Churches and the Broad Terrain of Civil Rights*. Albany, NY: State University of New York, 2013.
Taylor, Clarence. *Black Religious Intellectuals: The Fight for Equality from Jim Crow to the 21st Century*. New York: Routledge, 2002.
Walton, Jonathan L. *Watch This! The Ethics and Aesthetics of Black Televangelism*. New York: New York University Press, 2009.
Williams, Deloris S. *Sisters in the Wilderness: The Challenge of Womanist God-Talk*. Maryknoll, NY: Orbis Books, 1993.

7 "Black Lives Matter"

Spiritual Strivings during the Twenty-First Century

In the new millennium, the Black middle class has grown and the number of Black people with college degrees has increased. Black people have ascended to the highest ranks in various fields, becoming college presidents, CEOs of major corporations, and owners of professional sports teams and television networks. After Barack Obama's historic election and tenure as the first Black president, some social and political conservatives, and neoliberals were apt to posit that America has entered a new post-racial period. For some, Obama's election provided a turning point in American history. Some perceived Obama as the fulfillment of King's dream, and felt that his election was confirmation that America is finally a meritocracy. Though Obama did not believe this, he upheld an optimistic political outlook that America was making steady progress in civil rights and was becoming a more inclusive society. The title of his memoir, *A Promised Land*, reverberated this perspective and his hopeful vision for the country.

Still, America has not yet and certainly is not under the administration of President Donald Trump close to becoming the land of promise many Black people long wished it would be. The emergence of the #BlackLivesMatter hashtag and movement during Obama's administration shattered the myth of post-racialism. Black people are yet striving for social justice and seeking to challenge systemic racism and other forms of oppression in the twenty-first. This chapter explores Black religious activists working within three emergent contemporary movements and organizations—Black Lives Matter, the Poor People's Campaign, and the Nap Ministry.[1] The chapter surveys how these groups are creatively drawing on ethical and religious resources and rituals to oppose systemic oppression during and post Obama's presidency. Ritual theorist Catherine Bell notes that humans possess agency and are "active creators of both cultural continuity and change rather than passive inheritors of a system who are conditioned from birth to replicate it."[2] While rituals can be a means of "maintaining the status quo," people can develop rituals and rework religious language to pursue social transformation. The innovative strivings of these three movements provide examples of how Black people's spiritual strivings remain dynamic and are responding to the rapidly advancing technologically world and information age in which we live.

Black Lives Matter

Three Black women—Alicia Garza, Patrice Cullors, and Opal Tometi—founded Black Lives Matter (BLM) in 2014 as a hashtag on social media following George Zimmerman's acquittal for the murder of Trayvon Martin, a seventeen-year-old Black youth.[3] Martin had walked to the convenience store to purchase snacks near his home in his

DOI: 10.4324/9781003359197-8

middle-class suburban community in Sanford, Florida. As Martin was walking back home, Zimmerman, a neighborhood watchman, called the police and told the dispatcher that Martin seemed suspicious. He judged him to be a troublemaker based on his skin color and clothing, especially his hoodie. Disregarding a directive from the 911 dispatcher, he confronted Martin. A scuffle subsequently ensued between the two, which tragically resulted in the teenager's death. Zimmerman shot Martin, who was unarmed and merely possessed a bag of Skittles and the iced tea he had purchased from the convenience store. After some pressure from activists, prosecutors charged Zimmerman with second-degree murder and manslaughter. Zimmerman's defense contended that their client acted in self-defense. Based on the evidence presented by his defense attorneys and Florida's stand-your-ground law, a jury of six women (five White and one Black/Hispanic) acquitted Zimmerman of the charges.[4] Many Black people who watched the highly televised trial perceived Martin as a victim of racial violence.

Alicia Garza was deeply troubled by the verdict. Having a brother close to Martin's age at the time, she empathized with his family. When she logged into Facebook the day after the jury's verdict, she posted an update entitled "A Love Letter to Black People." She expressed, "I continue to be surprised at how little Black lives matter." She concluded her letter by affirming: "Our lives matter."[5] The letter moved Garza's friend and an experienced community organizer and advocate, Patrice Cullors, to share the post with her social media connections using the #blacklivesmatters hashtag. She posted, "[T]win, #BLACKLIVESMATTER campaign? Can we discuss this? i have ideas. I am thinking we can do a whole social media/all out in the streets organizing effort."[6] Her post gained wide traction and resonated with numerous people incensed with Zimmerman's acquittal.[7] Opal Tometi, director of an immigrant rights organization, informed Garza that she wanted to become involved in organizing the movement. Garza, Cullors, and Tometi worked in the Black Organizing for Leadership Network (BOLD). They formed the first BLM chapter in Los Angeles during the summer of 2013.

BLM distinguished itself from the Movement of the 1950s and 1960s. The three founders, all women of color, and two of them Black queer women, insisted that Black liberation is not merely about combatting anti-racism but also about resisting internal oppressions within social activist movements. Garza stressed that BLM opposes "keeping straight cis Black men in the front of the movement while our sisters, queer and trans and disabled folk take up roles in the background or not at all."[8] BLM rejects the hierarchical leadership structure typified by King's SCLC. Black millennials comprise much of the leadership of the organization. In line with Baker's vision and critique of King discussed in Chapter 5, BLM embraces a decentralized structure that empowers local leaders to take charge. In contrast to King, who was at the forefront of the movement and frequently addressed the media, the initial founders were not pressing to be in the media limelight during BLM protests. They worked behind the scenes, allowing local activists to lead.

Besides Baker's community organizing model, Black organizations such as the Combahee River Collective (CRC) and the Black Radical Congress (BRC) informed the development of BLM. Formed in 1974 in Boston, Massachusetts, the CRC was a Black feminist lesbian organization that emphasized addressing intersecting racial, sexual, heterosexual, and class oppressions faced by Black women. Established in 1998 in Chicago, the BRC aimed to foster dialogue among Black intellectuals and activists regarding "radical and democratic solutions" and strategies for pursuing social justice.[9] In line with the CRC, BLM stresses the need to combat intersecting systems of oppression and multiple forms of violence against Black bodies. The organization addresses the violence experienced by poor, incarcerated, "undocumented," LGBTQ+, and disabled Black people.[10] Similar to the BRC, BLM upholds radical "abolitionist politics," which insists that the government should not merely reform the criminal justice system but should divest from the prison industrial complex and invest in restorative justice programs.[11] Its current mission is to work "inside and outside of the system to heal the past, re-imagine the present, and invest in the future of Black lives through policy change, investment in our communities, and a commitment to arts and culture." The Foundation envisions "a future that is fully divested from police, prison, and all punishment paradigms to be replaced with investment into justice, joy, and culture."[12]

BLM became more than a social media hashtag in 2014 following the death of Michael Brown, an eighteen-year-old teenager killed by Darren Wilson, a White police officer in Ferguson, Missouri. In August and September of 2014, in response to Brown's death, BLM mobilized hundreds of activists from eighteen different cities to travel to Ferguson to participate in demonstrations. They joined a chorus of local community activist groups and historic organizations, such as the NAACP, in protesting Brown's death. Ferguson catapulted BLM from being a movement in cyberspace to one on the streets.

BLM's Alliances with Religious Leaders in Ferguson

In *Ferguson and Faith: Sparking Leadership and Community*, Leah Gunning Francis interviewed twenty-four faith leaders of various religious groups (Protestant, Catholic, Unitarian Universalist, and Jewish) who participated in protests and several young local activists. She uncovered how many BLM activists were skeptical and suspicious of churches and religious institutions. She underscored how some religious leaders established trust and a rapport with BLM activists.

First, activists' distrust stemmed from their presuppositions about religious leaders based on hurtful experiences in churches. For example, some activists had experienced rejection within the church on account of their sexual orientation. Same-sex-loving activists found sermons that some pastors delivered with homophobic slurs offensive. Second, some activists were suspicious that clergy would try to use BLM to bolster their ministerial or political careers instead of to advance social justice for Blacks in their communities.[13] They were skeptical as to whether Black religious folks, especially Christians' care for impoverished Black people extended beyond charitable outreach such as organizing food and clothing drives. Sincere concern for Black life means working for policy changes that can lead to restorative and social justice. Third, some BLM activists expressed criticism of Black Christians' respectability politics (see Chapter 2). A young activist explained that too many pastors and church leaders told youth "to pull up your pants" and "be more respectable" rather than advocating for them.[14] Ferguson BLM activist Rapper Tef Poe refused to kowtow to Black church leaders seeking to organize a rally in Ferguson. He shouted, "This ain't your grandparents' civil rights movement!" When Reverend Sharpton and the National Action Network marched in Washington DC on December 13, 2014, to protest the police slaying of Black youth, several organizers from Ferguson who were troubled by the exclusion of young activists on the program charged the stage, saying, "We the youth did not elect Al Sharpton to be our spokesperson."[15] The younger activists resisted respectability politics and held that ordinary youth on the streets with baggy pants could lead the struggle.

Pastor Michael McBride, a local pastor who became involved in the movement in Ferguson, summed up Black youth's criticism by acknowledging the weak "theological imaginations" of religious institutions that have upheld the status quo by responding to racial violence with the "heretical prosperity gospel and a cheap forgiveness."[16] Many Black millennial activists were exposed to prosperity televangelists via television (see Chapter 6). Though many prosperity ministers saw themselves empowering impoverished people, they garnered a reputation for exploiting poor folks. Cheap forgiveness insists that racial healing and reconciliation will come without reparations or penitence from perpetrators of wrongdoing.[17] It asserts that the victims of injustice must forgive and let bygones be bygones.

Many Ferguson activists had attended churches where religious leaders were not trained in progressive theologies of liberation. They learned about the basic precepts of Black liberation theology from religious leaders involved in the Ferguson Movement (see Chapter 6).[18] Alexis Templeton, a BLM activist in Ferguson, appreciated clergy such as Traci Blackmon, Rabbi Susan, and Starsky Wilson for exposing her to a different model of church and theology contrary to traditional, "biblical literalist" evangelicalism and the prosperity gospel.[19]

Despite initial tension between young Black activists and religious leaders in Ferguson, BLM activists and Black religious leaders were able to collaborate once clergy humbly allowed local activists to take the lead instead of commandeering leadership.[20] Shaun Jones, assistant pastor of Mt. Zion Baptist Church Complex in St. Louis, reflected:

> We approached them with humility, not with position, not with title. We came with the idea that we're not better than you, but want to learn from you. Your passion, your commitment, your sacrifice has inspired us ... By no means have we, as a church, tried to own this movement. We've tried to say that we can be a part of this movement, we have a part to play.[21]

Jamell Spann respected the clergy for being present, supportive, and allowing the youth to lead. He expressed, "They didn't come with any terms or conditions. They didn't try to impose what they thought on any of us."[22]

BLM activists organized and led most of the demonstrations. Local clergy orchestrated a protest march on Monday, October 13, from the Wellspring Church to the Ferguson police station, and they led a rally at the police station.[23] Rather than taking charge of the movement, religious folks from various faith traditions (Christians, Jews, Muslims, Unitarian Universalists, etc.), by and large, showed up to support BLM protestors. Traci Blackmon, pastor of Christ the King United Church of Christ in Florissant, Missouri, ministered to the traumatized residents at the apartment building near where Brown had been killed. The clergy participated in prayer demonstrations. They kneeled and prayed on the streets for activists engaging the Ferguson police. Clergy opened the doors of their churches to BLM activists so they could have the meeting space they needed to plan and organize events. Starsky Wilson welcomed BLM activists who poured into Ferguson via the freedom rides to have two events at St. John's United Church of Christ. He also welcomed stranded freedom riders who could not secure hotels at his church. Pastor Michael McBride also joined the Ferguson Movement. He had played a leadership role in the Lifelines to Healing/LIVE Free Campaign, a national organization that aimed to reduce gun violence in urban communities. When he arrived on the scene, McBride acknowledged the revolutionary work the activists were spearheading in the streets of Ferguson. Granting that many of the activists were probably not affiliated with a church, McBride asserted that "Black Jesus... the prophet, the healer, the liberator, the organizer, the exorcist of both individuals and systems" was present in Ferguson before he and other clergy arrived.[24]

BLM's Religious Eclecticism

While McBride interpreted BLM activists as doing the work of "Black Jesus," BLM is not a Christian religious movement. Religion and spirituality's influence on BLM activism has been explored recently by academics and religious scholars such as Hebah Farrag, assistant director of research at the University of Southern California Center for Religion and Civic Culture. Farrag has interviewed Patrice Cullors, one of the founders of BLM, who was reared in the Jehovah's Witness tradition and later embraced Ifà, a religion originating in Nigeria. Cullors led a ritual at the UCLA Fowler Museum on June 13, 2020, drawing on her religious belief in ancestral veneration. As she ripped paper that had the words inscribed "police" and "white racism," she played "a recorded prayer" for the recent victims of police violence. She described this ritual as "sanctifying the names of the victims of American racism."[25] The ritual reiterated the meaning and value of Blacks' lives. She explained:

> I feel like part of the story in the building of BLM was about remembering — and remembering our people, not based off of a white supremacist memory, which would be about slandering them and putting their names in the newspaper and showing their mugshots ... But, instead remembering them from the place that their mothers and their fathers and their family would want us to remember them in.[26]

BLM calls out the names of the deceased to remember them and conjure their spirits. In addition, BLM has facilitated libation ceremonies during memorials and rallies. Libation rituals, such as pouring drink offerings to deities or in honor of deceased ancestors, date back to the ancient Egyptians.[27] Melina Abdulla, a California State University professor who co-founded the Los Angeles Chapter of BLM, led a libation ceremony during a defund the police protest event on June 2, 2020. She poured an alcoholic drink on the ground as she led the group in saying the names of recent victims of racial injustice, followed by freedom fighters who devoted their lives to social justice: "George Floyd. Asé. Philandro Castille. Asé. Andrew Joseph. Asé. Michael Brown. Asé. Erika Garner. Asé. Harriet Tubman. Asé. Malcolm X. Asé. Martin Luther King. Asé."[28] The term "Asé" is a term that derives from the Yoruba tradition in Nigeria. It is an affirmation akin to the word "Amen" that often concludes Christian prayers, which means "let it be so."

Abdullah and Cullors have incorporated African cosmologies, such as Ifà spirituality and libation ceremonies, into BLM rituals. Yet, BLM activists are religiously diverse. Some activists are atheists and do not have ties to any specific religious group. Nyle Fort, a BLM activist who participated in a BLM freedom ride from New York City to Ferguson after he completed seminary training, suggests that BLM activists are religiously eclectic and draw on a wide gamut of spiritual practices such as "ancestral worship, call-and-response, chanting, libation, prayer, mysticism, the lighting of incense."[29] BLM also improvises new religious practices and rituals to pursue justice and affirm the sacredness of Black life.[30] Fort employs religious language to paint a picture of a scene in which activists met at a shrine to commemorate those who were killed, noting:

> A few people lit candles. Some replaced soiled teddy bears and handed out water, while others stood in silence. Many of us wept. And after a few moments, we all joined hands and formed a circle around the shrine. Children, elders, parents, pro-testers, clergy, residents, out-of-towners, queer organizers, white activists, Black kids from the neighborhood. It felt like an altar call. Except salvation was not about joining a church or having faith in a higher power. It was about believing that every life is holy and joining a movement that protects the living while mourning the dead.[31]

Fort describes the memorial event as similar to "an altar call." In the Christian tradition, an altar call invites persons to come forward, make a public profession of their faith in Christ, and accept the offer to join the Christian community. Fort felt that the encircled participants at the shrine were a religious community on one accord about the sacred-ness of Black life. The shrine was reconstituted into an altar. The altar was a location to mourn the Blacks who lost their sacred lives and a site for dedicating themselves to the movement to advocate for justice.[32] BLM names and celebrates the American impos-sible, the oxymoron—"Blackness as sacred."[33] According to Biko Gray, "Black life is sacred because it is impossible and impossibly lived because it knows that attending to the horizon will necessarily benefit 'all people.'"[34] BLM's push for "the unthought, yet indispensable, horizon" in America and the world is what fundamentally constitutes its religious nature.[35]

Figure 7.1. One year anniversary of the murder of George Floyd. Attendees are kneeling to com-memorate and pay homage to Floyd and other Black people who have died as a result of police violence. May 25, 2021.
Courtesy of Fibonacci Blue, Flickr

Many people have generally embraced BLM as a social rather than a religious movement.[36] Since Ferguson, BLM has organized more than thirty local chapters in the United States.[37] Many men and women and professional and college athletes have used their platforms to affirm the Black Lives Matter slogan and support the organization's call for racial justice. BLM became a nonprofit, the Black Lives Matter Global Network Foundation, Inc., in 2017.

It seems that Christian activists who endorse BLM primarily uphold the organization's commitment to resisting state-sanctioned violence against Black people. In this vein, womanist theologian Kelly Brown Douglas has written multiple books in line with Black Lives Matter, including *Stand Your Ground: Black Bodies and the Justice of God* and *Resurrection Hope: A Future Where Black Lives Matter*. She published the former shortly after the death of Trayvon Martin and the genesis of BLM. She traces how people of faith have resisted racial violence and dehumanization and upheld the dignity and value of Black people made in the divine image.[38] The latter book was published in 2021, following the deaths of African Americans such as Ahmaud Arbery on February 23, 2020, Breonna Taylor on March 13, 2020, and George Floyd on May 25, 2020. In *Resurrection Hope*, Douglass theologically grapples with the meaning of the cross and resurrection in the age of Black Lives Matter.

In addition to Christians of diverse races, Muslim Americans, especially Black Muslims, have publicly affirmed and supported the BLM movement. Support for the organization increased among Muslims across racial lines following the horrific viral video of George Floyd's murder. This incident stimulated Muslims affiliated with more than 35 national Muslim civil rights organizations and groups to issue a "joint statement against police violence."[39] Their statement mourned the numerous Black people, including Black Muslims such as Marcellus "Khalifa" Williams, who have died as a result of state-sanctioned violence. They called for a host of reforms to the criminal justice system, including but not limited to prohibiting chokeholds, no-knock warrants, and racial profiling and reallocating "funding into community health, education, employment and housing programs." In line with BLM, they concluded, "If this deep-seated discrimination cannot be done away with through reform, then these systems will need to be abolished and reimagined entirely."[40] Floyd's murder inspired people of various faiths to stand in solidarity with BLM and even join demonstrations. It remains to be seen whether the solidarity between traditional and nontraditional religious groups with BLM will be sustained.

The Poor Peoples Campaign: National Call for Moral Revival

Reverend Dr. Liz Theoharis and Reverend Dr. William Barber II serve as co-chairs of the Poor People's Campaign: National Call for Moral Revival. Similar to BLM, the initiative is multiracial and interfaith. The National Call for Moral Revival was inspired by the original Poor People's campaign that SCLC organized in 1968 to galvanize people of diverse races and ethnicities to nonviolently protest economic injustice in Washington, DC. Thousands of protestors marched demanding an Economic Bill of Rights that would guarantee jobs and end discrimination in housing. Protestors also built shanty tents near the Capitol grounds and named the area Resurrection City. Some activists camped out for days until a rainstorm muddied the area and made the temporary shelters unsafe and unsanitary. The demonstrations lasted from March to June. The campaign was short-lived and abruptly ended with police forcing protestors to abandon their tents and leave. Police arrested those who refused to comply, including Reverend Ralph Abernathy. To put it simply, the campaign failed to reach its ultimate goals. It did not persuade Congress to pass an economic Bill of Rights for the Disadvantaged or influence the government to redirect funds from the war economy toward government programs that could potentially reduce, if not eradicate, poverty. Nevertheless, the campaign's most enduring legacy was facilitating interracial organizing among poor and working-class people.

Embracing the original campaign's emphasis on interfaith and interethnic organizing, Barber and Theoharis stress that persons affected by poverty and activists from faith communities must continue collaborating to redeem and reform America in contemporary times. They stress that "moral-fusion organizing" is a proven strategy that undergirded the successes of the abolitionist, civil rights, and anti-apartheid movements.[41] Their co-leadership signifies the racial diversity they seek to advance in the New Poor People's Campaign. Theoharis is a White woman, ordained minister in the Presbyterian Church (USA), and Executive Director of the Kairos Center for Religions, Rights, and Social Justice at Union Theological Seminary. Founded in 2013, the Kairos Center gives seminaries and theological institutions resources to resist and mobilize against racism and poverty. She has worked with several unions and grassroots organizations, including but not limited to the National Union of the Homeless, the National Welfare Rights Union, and Domestic Workers United.[42] Barber is a Black man who has served as pastor of the Greenleaf Christian Church in Goldsboro, North Carolina.[43] He also has been a leader in multiple civil rights organizations. He ran successfully for president of the state branch chapter of the National Association for the Advancement of Colored People in North Carolina. He served as chair of the political action committee of the NAACP's National Board.[44] In 2015, he founded Repairers of the Breach, an organization committed to training and mobilizing people of diverse faith traditions to advance "a moral policy agenda" that elevates American democratic values and moral principles shared by diverse religious traditions. Barber also has a disability. At thirty years of age, he was diagnosed with ankylosing spondylitis, an inflammatory arthritis of the spine that influences severe pain and immobility.[45] Barber had to use a walker for years during his early ministerial career at Greenleaf Church. The diversity of the Poor Peoples Campaign's leadership contributes to the socio-economically diverse people who have attended demonstrations.

Barber and Theoharis hold that morality is the glue that fuses people to collaborate across their lines of difference. Barber accents morality because "issues that are at the heart of all our religious traditions" are "truth, justice, love, and mercy."[46] These are moral values that cut across multiple religions.[47] Moral fusion organizing is mobilizing people to stand together on moral grounds so that they can strive to access the political power necessary to establish justice and ensure that governmental powers respect the interests of the working class and not merely the wealthy and powerful elites.[48]

Prior to establishing the Poor People's Campaign, Barber employed moral fusion organizing as president of the North Carolina chapter of the NAACP. He strove to inspire people of diverse races to join the organization. Al McSurely, a White civil rights attorney, accepted Barber's invitation to become the legal redress chair of the North Carolina Branch. In 2006, Barber also invited collaborators from groups focusing on diverse issues such as labor, educational inequality, gay rights, prison reform, and other areas to form a broad coalition. During a retreat, the activists, academics, and various leaders who represented sixteen different organizations agreed upon a fourteen-point

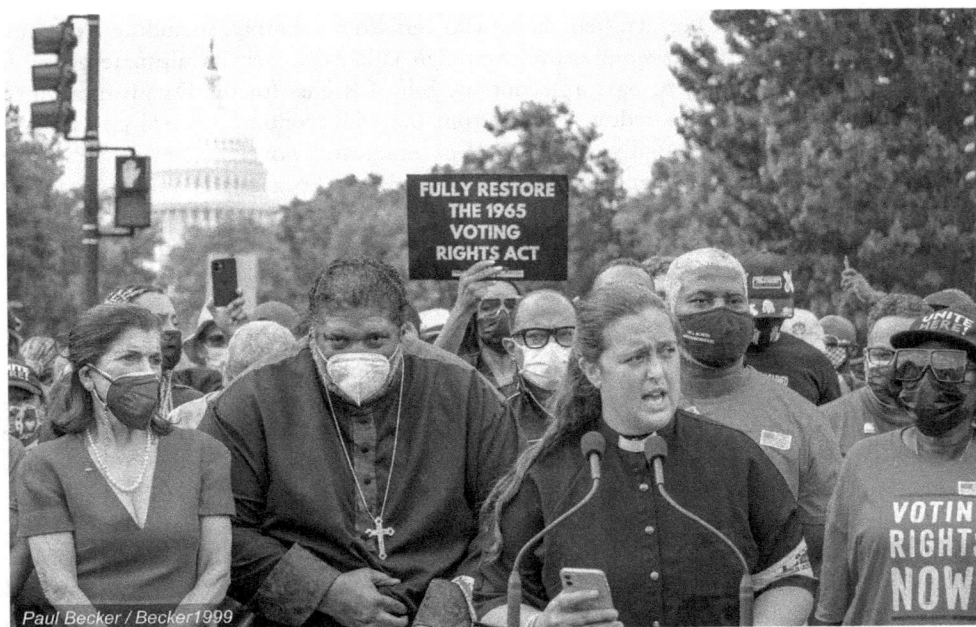

Figure 7.2. An image of a Poor Peoples Campaign Rally and march at Union Station in Washington DC on August 3, 2021. Rev. Liz Theoharis is speaking to attendees in front of the microphone. Rev. William Barber is immediately to the left, wearing a black shirt and a gold necklace with a large gold cross.
Courtesy of Paul Becker, Flickr

agenda and a list of demands including but not limited to raising the salary of North Carolina teachers to the national average, accepting Medicaid expansion under Obama's Affordable Healthcare program, total funding for programs designed to aid at-risk students, and immigration reform. They led a protest march through downtown that ended at the state capitol. Once they arrived there, they dramatically presented their fourteen-point agenda on a fourteen-foot-tall placard. They invited diverse participants to share their stories of hardship and struggle. The coalition also focused on ensuring that working-class people had access to the ballot. In 2008, their voter registration and mobilization efforts helped Barack Obama win the state's electoral college votes and other progressive candidates who supported policies helpful to the working class. Al McSurely named the new movement the Historic Thousand on Jones Street (HKonJ).[49]

HKonJ faced opposition during the 2010 midterm elections from political conservatives who were dissatisfied with Obama's election and the loss of political power at the local and state levels. According to Barber, political conservatives attempted to sow division in the coalition by seeking to influence evangelical Christians to stand against gays and lesbians. Upon persuading Christian conservatives to jump on their bandwagon, they regained power in the North Carolina State Legislature; they overturned many policies Barber's coalition helped advance, such as the Racial Justice Act, public financing for judicial elections, and higher taxes for the wealthy.[50] The state legislature proposed legislation that many activists deemed to be a blatant attempt at voter suppression following Obama's election as president in 2008. For example, the legislature proposed reducing early voting times, prohibiting on-site registration during the early voting period, and ending the granting of voting rights to ex-prisoners.[51]

After unsuccessfully negotiating with political officials to address oppressive laws, HKonJ turned to civil disobedience, spearheading a series of Moral Monday protests. The first Moral Monday protest occurred in the North Carolina capitol chambers in the spring of 2013. The police arrested seventeen demonstrators. During one protest, Barber read scriptures and cited statistics about North Carolina's poverty. He criticized the North Carolina legislature for not expanding Medicaid and health benefits for impoverished people. The number of activists law enforcement officers detained during Moral Mondays swelled to a total of more than 1,000. Demonstrators sang freedom songs and publicly discussed their grievances.[52]

Building on his activism in North Carolina, Barber aimed to expand the fusion organizing employed in North Carolina to other states. In 2018 Barber and Theoharis kicked off the National Call for Moral Revival with large-scale direct action campaigns occurring in roughly forty states for forty days.[53] The initiative endeavored to unite impoverished and working-class people across racial lines nationwide because 43 percent of Americans (approximately 140 million people) struggle to make ends meet, and live from paycheck to paycheck. Poverty is a widespread, systemic concern that is not restricted to racial minorities. According to statistics compiled by the Poor People Campaign, about 33.5 percent of White people (65 million people) are poor. Poor white people constitute the largest demographic group of impoverished Americans in absolute numbers. Roughly 59.7 percent of Black people (23.7 million people) are poor. Nearly 64 percent of the Latinx community (8 million people) are poor. About 59% of Indigenous people (2.14 million people) are poor. Lacking access to quality health care, housing, and other necessities, impoverished people have higher morbidity and mortality rates. They are more likely to die from unmanaged chronic ailments such as high blood pressure and diabetes. During the COVID-19 pandemic, poor people were especially vulnerable to dying of the virus.[54] Amid the pandemic, National Call for Moral Revival leaders organized a massive gathering of working-class and poor people on social media platforms. In June 2020, the campaign galvanized nearly 150,000 people to wear face masks and participate in a nonviolent rally in Washington, DC, on Pennsylvania Avenue.[55]

The renowned philosopher and public intellectual Cornel West described Barber as "the only King-like figure we have in the country right now."[56] Reverend Barber's persona and slow, southern, style of speaking and preaching is similar to Dr. King.[57] In contrast to King, who embraced a charismatic leadership model, Barber has endeavored to avoid becoming the key spokesperson for the emerging movement. He has declined speaking opportunities: "I started telling folks who called that I wouldn't come speak at a press conference, but I would bring a team to teach and train others in moral fusion organizing."[58] Barber seems to embrace elements of Baker's community organizing model discussed in Chapter 5. He reflected, "Our victories in the timeless cause of love and democracy have always required the devotions of thousands of ordinary people, local communities, grassroots groups, prophetic churches, and organizing traditions."[59] He is adamant that "No single leader or organization can orchestrate" America's Third Reconstruction.[60] Barber views the Third Reconstruction as an expansion of the First and Second Reconstructions, which failed to meet the ultimate goal of establishing a just society or a beloved community. He has adamantly insisted that "fusion organizing always takes a long view" and requires a sustained and collective effort.[61]

The Poor People's Campaign Creative Adoption of Religious Discourse and Rituals

The Poor People's campaign is putatively interfaith since the leaders, Barber and Theo-haris, are Protestant Christian ministers. Still, it welcomes people of diverse faiths to participate and aims to advance a moral agenda based on perennial moral values. Each Moral Monday protest "concluded with a sermon and an altar call."[62] Barber explains:

> Every week when I was finished preaching, I invited people to come forward and make a public profession of their faith in a new North Carolina by exercising their constitutional right to petition their legislators in the General Assembly. They knew, of course, that they were risking arrest. Each person who had decided to make this public witness wore an armband to signify that they'd spent the afternoon doing nonviolence training at a local church.[63]

Barber's altar call resembles the description Fort provided of the BLM altar-memorial. Barber expanded the traditional meaning of the altar call beyond the traditional Christian understanding, in which an individual decides to convert to Christianity. Barber invited people to come forward and profess their faith in their capacity to be a change agent in North Carolina. Though he was drawing on the Christian ritual of public confession, Barber's reformulated altar call focused on allowing people to affirm faith in their capacity to influence social justice. The armband enabled them to outwardly express and symbolize this hope and perhaps inspire others to believe in the power of collective and coercive action.

Barber described Moral Mondays as akin to an "evangelistic and revivalist" moment.[64] This language is metaphorical rather than literal. The moral revival movement is not equivalent to the Great Awakening or Pentecostal revivals discussed in prior chapters. Rather than a traditional spiritual revival, Barber ostensibly refers to conscientization, a concept developed by Paulo Freire, a Brazilian social theorist. It relates to enabling persons to see the social and political contradictions that underly systemic injustice and social disparity. This new understanding influences discomfort with the status quo and inspires commitment to resist social evil. It arouses people from the slumber of social and political apathy and passivity. Civil disobedience is a conduit for conscientization or critical consciousness formation in society. Although some politicians such as Senator Thom Goolsby referred to Moral Mondays as "Moron Mondays" and ostensibly ignored the protests, Barber explained that nonviolent direct action influenced some Republicans in North Carolina to see the injustice with their policies and to vote against "draconian budgets."[65]

Persons from marginalized communities who engage in civil disobedience have been converted to a new way of seeing the world and themselves. They can no longer tolerate injustice and are awakened to their capacity to be change agents. Barber asserts that engaging in civil disobedience enables participants to recognize their power and influence. Bob Zellner, a civil rights activist who served as "field secretary for the Student Nonviolent Coordinating Committee" and who resides in Wilson, North Carolina, affirmed the Moral Monday Movement, saying: "We've been waiting for a renewal of the civil rights movement, and this is it … It really caught on like in the old days."[66] Yet, it is essential to clarify that the New Poor People's Campaign is not a carbon copy of the past civil rights initiative. The National Call for Moral Revival is distinct and seeks to extend and expand the previous movement.

The Nap Ministry

In contrast to the New Poor People's Campaign, the Nap Ministry offers a novel approach to challenging racism and capitalism in the twenty-first century. Tricia Hersey, the founder of the Nap Ministry, is an African American woman performance and teaching artist, poet, theologian, former chaplain, and community organizer. She experienced burnout while pursuing her master's degree at Emory University's Candler School of Theology, a predominantly White institution. She overloaded her schedule by taking six graduate-level courses. She volunteered time and mental energy as a community organizer to combat state-sanctioned violence against Black people.[67] As if this was not enough, she was traumatized after being robbed while visiting a gas station with her son.[68] Hersey coped with her pain by taking naps at various times of the day and in different locations on campus. After recovering, she became interested in the restorative and resistance power of rest. She began to see exhaustion as a social justice concern affecting many Americans entangled in grind culture, defined as a hegemonic cultural system rooted in capitalism that bolsters overworking, promotes unhealthy infatuation with being productive at all costs, and prioritizes profits over people.[69]

Based on Hersey's analysis, many Black people who embrace grind culture unconsciously accept working harder than White people as expected. They often fail to grasp how this is potentially harmful. Ta-Nehisi Coates explains why this viewpoint is problematic in his bestselling book *Between the World and Me*:

> All my life I'd heard people tell their black boys and black girls to be "twice as good," which is to say "accept half as much." These words would be spoken with a veneer of religious nobility, as though they evidenced some unspoken quality, some undetected courage, when in fact all they evidenced was the gun to our head and the hand in our pocket. This is how we lose our softness. This how they steal our right to smile. No one told those little white children, with their tricycles, to be twice as good … It seemed to me that our own rules redoubled plunder. It struck me that perhaps the defining feature of being drafted into the black race was the inescapable robbery of time because the moment we spent readying the mask or readying ourselves to accept half as much could not be recovered. The robbery of time is not measured in lifespans but in moments.[70]

Coates insists that encouraging Black people to outwork Whites is essentially "doubling down" on the racism Black people have experienced in a capitalistic system that has often not paid or adequately compensated them for their labor. Overworked Black people have frequently been robbed of "time" and have been too busy to experience fleeting moments with their loved ones.

In line with Coates's reflection, Hersey's critique of grind culture is grounded in the experiences of Black people during slavery. To fuel the plantation economy, White planters often forced enslaved Black people to push their bodies beyond the limits. They labored from sunup to sundown and were given limited time off. Enslaved Black people even had to work the entire day on Sunday, which is a day of sabbath in the Christian tradition. Instead of resting, they worked through "binding wheat, taking up hemp, stemming tobacco and corn."[71]

Though the system of plantation slavery ended more than a century and a half ago, Black Americans are still victims of grind culture. They are more likely than other racial groups to suffer from sleep deprivation. Hersey poignantly explained how her father was a casualty. He pushed himself to the limit while working full-time for the Union Pacific Railroad Company and serving as an assistant pastor of Robbins Church of God in Christ.[72] During his days off from the railroad company, her father was responsive to the needs of parishioners and served the church on weekends. Suffering from chronic conditions such as diabetes, heart disease, and high blood pressure, he died at the tender age of fifty-five after having a triple bypass procedure. Besides his underlying health conditions, Hersey contends that grind culture was the culprit for her father's early death. Like many working-class Black people, he frequently worked overtime to justify his worth at work and to provide for his family's needs.

In developing her manifesto, Hersey draws on various sources, including Black history, somatics, sleep medicine research, Black liberation theology, womanist theology, and Afrofuturism. She reinterprets and revalorizes the meaning of rest, asserting that people's sense of self-worth and meaning should not be solely based on what they produce. She contends that the cultural obsession with "productivity" causes many Americans to feel guilty about pausing and resting. This, in turn, prevents them from having the rest they need to develop creative plans to resist intersecting systems of oppression.[73] Rest is necessary to reclaim what capitalism has stolen—human's connection to their bodies, spirit, and communities. Rest allows space to dream and engage in the spiritual realm. It enables healing from past hurts and traumas.

Hersey draws on the narratives of Black maroons to further advance her thesis. Maroons were communities of runaway enslaved Black people who lived in the backwoods of the South. They are distinct from enslaved Blacks who moved to free territory in the North or Canada upon escaping bondage. Maroons formed free communities under the nose of the slave system before the Civil War when the system was yet intact. The maroons inspire Hersey's vision of the possibility that Blacks can live and thrive in their capitalistic context. They refused to abide by the rules of plantation capitalism. They managed to resist the system before it ended. She posits that those living within the American capitalistic system must "reimagine rest" while capitalism reigns.[74]

Hersey is also profoundly inspired by Afro-futurism, which imagines a socially just and free world where many lingering and longstanding social concerns that have plagued Black people for millennia no longer exist. She acknowledges Sun Ra, the father of Afrofuturism, for daring to dream of the impossible. She argues that "deprogramming from grind culture" requires using the imagination and learning to dream with others in a community context. She states, "Community care will save us, and we can dream up all the ways to manifest and strategize the care of our communities."[75]

Collective Napping Experiences in Atlanta and Beyond

Hersey developed the Nap Ministry and organized the first "Collective Napping Experiences" in Atlanta in 2016 while completing her master's thesis. About fifty people in the Emory University community attended the first nap experience, initially a simple performance arts exercise. Though open to everyone, most attendees at the first and subsequent napping experience have been Black women. This is likely because Black women have been vulnerable to suffering burnout. The dominant culture has wrongly stereotyped them as able to "withstand more pressure and pain and physical labour."[76] Subsequently, Black women have often internalized these racist assumptions and pushed themselves beyond their limits. Yet, the Nap Ministry not only targets or attracts Black women. People of diverse hues have been drawn to the Nap Ministry because grind culture has negatively affected Americans from all walks of life.

During her first organized nap experience, Hersey curated a space with yoga mats, couch-like cushions, pillows, and blankets on the floor. She organized a sleep altar that included candles, cotton extracted from Southern farms where numerous Black people once labored, and a book replete with narrative excerpts and "testimonies of enslaved people."[77] The cotton ostensibly served as a reminder to Black people of their right to rest, especially given the forced labor of their ancestors. She welcomed attendees to snuggle up in blankets as she dimmed the lights in the room and played relaxing music. While moving around the space and encouraging persons to experience sacred rest for about an hour, she softly asserted, "This is a resistance. This is our protest."[78] After attendees awoke from the community nap session, she concluded with a debriefing conversation, inviting attendees to discuss their experiences and to disclose any epiphanies they had.[79]

A thirty-nine-year-old woman who attended an event in Atlanta, Dominique Hollo-man, expressed that her forty-minute nap helped her "decompress and eliminate dis-tractions preventing her from focusing on important matters" and enabled her to recognize the need to reduce stress by saying, "No."[80] Constance Collier-Mercado, another frequent attendee at napping experiences, explained that the experience helped her feel "productive" and connected to her community.[81]

Since the first event in Atlanta in 2016, Hersey has led nap events in Colorado, Chicago, and other states. Her monthly napping experiences have been free of charge and have occurred in "libraries, yoga studios, art galleries, and outdoor spaces."[82] She and her team have also organized virtual nap events. The Nap Ministry grew extensively on social media during the COVID-19 pandemic and amid the Great Resignation when millions of American workers were quitting their jobs due to inadequate compensation, limited opportunity for career advancement, and experience of disrespect on the job.[83] Workers also complained of long work hours and being unfulfilled. The pandemic allowed many Americans to pause, daydream, think about their lives and careers, and spend more time at home with their families. It provided rich soil for the Nap Ministry to flourish, forcing Americans to slow down and reflect. Devon Gates, a student at Harvard College and Berklee College of Music who served as an intern with the Nap Ministry, explains how COVID-19 influenced him to reflect "for the first time why (and for whom) I and my peers are working so hard—often to the detriment of our mental and physical health—and how that can not only be normalized, but also glorified."[84]

Though it is not a church with a traditional membership roster, the growth of the Nap Ministry can be evidenced by its 600,000 Instagram and Twitter followers. Fur-thermore, Hersey has lectured, presented, and facilitated napping experiences at schools such as Chicago's School of Art Institute, DePaul University, MIT, and Brown Uni-versity.[85] She has also engaged institutions such as Google Global and the United States Peace Corps. The Nap Ministry has a hotline number, which includes a "recorded rest message" of Hersey affirming the healing power of naps and inviting callers to seize time to rest, heal, and resist.[86]

The Nap Ministry's Adaptation of Christian Discourse and Rituals

It is fair to question if the Nap Ministry is a religion akin to other innovative Black religious movements explored. This is a reasonable question given that Michael Render, popularly known as "Killer Mike," a politically outspoken renowned Grammy award-winning rapper based in Atlanta, comically introduced a new religion, "The Church of Sleep," in his *Trigger Warning* Netflix series in 2019. He uplifts the Church of Sleep as a religion. He assigns his fabricated religion a messiah and a sacred text, the Book of Sleep. Members of the Church of Sleep engaged in the ritual of taking naps. Given Mike's connection to Atlanta, it is conceivable that he may have heard of the Nap Ministry, which was gaining traction years before the production of his show. Mike's Netflix show has no formal tie to the Nap Ministry. In his commentary about the show, Mike has expressed that he believes Black people should reject White Jesus and religions that have condoned racial oppression. He contends they should invent religions that center on Black people and that help them see their divinity.[87]

Rather than seeking to establish a new religion, Hersey describes the Nap Ministry as spiritual instead of religious. Although the movement is not affiliated with a specific denomination or religious institution, and she does not advance particular doctrines, it falls under the umbrella of religion based on the definition of religion provided in this book, which centers Black people's push for life meaning amid their oppressive American context. Furthermore, Hersey employs traditional religious language to describe herself and the organization's programming. For example, she named the organization the Nap Ministry and assumed the title, the Nap Bishop. Traditionally, a bishop is a high-ranking clergy member in an episcopal system that oversees churches and appoints pastors, priests, and ministers. Growing up in the Church of God in Christ, Hersey knew that ministers who became bishops had achieved that rank typically because they had devoted their lives to the church. Hersey is not a bishop in the traditional sense. It seems she refers to herself as the Nap Bishop to stress her devotion to advancing her message and addressing the burnout workers far and wide are experiencing as a result of global capitalism.

Hersey also named the event space the organization acquired to hold napping experiences in Atlanta's Grant Park Community "The Nap Temple."[88] Traditionally, a temple is a sacred space designated for religious meetings, worship, and spiritual communion with the divine. Perhaps she adopted the language "Nap Temple" instead of "Nap Studio," which associates with her performance arts background, to emphasize that rest is a sacred activity. It is a means of experiencing the Divine. Employing other traditional religious terms such as "invocation" and "spirit of rest," she further accentuates the sacredness of rest:

> At each nap experience, I read the Nap Ministry invocation as an open invitation to rest. Right at the moment before an individual drifts off into a dream state, while between the awake and sleep worlds, I begin slowly and softly with the opening line, "The doors of the nap temple are open" … For forty minutes the soundtrack plays, and we wait for the spirit of rest to show up. It always does. Rest has never failed us.[89]

The Nap Ministry's rituals parallel the religious liturgy of a Christian church, which includes elements such as an Invocation to Worship and an invitation to Christian discipleship. During the invitation to discipleship, a minister may say, "The doors of the church are open." Attendees at Collective Nap Experiences who were reared in the church probably understand Hersey's play on words. She clearly draws on Christian language to encourage people to reflect on the sacred quality of rest. She capitalizes

"Rest" to highlight that it is a noble aspect of the divine nature. Just as God is personified in Scripture as Love, Holiness, Truth, and other noble virtues, Hersey reworks scriptural language in her assertion that "Rest [God] has never failed us" (1 Corinthians 13:8).

Similar to the diverse religious traditions Black people have created and refashioned throughout Black History, Black Lives Matter, the Poor People's Campaign, and the Nap Ministry reflect Black people's creative agency as they continuously strive to pursue a more equitable future. These movements innovate with (and, in some cases, beyond) traditional religious orientations. Though they build on past movements, they have all endeavored to provide fresh responses to the vast array of systemic challenges oppressed people face today. They demonstrate the ever-evolving ways contemporary Black Americans use religious language and rituals to challenge social injustices.

Review and Discussion Questions

1 How have BLM activists challenged traditional religions such as Christianity?
2 Is BLM only a political movement? What constitutes BLM as religious? How have BLM activists cooperated with religious organizations and incorporated religious rituals?
3 Is the National Call for Moral Revival merely a replication of the Poor People's Campaign organized by SCLC in 1968? How is the movement seeking to respond in a unique fashion to contemporary social injustices?
4 How does Tricia Hersey's Nap Ministry challenge traditional notions of productivity within capitalism? How do the religious rituals and language she incorporates reshape rest as sacred?

Notes

1 These three organizations are by no means exhaustive of the plethora of religious civil rights organizations pursuing social justice today. Furthermore, as these movements are yet unfolding, full histories of these movements remain to be written. I draw on descriptions of the movements by founders, organizational websites, recent works by anthropologists, and articles written by newspaper reporters.
2 Catherine Bell, "Performance," cited in Mark C. Taylor, *Critical Terms for Religious Studies* (Chicago, IL: University of Chicago Press, 1998), 209.
3 Cicley Gay, D'shane Parker, and Shalomyah Bowers currently serve on the Board of Directors of the Black Lives Matter Global Network Foundation, a nonprofit organization with numerous chapters throughout the country.
4 K. Fasching-Warner and N. D. Hartlep, eds., *The Assault on Communities of Color* (Lanham, MD: Rowman & Littlefield), 14; Dewey M. Clayton, "Black Lives Matter and the Civil Rights Movement," *Journal of Black Studies*, 49, no. 5 (July 2018), 453, www.jstor.org/stable/10.2307/26574572.
5 E. Day, "#BlackLivesMatter: The Birth of a New Civil Rights Movement," *The Guardian*, July 19, 2015, retrieved from www.theguardian.com/world/2015/jul/19/blacklivesmatter-birth-civil-rights-movement; Dewey M. Clayton, "Black Lives Matter and the Civil Rights Movement," *Journal of Black Studies*, 49, no. 5 (July 2018), 453.
6 Camille Squires and Alice Markham-Cantor, "The Beginning," January 31, 2022, retrieved from https://nymag.com/article/black-lives-matter-2022.html.
7 Dewey M. Clayton, "Black Lives Matter and the Civil Rights Movement," *Journal of Black Studies*, 49, no. 5 (July 2018); J. Cobb, "The Matter of Black Lives," *The New Yorker*, March 14, 2016, retrieved from www.newyorker.com/magazine/2016/03/14/where-is-black-lives-matter-headed.
8 Alice Garza, "A Herstory of the #BlackLivesMatter Movement," *The Feminist Wire*, October 7, 2014, http://thefeministwire.com/2014/10/blacklivesmatter-2; cited in Darrius D. Hills and

Tommy J. Curry, "Cries of the Unheard: State Violence, Black Bodies, and Martin Luther King's Black Power" *Journal of Africana Religions*, 3, no. 4 (2015): 459.

9 Combahee River Collective Statement (1977), retrieved from www.blackpast.org/african-am erican-history/combahee-river-collective-statement-1977; Mission Statement of the Black Radical Congress (BRC), retrieved from https://web.archive.org/web/20070202101427/www. blackradicalcongress.org/mission.html.

10 Barbara Ransby, *Making All Black Lives Matter: Reimagining Freedom in the Twenty-First Century* (University of California Press, 2018), 159.

11 Barbara Ransby, *Making All Black Lives Matter: Reimagining Freedom in the Twenty-First Century* (University of California Press, 2018), 132.

12 "BLM Transparency Center," retrieved from https://blacklivesmatter.com/transparency.

13 Chanequa Walker-Barnes, "Response to Rev. Michael McBride Plenary, 'Conversions in the Age of Trump'" *Journal of Pastoral Theology* 29: 1 (2018), 15; Leah Gunning Francis, *Ferguson and Faith: Sparking Leadership and Awakening Community* (Des Peres, MO: Chalice Press, 2015), 62.

14 Leah Gunning Francis, *Ferguson and Faith: Sparking Leadership and Awakening Community* (Des Peres, MO: Chalice Press, 2015), 97.

15 Gene Demby, "The Birth of a New Civil Rights Movement," *Politico Magazine*, December 31, 2014, accessed December 30, 2017, www.politico.com/magazine/story/2014/12/ferguson-new-ci vil-rights-movement-113906.

16 Michael McBride, "Conversion in the Age of Trump" *Journal of Pastoral Theology*, 29, no. 1 (2019): 10, doi:10.1080/10649867.2019.1603919

17 Cheap forgiveness is a spinoff of German theologian Dietrich Bonhoeffer's theology of cheap grace, which stresses the cost of being a disciple of Jesus Christ and of bearing the cross.

18 Michael McBride, "Conversion in the Age of Trump" *Journal of Pastoral Theology*, 29, no. 1 (2019): 20.

19 Leah Gunning Francis, *Ferguson and Faith: Sparking Leadership and Awakening Community* (Des Peres, MO: Chalice Press, 2015), 62–63.

20 Walker-Barnes, "Response to Rev. Michael McBride Plenary," 15.

21 Leah Gunning Francis, *Ferguson and Faith: Sparking Leadership and Awakening Community* (Des Peres, MO: Chalice Press, 2015), 51.

22 Leah Gunning Francis, *Ferguson and Faith: Sparking Leadership and Awakening Community* (Des Peres, MO: Chalice Press, 2015), 66, 70.

23 Leah Gunning Francis, *Ferguson and Faith: Sparking Leadership and Awakening Community* (Des Peres, MO: Chalice Press, 2015), 94.

24 Michael McBride, "Conversion in the Age of Trump" *Journal of Pastoral Theology*, 29, no. 1 (2019): 7–8. The individuals mentioned in this chapter are by no means an exhaustive list of all religious persons who supported the movement in Ferguson.

25 Alejandra Molina, "Black Lives Matter is 'a Spiritual Movement,' Says Co-founder Patrisse Cullors," *Religion News Service*, June 15, 2020, retrieved from https://religionnews.com/2020/ 06/15/why-black-lives-matter-is-a-spiritual-movement-says-blm-co-founder-patrisse-cullors.

26 Alejandra Molina, "Black Lives Matter is 'a Spiritual Movement,' Says Co-founder Patrisse Cullors," *Religion News Service*, June 15, 2020, retrieved from https://religionnews.com/2020/ 06/15/why-black-lives-matter-is-a-spiritual-movement-says-blm-co-founder-patrisse-cullors.

27 Kimani S. Nehuri, *Libation: An Afrikan Ritual of Heritage in Circle of Life* (Lanham, MD: University Press of America, 2015).

28 Hebah Farrag, "The Fight for Black Lives is a Spiritual Movement," June 9, 2020, Berkley Form, retrieved from https://berkleycenter.georgetown.edu/responses/the-fight-for-black-live s-is-a-spiritual-movement.

29 Nyle Fort, "Black Lives Matter: The Religion of Protest," January 31, 2022, retrieved from www.thecut.com/2022/01/black-lives-matter-religion-spirituality.html?_gl=1*7zwbl4*_ga*MTg 5NTk3NzIzLjE3MDIyNTAwNTk.*_ga_DNE38RK1HX*MTcwMjI1MDc5Ny4xLjAuMTcw MjI1MDgwNS41Mi4wLjA.#_ga=2.168920033.1367005928.1702250059-189597723.1702250059.

30 Nyle Fort, "Black Lives Matter: The Religion of Protest," January 31, 2022, retrieved from www.thecut.com/2022/01/black-lives-matter-religion-spirituality.html?_gl=1*7zwbl4*_ga*MTg 5NTk3NzIzLjE3MDIyNTAwNTk.*_ga_DNE38RK1HX*MTcwMjI1MDc5Ny4xLjAuMTcw MjI1MDgwNS41Mi4wLjA.#_ga=2.168920033.1367005928.1702250059-189597723.1702250059.

31 Nyle Fort, "Black Lives Matter: The Religion of Protest," January 31, 2022, retrieved from www.thecut.com/2022/01/black-lives-matter-religion-spirituality.html?_gl=1*7zwbl4*_ga*MTg 5NTk3NzIzLjE3MDIyNTAwNTk.*_ga_DNE38RK1HX*MTcwMjI1MDc5Ny4xLjAuMTcw MjI1MDgwNS41Mi4wLjA.#_ga=2.168920033.1367005928.1702250059-189597723.1702250059.

32 Hebah Farrag, "The Fight for Black Lives is a Spiritual Movement," June 9, 2020, Berkley Form, retrieved from https://berkleycenter.georgetown.edu/responses/the-fight-for-black-live s-is-a-spiritual-movement.

33 Biko Mandela Gray, "Religion in/and Black Lives Matter: Celebrating the impossible" *Religion Compass* 13, no. 1 (2019), 2, doi:10.1111/rec3.12293. See also Biko Mandela Gray, *Black Life Matter: Blackness, Religion, and the Subject* (Durham, NC: Duke University Press, 2022).

34 Biko Mandela Gray, "Religion in/and Black Lives Matter: Celebrating the impossible" *Religion Compass* 13, no. 1 (2019), 8.

35 Biko Mandela Gray, "Religion in/and Black Lives Matter: Celebrating the impossible" *Religion Compass* 13, no. 1 (2019), 8.

36 Kevin C. Winstead, "Black Catholicism and Black Lives Matter: the process toward joining a movement" *Ethnic and Racial Studies* Vol. 40, No. 11 (2017): 1855–1863, doi:10.1080/ 01419870.2017.1334932

37 J. Cobb, "The Matter of Black Lives," *The New Yorker*, March 14, 2016, retrieved from www.newyorker.com/magazine/2016/03/14/where-is-black-lives-matter-headed.

38 Kelly Brown Douglas, *Stand Your Ground: Black Bodies and the Justice of God* (Maryknoll, NY: Orbis Books, 2015), 141–159; Maria Teresa Davila, "Discussing Racial Justice in Light of 2016: Black Lives Matter, a Trump Presidency, and the Continued Struggle for Justice," *Journal of Religious Ethics*, 45, no. 4 (2017): 769–770.

39 Muslim Advocates, "Joint Statement Against Anti-Black Police Violence: Black Lives Matter, An American Muslim Community Statement Against Police Violence," Washington, DC, retrieved from https://muslimadvocates.org/joint-statement-against-anti-black-police-violence; Donna Auston, "Prayer, Protest, and Police Brutality: Black Muslim Spiritual Resistance in the Ferguson Era," *Transforming Anthropology*, 25, no. 1 (2017), 11–22.

40 Muslim Advocates, "Joint Statement Against Anti-Black Police Violence: Black Lives Matter, An American Muslim Community Statement Against Police Violence," Washington, DC, retrieved from https://muslimadvocates.org/joint-statement-against-anti-black-police-violence.

41 William J. Barber II, *We Are Called to Be a Movement* (New York: Workman Publishing, 2020), 69–71.

42 Kairos Center for Religion, Rights & Social Justice, retrieved from https://kairoscenter.org/p rojects/poor-peoples-campaign.

43 William J. Barber II and Jonathan Wilson-Hartgrove, *The Third Reconstruction: How a Moral Movement is Overcoming the Politics of Division and Fear* (Boston, MA: Beacon Press, 2016), 38.

44 Associated Press, "Moral Monday Leader Inspires Protests Arrests and Action," July 27, 2015, retrieved from https://abc11.com/moral-monday-protests-arrests-barber/885064.

45 William J. Barber II and Jonathan Wilson-Hartgrove, *The Third Reconstruction: How a Moral Movement is Overcoming the Politics of Division and Fear* (Boston, MA: Beacon Press, 2016), 31.

46 William J. Barber II and Jonathan Wilson-Hartgrove, *The Third Reconstruction: How a Moral Movement is Overcoming the Politics of Division and Fear* (Boston, MA: Beacon Press, 2016), xv.

47 William J. Barber II and Jonathan Wilson-Hartgrove, *The Third Reconstruction: How a Moral Movement is Overcoming the Politics of Division and Fear* (Boston, MA: Beacon Press, 2016), 13.

48 William J. Barber II and Jonathan Wilson-Hartgrove, *The Third Reconstruction: How a Moral Movement is Overcoming the Politics of Division and Fear* (Boston, MA: Beacon Press, 2016), 28.

49 William J. Barber II and Jonathan Wilson-Hartgrove, *The Third Reconstruction: How a Moral Movement is Overcoming the Politics of Division and Fear* (Boston, MA: Beacon Press, 2016), 47–61.

50 William J. Barber II and Jonathan Wilson-Hartgrove, *The Third Reconstruction: How a Moral Movement is Overcoming the Politics of Division and Fear* (Boston, MA: Beacon Press, 2016), 88, 98.

51 Ari Berman, "North Carolina's Moral Mondays" *The Nation*, July 17, 2013, retrieved from www.thenation.com/article/archive/north-carolinas-moral-mondays.

52 William J. Barber II and Jonathan Wilson-Hartgrove, *The Third Reconstruction: How a Moral Movement is Overcoming the Politics of Division and Fear* (Boston, MA: Beacon Press, 2016), x, 77, 80–81, 101; William J. Barber, "Our Message to North Carolina's GOP: 'Moral Mondays' Are Here to Stay," *The Guardian*, June 10, 2013, retrieved from www.theguardian.com/commentisfree/2013/jun/10/north-carolina-gop-moral-mondays.

53 William J. Barber II, *We Are Called to Be a Movement* (New York: Workman Publishing, 2020), 56, 88–89.

54 William J. Barber II, *We Are Called to Be a Movement* (New York: Workman Publishing, 2020), 40–43.

55 William J. Barber II and Liz Theoharis, "The Poor People's Campaign Launched on Mother's Day 2018," *The Nation*, May 14, 2023, retrieved from www.thenation.com/article/society/mothers-day-poverty-justice; Union Theological Seminary, "A Conversation with Rev. Dr. Liz Theolharis," retrieved May 15, 2024 from https://utsnyc.edu/spotlight-liz-theoharis.

56 Associated Press, "Moral Monday Leader Inspires Protests, Arrests and Action" ABC11 News, July 27, 2015, Retrieved from https://abc11.com/moral-monday-protests-arrests-barber/885064.

57 Associated Press, "Moral Monday Leader Inspires Protests, Arrests and Action" ABC11 News, July 27, 2015, Retrieved from https://abc11.com/moral-monday-protests-arrests-barber/885064.

58 William J. Barber II and Jonathan Wilson-Hartgrove, *The Third Reconstruction: How a Moral Movement is Overcoming the Politics of Division and Fear* (Boston, MA: Beacon Press, 2016), 114.

59 William J. Barber II, *We Are Called to Be a Movement* (New York: Workman Publishing, 2020), 88–89.

60 William J. Barber II and Jonathan Wilson-Hartgrove, *The Third Reconstruction: How a Moral Movement is Overcoming the Politics of Division and Fear* (Boston, MA: Beacon Press, 2016), 127.

61 William J. Barber II and Jonathan Wilson-Hartgrove, *The Third Reconstruction: How a Moral Movement is Overcoming the Politics of Division and Fear* (Boston, MA: Beacon Press, 2016), 114.

62 William J. Barber II and Jonathan Wilson-Hartgrove, *The Third Reconstruction: How a Moral Movement is Overcoming the Politics of Division and Fear* (Boston, MA: Beacon Press, 2016), 105.

63 William J. Barber II and Jonathan Wilson-Hartgrove, *The Third Reconstruction: How a Moral Movement is Overcoming the Politics of Division and Fear* (Boston, MA: Beacon Press, 2016), 106.

64 Lynn Stuart Parramore, "The Man Behind Moral Mondays," *The American Prospect*, June 18, 2013. https://prospect.org/power/man-behind-moral-mondays.

65 Lynn Stuart Parramore, "The Man Behind Moral Mondays," *The American Prospect*, June 18, 2013. https://prospect.org/power/man-behind-moral-mondays.

66 Ari Berman, "North Carolina's Moral Mondays" *The Nation*, July 17, 2013, retrieved from www.thenation.com/article/archive/north-carolinas-moral-mondays.

67 Najia Parker, "Nap Ministry Redefines Resistance by Resting," *The Atlanta Journal Constitution*, February 27, 2023, retrieved from www.ajc.com/news/martin-luther-king-jr/nap-ministry-redefines-resistance-by-resting/GJFF2TSLSRHTXHYMSN6X3K6ZO4.

68 Gray Chapman, "The Atlanta Nap Ministry Preaches the Liberating Power of Rest," *Atlanta Magazine*, April 29, 2019, retrieved from www.atlantamagazine.com/health/the-atlanta-nap-ministry-preaches-the-liberating-power-of-rest.

69 Tricia Hersey, *Rest is Resistance: A Manifesto* (New York: Little, Brown Spark, 2022), 12.

70 Ta-Nehisi Coates, *Between the World and Me* (New York: Spiegel & Grau, 2015), 90.

71 Tricia Hersey, *Rest is Resistance: A Manifesto* (New York: Little, Brown Spark, 2022), 37.

72 Tricia Hersey, *Rest is Resistance: A Manifesto* (New York: Little, Brown Spark, 2022), 49.

73 Tricia Hersey, *Rest is Resistance: A Manifesto* (New York: Little, Brown Spark, 2022), 7, 98.

74 Tricia Hersey, *Rest is Resistance: A Manifesto* (New York: Little, Brown Spark, 2022), 135; Sylvian A. Diouf, *Slavery's Exiles: The Story of the American Maroons* (New York: New York University Press, 2014).

75 Tricia Hersey, *Rest is Resistance: A Manifesto* (New York: Little, Brown Spark, 2022), 177–188.

76 "Nap Ministry: An Act of Rebellion?" *Church Times*, August 4, 2023, retrieved from www. churchtimes.co.uk/articles/2023/4-august/features/features/nap-ministry-an-act-of-rebellion.

77 Gray Chapman, "The Atlanta Nap Ministry Preaches the Liberating Power of Rest," *Atlanta Magazine*, April 29, 2019, retrieved from www.atlantamagazine.com/health/the-atlanta-nap -ministry-preaches-the-liberating-power-of-rest.

78 Kelundra Smith, "The Power of Naps," *Emory Magazine*, Summer 2023, https://news.emory. edu/features/2023/07/emag-power-of-naps-13-07-23/index.html; Nicquel Terry Ellis, "Atlanta Woman has an Antidote for Burnout-Napping for Self-Care and Social Justice," *USA Today*, September 9, 2019, retrieved from www.usatoday.com/story/news/nation/2019/08/31/nap-min istry-provides-safe-space-rest-and-self-care-atlanta/1840035001.

79 Gray Chapman, "The Atlanta Nap Ministry Preaches the Liberating Power of Rest," *Atlanta Magazine*, April 29, 2019, retrieved from www.atlantamagazine.com/health/the-atlanta-nap -ministry-preaches-the-liberating-power-of-rest.

80 Nicquel Terry Ellis, "Atlanta Woman has an Antidote for Burnout-Napping for Self-Care and Social Justice," *USA Today*, September 9, 2019, retrieved from www.usatoday.com/story/news/na tion/2019/08/31/nap-ministry-provides-safe-space-rest-and-self-care-atlanta/1840035001.

81 Nicquel Terry Ellis, "Atlanta Woman has an Antidote for Burnout-Napping for Self-Care and Social Justice," *USA Today*, September 9, 2019, retrieved from www.usatoday.com/story/news/na tion/2019/08/31/nap-ministry-provides-safe-space-rest-and-self-care-atlanta/1840035001.

82 Nicquel Terry Ellis, "Atlanta Woman has an Antidote for Burnout-Napping for Self-Care and Social Justice," *USA Today*, September 9, 2019, retrieved from www.usatoday.com/story/news/na tion/2019/08/31/nap-ministry-provides-safe-space-rest-and-self-care-atlanta/1840035001.

83 Kim Parker and Juliana Menasche Horowitz, "Majority of Workers Who Quit a Job in 2021, Cite Low Pay, No Opportunities for Advancement, Feeling Disrespected," *Pew Research Center*, March 9, 2022.

84 Meloynce McAfee, "The Nap Bishop is Spreading the Good Word: Rest," *New York Times*, October 13, 2022, retrieved from www.nytimes.com/2022/10/13/well/live/nap-ministry-bishop -tricia-hersey.html.

85 "About Tricia Hersey," retrieved May 1, 2024 from www.triciahersey.com/about.html.

86 L'oreal Thompson Payton, "I Called the Nap Ministry Hotline That Encourages Breaks and Here's What Happened," *Fortune* October 8, 2022, retrieved from https://fortune.com/well/ 2022/10/08/tricia-hersey-nap-ministry-hotline.

87 Marjua Estevez, "Killer Mike Thinks Christianity Does Black People More Harm Than Good—Q&A Reveals Why," *BET*, February 8, 2019, retrieved from www.bet.com/article/ vshuk0/killer-mike-says-christianity-is-damaging-to-black-people.

88 Najia Parker, "Nap Ministry Redefines Resistance by Resting," *The Atlanta Constitution*, February 27, 2023.

89 Tricia Hersey, *Rest is Resistance: A Manifesto* (New York: Little, Brown Spark, 2022), 111.

Further Readings

Barber, William J., II, and Jonathan Wilson-Hartgrove. *The Third Reconstruction: How a Moral Movement Is Overcoming the Politics of Division and Fear*. Boston, MA: Beacon Press, 2016.

De La Torre, Miguel A., ed. *Faith and Resistance in the Age of Trump*. Maryknoll, NY: Orbis Books, 2017.

Douglas, Kelly Brown. *Resurrection Hope: A Future Where Black Lives Matter*. Maryknoll, NY: Orbis Books, 2021.

Douglas, Kelly Brown. *Stand Your Ground: Black Bodies and the Justice of God*. Maryknoll, NY: Orbis Books, 2015.

Floyd-Thomas, Stacey M. *Religion, Race, and COVID-19: Confronting White Supremacy in the Pandemic*. New York: New York University Press, 2022.

Floyd-Thomas, Juan M. and Anthony B. Pinn, eds. *Religion in the Age of Obama*. New York: Bloomsbury, 2018.

Francis, Leah Gunning. *Ferguson and Faith: Sparking Leadership and Awakening Community*. Des Peres, MO: Chalice Press, 2015.

Gray, Biko Mandela. *Black Life Matter: Blackness, Religion, and the Subject*. Durham, NC: Duke University Press, 2022.

Hersey, Tricia. *Rest is Resistance: A Manifesto*. New York: Little, Brown Spark, 2022.

Johnson, Andre E., and Amanda Nell Edgar. *The Summer of 2020: George Floyd and the Resurgence of the Black Lives Matter Movement*. Jackson, MS: University Press of Mississippi, 2024.

8 Conclusion

Since arriving in America aboard slave vessels, people of African descent have been reinterpreting and remaking religions. Indeed, as I have discussed throughout this book, numerous Black Americans have long adhered to traditional religions that have been around for millennia. For example, Black Christians, Black Muslims, and Black Buddhists esteem ancient sacred texts and follow longstanding religious practices. Still, Black people have continuously modified and reorganized established religions based on shifting social and historical contexts.

One way of respecting this mutable nature of Black religions is through attending to developments in Black musical history. The aesthetics and sounds of Black people have changed with the times. Many of the diverse religious responses to the problem of racial exclusion or to the challenge of double consciousness discussed throughout this book have been expressed in popular Black music, drawing on Black people's lived experiences. From the spirituals to hip-hop, the changing nature of Black music indicates the mental and spiritual shifts Black people have made to survive in America.[1] They have persistently created new music and songs to adjust to changing times and circumstances.

The spirituals, also called slave and sorrow songs, were born during the era of Black enslavement. They permitted enslaved people of African descent to uphold "the universal dimensions of the human spirit and its transcendence over the vicissitudes of life."[2] Some spirituals had double meanings. For example, in the spiritual "Bound for Canaan," Canaan referred to Black people's hope to live eternally in heaven *and* escape to freedom either in the North or Canada.[3] Spirituals such as "Go Down Moses" and "Steal Away" were mere sacred songs to enslavers. However, to many enslaved Black people, they were calls to attend a secret worship service. Such songs also put some enslaved Blacks on notice of the arrival of conductors for the Underground Railroad. After the abolition of slavery, these double meanings of the spirituals no longer remained relevant.

In response to continuing racial oppression following the Civil War and the demise of Reconstruction, Black people developed the blues. Although the blues likely originated during the antebellum era and enslaved Blacks sang blues songs when working in the fields and in the slave quarters, this form of music flowered during the Reconstruction and the early Jim Crow era. Like the spirituals, the blues had deep layers of meaning that Whites and some Blacks failed to grasp.[4] Through the blues, Black people expressed their feelings and emotions about their everyday life struggles, circumstances, and relationships. For example, blues music touched upon nineteenth and early twentieth century African Americans' experiences with imprisonment, storms, Tuberculosis, "Greyhound buses," and the "boll weevil."[5] The music was responsive to the times in which the various artists lived.

DOI: 10.4324/9781003359197-9

The gospel blues came of age during the Great Migration era (see Chapter 4). Since then, gospel artists have constantly reshaped the music to address the social needs of Black Americans. For example, Blacks remade gospel hymns into freedom songs during the civil rights era. Bernice Johnson Reagan, a freedom singer, states, "We cherished the ability to create new songs as we experienced different events."[6] She mentions how freedom singers remade Mahalia Jackson's "Rockin' Jerusalem" into a freedom song. They replaced "Oh Mary, Oh Martha" with "Oh Pritchett, Oh Kelly." These directly referenced civic leaders during the Civil Rights Movement in Albany, Georgia. Laurie Pritchett served as police chief, and Asa Kelly was the mayor. The freedom singers replaced the solo lead "Jerusalem" in Jackson's original song with "Freedom." They substituted the words "Church getting higher" with "bails gets higher" and swapped "rockin' Jerusalem" with "prayin' in jail."[7] Many freedom songs were explicitly tied to the context of civil rights. Often sung in jail cells, during civil rights demonstrations, and in mass meetings, freedom songs gave activists hope and inspiration to strive for social justice against the odds.

Rap music developed in New York City in the late 1970s. Rap is one of the elements of hip-hop culture's broader terrain, including other artistic components such as break dancing, deejaying, graffiti, and knowledge. Deejays employed "high-tech conjuration" to awaken the spirit of Black ancestors and address the realities of urban youth in the post-civil rights era impacted by deindustrialization and poverty.[8] DJ Kool Herc, an immigrant born in Kingston, Jamaica, introduced the turntablism technique, which manipulated sounds by mixing and scratching vinyl records. Deejays creatively utilized existing technology to engineer new beats and sounds. Though often viewed as mere secular music like the blues, religious themes are inherent in the lyrics of rap music, and many rappers have explicit ties to various Black religious traditions, including but not limited to Christianity, Islam, and Rastafarianism. For example, Kanye West's popular rap song "Jesus Walks" reflects his roots in the Christian tradition. The song's message encouraged oppressed individuals to maintain hope that Jesus abides with them. KRS-One, whose name means Knowledge Reigns Supremes Over Nearly Everyone, also produced several hit songs during the 1980s and 1990s, such as "Health, Wealth, Self" and "My Philosophy." Like other figures discussed in this book, KRS-One is a religious innovator. In 2009, he founded the Temple of Hip Hop and wrote a text called *The Gospel of Hip-Hop: The First Instrument*, in which he offers members of Hip Hop culture a philosophical guide to living a meaningful life derived from the culture.[9] Over the years, different styles of rap have continued to emerge, including but not limited to conscious, gangsta, mumble, chopped and screwed, trap, and even gospel rap. Rap, as with other forms of music Black Americans have produced, is ever-changing.

The point with these few examples is that the lyrics and sounds Black artists have created over generations have been informed by historical situations and contexts. Rather than simply singing the same tunes, Black musicians have continuously manufactured and produced new sounds and remixed established genres in response to changing circumstances and times. Likewise, Black people across the religious spectrum discussed in this book have perpetually developed creative religious responses to social injustice filtered through the Black experience. Black human agency has always informed Black religions. Even among Black religious organizations like Black Pentecostals and the Nation of Islam, religious organizations that strongly accentuate Divine agency, the founders and members of these traditions developed innovative responses to social injustice grounded in their respective historical contexts (See Chapters 3 and 4). For example, the interracial Azusa Street revival was extraordinary because it occurred during the early Jim Crow America. While some may contend that the revival was purely divinely inspired and spiritually driven, Seymour's experiences with racial segregation contributed to his vision and leadership of the Pentecostal movement.

Despite Black people's diverse, ingenious, forceful religious responses to social injustice over the centuries, it may be disheartening to acknowledge that social inequities persist in the twenty-first century. None of the religious groups or orientations discussed have managed to obliterate oppression. The hag of white supremacy has repeatedly shape-shifted and continues to ride and terrorize Black Americans in contemporary times (see Chapter 1). Not only are the pharaohs "on both sides of the blood-red waters," as Garnet poignantly pinpointed in the nineteenth century, but critical race scholars have also determined that pharaohs (white supremacy, patriarchy, heterosexism, and other hegemonic systems) are imbedded in American social structures. The pharaohs in positions of political power today are seeking to turn back the clock on advancements in social justice and undercut efforts to promote diversity, equity, and inclusion.

Nevertheless, throughout American history, Black religions have helped numerous Black people maintain hope. Written by James Weldon Johnson in 1900 during the thick of the Jim Crow era, the poem "Lift Every Voice and Sing," which was later converted into a song, gave Americans hope and inspiration to continue pursuing justice against the odds. In one verse, he expressed, "Sing a song full of the faith that the dark past has taught us, Sing a song full of the hope that the present has brought us." Johnson reminds us that victories against "dark" past diabolic systems are lessons that the most insurmountable hardships can be overcome. The achievements of past Black activists may enthuse us to hold fast to faith. The poem also affirms that the present is a gift pregnant with possibilities for every American generation to reconsider what erecting a more just country means and to reflect afresh on the values and ethics that will guide them in improving and refashioning America and the world. The present provides the precious opportunity to join the ancestors in perpetual spiritual striving for social justice.

Notes

1 Anthony B. Pinn, *Noise and Spirit: The Religious and Spiritual Sensibilities of Rap Music* (New York: New York University Press, 2003), 8; James H. Cone, *The Spirituals and the Blues: An Interpretation* (New York: Seabury Press, 1972), 6, 109.
2 James H. Cone, *The Spirituals and the Blues: An Interpretation* (New York: Seabury Press, 1972), 12–17, 112.
3 James H. Cone, *The Spirituals and the Blues: An Interpretation* (New York: Seabury Press, 1972), 88.
4 Anthony B. Pinn, *Noise and Spirit: The Religious and Spiritual Sensibilities of Rap Music* (New York: New York University Press, 2003), 3–6.; James H. Cone, *The Spirituals and the Blues: An Interpretation* (New York: Seabury Press, 1972), 112–113.
5 James H. Cone, *The Spirituals and the Blues: An Interpretation* (New York: Seabury Press, 1972), 120–121.
6 Bernice Johnson Reagon, *If You Don't Go, Don't Hinder Me: The African American Sacred Song Tradition* (Lincoln, NE: University of Nebraska Press, 2001), 82.
7 Bernice Johnson Reagon, *If You Don't Go, Don't Hinder Me: The African American Sacred Song Tradition* (Lincoln, NE: University of Nebraska Press, 2001), 96.
8 Anthony B. Pinn, *Noise and Spirit: The Religious and Spiritual Sensibilities of Rap Music* (New York: New York University Press, 2003), 13.
9 The Temple of Hip Hop is a "ministry, archive, school, and society." To learn more about KRS-One's initiative, visit Temple of Hip Hop's website at www.thetempleofhiphop.org.

Further Readings

Barlow, William. *Looking Up at Down: The Emergence of Blues Culture*. Philadelphia, PA: Temple University Press, 2010.

Booker, Vaughn A. *Lift Every Voice and Swing: Black Musicians and Religious Culture in the Jazz Century*. New York: New York University Press, 2020.

Chang, Jeff. *Can't Stop, Won't Stop: A History of the Hip-Hop Generation*. New York: Picador, 2005.

Cone, James H. *The Spirituals and the Blues: An Interpretation*. New York: Seabury Press, 1972.

Fisher, Miles Mark. *Negro Slave Songs in the United States*. New York: Carol Publishing Group, 1990.

Harold, Claudrena N. *When Sunday Comes: Gospel Music in the Soul and Hip-Hop Eras*. Urbana, IL: University of Illinois Press, 2020.

Gussow, Adam. *Beyond the Crossroads: The Devil and the Blues Tradition*. Chapel Hill, NC: University of North Carolina Press, 2017.

KRS-One. *The Gospel of Hip Hop: The First Instrument*. Brooklyn, NY: Powerhouse Books, 2009.

Pinn, Anthony. *Noise and Spirit: The Religious and Spiritual Sensibilities of Rap Music*. New York: New York University Press, 2003.

Reagon, Bernice Johnson. *If You Don't Go, Don't Hinder Me: The African American Sacred Song Tradition*. Lincoln, NE: University of Nebraska Press, 2001.

Thorpe, Earl E. *African Americans and the Sacred: Spirituals, Slave Religion and Symbolism*. Durham, NC: Harrington Publications, 1982.

Bibliography

Alexander, Estrelda. *Black Fire: One Hundred Years of Black Pentecostalism.* Downers Grove, IL: Intervarsity Press, 2011.

Alexander, Estrelda. *The Women of Azusa Street.* Cleveland, OH: The Pilgrim Press, 2005.

Ali, Noble Drew. *The Holy Koran of the Moorish Science Temple of America.* Baltimore, MD: n. p., 1978.

Allen, Richard. *The Life, Experience, and Gospel Labours of the Rt. Rev. Richard Allen.* Philadelphia, PA: Martin & Bolden, 1833.

Anderson, Robert. *From Slavery to Affluence: Memories of Robert Anderson, Ex-Slave.* Hemingford, NE: Hemingford Ledger, 1927.

Anderson, Robert Mapes. *Vision of the Disinherited: The Making of American Pentecostalism.* New York: Oxford University Press, 1979.

Associated Press. "Moral Monday Leader Inspires Protests, Arrests, and Action." *ABC 11 News*, July 27, 2015. https://abc11.com/moral-monday-protests-arrests-barber/885064/.

Attanasi, Katherine, and Amos Young, eds. *Pentecostalism and Prosperity: The Socio-Economics of the Global Charismatic Movement.* New York: Palgrave Macmillan, 2012.

Auston, Donna. "Prayer, Protest, and Police Brutality: Black Muslim Spiritual Resistance in the Ferguson Era." *Transforming Anthropology* 25, no. 1 (2017): 11–22. doi:10.1111/traa.12095.

Baer, Hans A. *The Black Spiritual Movement: A Religious Response to Racism.* Knoxville, TN: University of Tennessee Press, 1984.

Baer, Hans A., and Merrill Singer. *African American Religion in the Twentieth Century: Varieties of Protest and Accommodation.* Knoxville, TN: University of Tennessee Press, 1992.

Baker, Ella. "Address at the Hattiesburg Freedom Day Rally." *Voices of Democracy*, January 21, 1964. Accessed from https://voicesofdemocracy.umd.edu/ella-baker-freedom-day-rally-speech-text/.

Ball, Charles. *A Narrative of the Life and Adventures of Charles Ball, a Black Man.* 3rd ed. Pittsburgh, PA: John T. Skyrock, 1854.

Barber, William J. II. "Our Message to North Carolina's GOP: 'Moral Mondays' Are Here to Stay." *The Guardian*, June 10, 2013. www.theguardian.com/commentisfree/2013/jun/10/north-carolina-gop-moral-mondays.

Barber, William J. II. *We Are Called to Be a Movement.* New York: Workman Publishing, 2020.

Barber, William J. II, and Liz Theoharis. "The Poor People's Campaign Launched on Mother's Day 2018." *The Nation*, May 14, 2023. www.thenation.com/article/society/mothers-day-poverty-justice/.

Barber, William J. II, and Jonathan Wilson-Hartgrove. *The Third Reconstruction: How a Moral Movement Is Overcoming the Politics of Division and Fear.* Boston, MA: Beacon Press, 2016.

Bartleman, Frank. *Azusa Street.* Plainfield, NJ: Logos International, 1980.

Bell, Bernard W. "President Barack Obama, the Rev. Dr. Jeremiah Wright, and the African American Jeremiadic Tradition." *The Massachusetts Review* 50, no. 3 (Autumn 2009): 452–473.

Berger, Peter L. *The Sacred Canopy: Elements of a Sociological Theory of Religion.* New York: Random House, 1967.

Berlin, Ira, Marc Favreau, and Steven F. Miller, eds. *Remembering Slavery: African Americans Talk about Their Personal Experiences of Slavery and Emancipation*. New York: New Press, 1998.

Berman, Ari. "North Carolina's Moral Mondays." *The Nation*, July 17, 2013. www.thenation.com/article/archive/north-carolinas-moral-mondays/.

Best, Wallace. "'The Right Achieved and the Wrong Way Conquered': J. H. Jackson, Martin Luther King, Jr., and the Conflict Over Civil Rights." *Religion and American Culture: A Journal of Interpretation* 16, no. 2 (Summer2006): 195–215. www.jstor.org/stable/10.1525/rac.2006.16.2.195.

Best, Wallace. *Passionately Human, No Less Divine: Religion and Culture in Black Chicago, 1915–1952*. Princeton, NJ: Princeton University Press, 2005.

Billingsley, Scott. *It's a New Day: Race and Gender in the Modern Charismatic Movement*. Tuscaloosa, AL: University of Alabama Press, 2008.

Boles, John. *Masters and Slaves in the House of the Lord: Race and Religion in the American South, 1740–1870*. Lexington, KY: University Press of Kentucky, 1988.

Boles, John. *The Great Revival: Beginnings of the Bible Belt*. Lexington, KY: University Press of Kentucky, 1996.

Booker, Vaughn. "Civil Rights Religion?: Rethinking 1950s and 1960s Political Activism for African American Religious History." *Journal of Africana Religions* 2, no. 2 (2014): 211–243. www.jstor.org/stable/10.5325/jafrireli.2.2.0211.

Brawley, Benjamin. *Social History of the American Negro*. New York: Macmillan, 1921.

Brekus, Catherine A. *Strangers and Pilgrims: Female Preaching in America, 1740–1845*. Chapel Hill, NC: University of North Carolina Press, 1998.

Brooks, Joanna. *American Lazarus: Religion and the Rise of African-American and Native American Literatures*. New York: Oxford University Press, 2003.

Brown, C.G. *C.H. Mason: A Man Greatly Used of God*. Memphis, TN: Church of God in Christ Publishing House, 1926.

Brown, David H. "Conjure/Doctors: An Exploration of a Black Discourse in America, Antebellum to 1940." *Folklore Forum* 19, no. 3 (1986): 3–46.

Brown, William Wells. *My Southern Home, or the South and Its People*. New York: n.p., 1880.

Butler, Anthea. *Women in the Church of God in Christ: Making a Sanctified World*. Chapel Hill, NC: University of North Carolina Press, 2007.

Byas, Lelia Mason. *Bishop C.H. Mason: Church of God in Christ Founder*. Memphis, TN: Church of God in Christ Publishing House, 1995.

Callahan, Allen Dwight. *The Talking Book: African Americans and the Bible*. New Haven, CT: Yale University Press, 2008.

Cannon, Katie G. *Black Womanist Ethics*. Atlanta, GA: Scholars Press, 1988.

Cannon, Katie G., and Anthony B. Pinn. *The Oxford Handbook of African American Theology*. New York: Oxford University Press, 2014.

CERCL Writing Collective. *Breaking Bread, Breaking Beats: Churches and Hip-Hop—A Basic Guide to Key Issues*. Minneapolis, MN: Fortress Press, 2014.

Chapman, Gray. "The Atlanta Nap Ministry Preaches the Liberating Power of Rest." *Atlanta Magazine*, April 29, 2019. www.atlantamagazine.com/health/the-atlanta-nap-ministry-preaches-the-liberating-power-of-rest/.

Chappell, David L. *A Stone of Hope: Prophetic Religion and the Death of Jim Crow*. Chapel Hill, NC: University of North Carolina Press, 2004.

Chireau, Yvonne Patricia. *Black Magic: Religion and the African American Conjuring Tradition*. Berkeley, CA: University of California Press, 2003.

Chism, Jonathan Langston. "'The Saints Go Marching': Black Pentecostal Critical Consciousness and the Political Protest Activism of Pastors and Leaders in the Church of God in Christ in the Civil Rights Era." *Pneuma*, 35 (2013): 7–24.

Chism, Jonathan Langston. *Saints in the Struggle: Church of God in Christ Activists in the Memphis Civil Rights Movement, 1954–1968*. New York: Lexington Books, 2019.

Church Times. "Nap Ministry: An Act of Rebellion?" August 4, 2023. www.churchtimes.co.uk/a rticles/2023/4-august/features/features/nap-ministry-an-act-of-rebellion.

Clayton, Dewey M. "Black Lives Matter and the Civil Rights Movement." *Journal of Black Studies* 49, no. 5 (2018): 448–480.

Coates, Ta-Nehisi. *Between the World and Me.* New York: Spiegel & Grau, 2015.

Cobb, Jelani. "The Matter of Black Lives." *The New Yorker*, March 14, 2016. Accessed from www.newyorker.com/magazine/2016/03/14/where-is-Black-lives-matter-headed.

Collier-Thomas, Bettye. *Daughters of Thunder: Black Women Preachers and Their Sermons, 1850–1979.* San Francisco, CA: Jossey-Bass Publishers, 1998.

Collier-Thomas, Bettye. *Jesus, Jobs, and Justice: African American Women and Religion.* New York: Alfred A. Knopf, 2010.

Colored Conventions Project. "Rachel Cliff." 2013. Accessed from https://coloredconventions.org/ Black-mobility/delegates/rachel-cliff/.

Cone, James H. *A Black Theology of Liberation.* Maryknoll, NY: Orbis Books, 1990. Originally published 1970.

Cone, James H. *Black Theology and Black Power.* Maryknoll, NY: Orbis Books, 1970.

Cone, James H. *God of the Oppressed.* New York: Harper & Row, 1975.

Cone, James H. *Martin & Malcolm & America: A Dream or a Nightmare.* Maryknoll, NY: Orbis Books, 1991.

Cone, James H., and Gayraud S. Wilmore, eds. *Black Theology: A Documentary History, Volume Two: 1980–1992.* Maryknoll, NY: Orbis Books, 1993.

Cooper, J. Valerie. *Word, Like Fire: Maria Stewart, the Bible, and the Rights of African Americans.* Charlottesville, VA: University of Virginia Press, 2011.

Cosmopolitan Community Church. "History of Cosmopolitan Community Church." Accessed from https://cosmocommchurch.org/a-rich-history/.

Cressler, Matthew J. *Authentically Black and Truly Catholic: The Rise of Black Catholicism in the Great Migration.* New York: NYU Press, 2017.

Curtis, Edward E. "Islamism and Its African American Muslim Critics: Black Muslims in the Era of the Arab Cold War." *American Quarterly* 59, no. 3 (2007): 683–709. doi:10.1353/ aq.2007.0054.

Curtis, Edward E. IV, and Danielle Brune Sigler, eds. *The New Black Gods: Arthur Huff Fauset and the Study of African American Religions.* Bloomington, IN: Indiana University Press, 2009.

Day, Elizabeth. "#BlackLivesMatter: The Birth of a New Civil Rights Movement." *The Guardian*, July 19, 2015. Accessed from www.theguardian.com/world/2015/jul/19/Blacklivesmatter-birth-civil-rights-movement.

Day, Keri. *Azusa Reimagined: A Radical Vision of Religious and Democratic Belonging.* Stanford, CA: Stanford University Press, 2020.

DeFord, Susan. "Gabriel's Rebellion." *Washington Post*, February 6, 2000. Retrieved from www. washingtonpost.com/archive/lifestyle/2000/02/06/gabriels-rebellion/33c9061a-e33d-4f18-bf02-fe3 cd294f5df/.

Delany, Martin R. *The Condition, Elevation, Emigration, and Destiny of the Colored People of the United States Politically Considered.* Philadelphia, PA: The Author, 1852.

Demby, Gene. "The Birth of a New Civil Rights Movement." *Politico Magazine*, December 31, 2014. Accessed from www.politico.com/magazine/story/2014/12/ferguson-new-civil-rights-movement-113906.

Diouf, Sylvian A. *Slavery's Exiles: The Story of the American Maroons.* New York: New York University Press, 2014.

Douglas, Kelly Brown. *Stand Your Ground: Black Bodies and the Justice of God.* Maryknoll, NY: Orbis Books, 2015.

Douglass, Frederick. *Narrative of the Life of Frederick Douglass: An American Slave.* Garden City, NY: Anchor Books, 1973. Originally published in 1845. https://hdl.handle.net/2022/2091.

Drake, St. Clair. *The Redemption of Africa and Black Religion.* Chicago, IL: Third World Press, 1970.

Du Bois, W.E.B. *The Negro Church*. Atlanta, GA: Atlanta University Press, 1903.

Du Bois, W.E.B. *The Souls of Black Folk*. Chicago, IL: A.C. McClurg & Co., 1903.

Dyson, Michael Eric. *April 4, 1968: Martin Luther King, Jr.'s Death and How It Changed America*. New York: Basic Books, 2009.

Ellis, Nicquel Terry. "Atlanta Woman Has an Antidote for Burnout—Napping for Self-Care and Social Justice." *USA Today*, September 9, 2019. www.usatoday.com/story/news/nation/2019/08/31/nap-ministry-provides-safe-space-rest-and-self-care-atlanta/1840035001/.

Emory News. "Power of Naps." July 13, 2023. https://news.emory.edu/features/2023/07/emag-power-of-naps-13-07-23/index.html.

Equiano, Olaudah. *The Interesting Narrative and Other Writings*. New York: Penguin, 1995.

Estevez, Marjua. "Killer Mike Thinks Christianity Does Black People More Harm Than Good – Q&A Reveals Why." BET, February 8, 2019. www.bet.com/article/vshuk0/killer-mike-says-christianity-is-damaging-to-black-people.

Fandrich, Ina J. *The Mysterious Voodoo Queen, Marie Laveaux: A Study of Powerful Female Leadership in Nineteenth Century New Orleans*. New York: Routledge, 2005.

Farrag, Hebah. "The Fight for Black Lives is a Spiritual Movement." *Berkley Forum*, June 9, 2020. https://berkleycenter.georgetown.edu/responses/the-fight-for-black-lives-is-a-spiritual-movement.

Fauset, Arthur Huff. *Black Gods of the Metropolis: Negro Religious Cults of the Urban North*. Philadelphia, PA: University of Pennsylvania Press, 2022. Originally published in 1944.

Ferris, William H. "Garvey and the Black Star Line." *Favorite Magazine*, July 1920.

Finkelman, Paul, ed. *Encyclopedia of African American History, 1896 to the Present: From the Age of Segregation to the Twenty-first Century*. New York: Oxford University Press, 2008.

Finley, Stephen C. *In and Out of This World: Material and Extraterrestrial Bodies in the Nation of Islam*. Durham, NC: Duke University Press, 2022.

Finley, Stephen, Margarita Guillory, and Hugh Page Jr., eds. *Esotericism in African American Religious Experience: There Is a Mystery*. Boston, MA: Brill, 2015.

Fitts, Leroy. *A History of Black Baptists*. Brentwood, TN: Broadman Press, 1985.

Floyd-Thomas, Stacey M. *Mining the Motherlode: Methods in Womanist Ethics*. Cleveland, OH: Pilgrim Press, 2006.

Fort, Nyle. "Black Lives Matter: The Religion of Protest." *The Cut*, January 31, 2022. www.thecut.com/2022/01/Black-lives-matter-religion-spirituality.html.

Francis, Leah Gunning. *Ferguson and Faith: Sparking Leadership and Awakening Community*. Des Peres, MO: Chalice Press, 2015.

Franklin, John Hope, and Alfred A. Moss, Jr. *From Slavery to Freedom: A History of African Americans*. 7th ed. New York: McGraw-Hill, 1994.

Frazier, Edward Franklin. *The Negro Church in America*. New York: Schocken Books, 1964.

Frodsham, Stanley H. *With Signs Following: The Story of the Pentecostal Revival in the Twentieth Century*. Springfield, MO: Gospel Publishing House, 1946.

Garza, Alice. "A Herstory of the #BlackLivesMatter Movement." *The Feminist Wire*, October 7, 2014. Accessed from http://thefeministwire.com/2014/10/Blacklivesmatter-2/.

Gates, Henry Louis, Jr. "Did African-American Slaves Rebel?" PBS. Accessed from www.pbs.org/wnet/african-americans-many-rivers-to-cross/history/did-african-american-slaves-rebel/.

Gates, Henry Louis, Jr. "What Was the Second Middle Passage?" *The Root*, January 28, 2013. Retrieved from www.theroot.com/what-was-the-2nd-middle-passage-1790895016.

Glaude, Eddie S. *Exodus!: Religion, Race, and Nation in Early Nineteenth-Century Black America*. Chicago: University of Chicago Press, 2000.

Glaude, Eddie S. *In a Shade of Blue: Pragmatism and the Politics of Black America*. Chicago, IL: University of Chicago Press, 2007.

Goff, James R. Jr., and Grant Wacker, eds. *Portraits of a Generation: Early Pentecostal Leaders*. Fayetteville, AR: University of Arkansas Press, 2002.

Gomez, Michael A. *Exchanging Our Country Marks: The Transformation of African Identities in the Colonial and Antebellum South*. Chapel Hill, NC: University of North Carolina Press, 1998.

Grant, Colin. *Negro with a Hat: The Rise and Fall of Marcus Garvey*. New York: Oxford University Press, 2008.

Grant, Jacquelyn. *White Women's Christ and Black Women's Jesus: Feminist Christology and Womanist Response*. Atlanta, GA: Scholars Press, 1988.

Gray, Biko Mandela. *Black Life Matter: Blackness, Religion, and the Subject*. Durham, NC: Duke University Press, 2022.

Gray, Biko Mandela. "Religion in/and Black Lives Matter: Celebrating the Impossible" *Religion Compass* 13, no. 1 (2019): 1–9. doi:10.1111/rec3.12293.

Griffith, R. Marie. *American Religions: A Documentary History*. New York: Oxford University Press, 2007.

Guillory, Margarita. *Spiritual and Social Transformation in African American Spiritual Churches*. Boston, MA: Brill, 2015.

Hall, Jacquelyn Dowd. "'I Train the People to Do Their Own Talking': Septima Clark and the Women in the Civil Rights Movement." *Southern Cultures* 12, no. 2 (May 20, 2010): 31–52.

Harris, Michael. *The Rise of Gospel Blues: The Music of Thomas Andrew Dorsey in the Urban Church*. New York: Oxford University Press, 1994.

Harrison, Milmon F. *Righteous Riches: The Word of Faith Movement in Contemporary African American Religion*. New York: Oxford University Press, 2005.

Hatcher, William E. *John Jasper: The Unmatched Negro Philosopher and Preacher*. New York: Fleming H. Revell Co., 1908.

Hersey, Tricia. *Rest is Resistance: A Manifesto*. New York: Little, Brown Spark, 2022.

Herskovits, Melville J. *The Myth of the Negro Past*. New York: Harper and Brothers, 1941.

Higginbotham, Evelyn Brooks. *Righteous Discontent: The Women's Movement in the Black Baptist Church, 1880–1920*. Cambridge, MA: Harvard University Press, 1993.

Hills, Darrius D., and Tommy J. Curry. "Cries of the Unheard: State Violence, Black Bodies, and Martin Luther King's Black Power." *Journal of Africana Religions* 3, no. 4 (2015): 453–469.

Hine, Darlene Clark, William C. Hine, and Stanley Harrold. *African Americans: A Concise History, Combined Volume*. New York: Pearson, 2014.

Horowitz, Mitch. *Occult America: The Secret History of How Mysticism Shaped Our Nation*. New York: Bantam Books, 2009.

Hutchinson, Earl Ofari. "The Vile Fascination with the Monkey Image of the Obamas (and African-Americans)." *HuffPost*, May 11, 2010. Accessed from www.huffpost.com/entry/the-vile-fascination-with_b_494985.

Jacobsen, Douglas. *Thinking in the Spirit: Theologies of the Early Pentecostal Movement*. Bloomington, IN: Indiana University Press, 2003.

Johnson, Sylvester A. *African American Religions, 1500–2000: Colonialism, Democracy, and Freedom*. New York: Cambridge University Press, 2015.

Johnson, Terrence L. *Tragic Soul-Life: W.E.B. Du Bois and the Moral Crisis Facing American Democracy*. New York: Oxford University Press, 2012.

Johnson, Walter. *Soul by Soul: Life Inside the Antebellum Slave Market*. Cambridge, MA: Harvard University Press, 2001.

Jones, Charles C. *A Catechism of Scripture Doctrine and Practice, for Families and Sabbath Schools, Designed Also for the Oral Instruction of Colored Persons*. 6th ed. New York: Leavitt, Trow and Company, 1837. Retrieved from https://babel.hathitrust.org/cgi/pt?id=njp.32101058495415&seq=5.

Jones, William R. *Is God a White Racist? A Preamble to Black Theology*. Garden City, NY: Anchor Press, 1998. Originally published 1973.

Joseph, Peniel E. *The Sword and the Shield: The Revolutionary Lives of Malcolm X and Martin Luther King Jr.* New York: Basic Books, 2020.

Kahn, Jonathan. *Divine Discontent: The Religious Imagination of W.E.B. Du Bois*. Oxford: Oxford University Press, 2009.

Kairos Center for Religion, Rights & Social Justice. "Poor People's Campaign." 2017. Accessed from https://kairoscenter.org/projects/poor-peoples-campaign/.

Katz, Bernard, ed. *The Negro and His Folklore in Nineteenth-Century Periodicals*. Austin, TX: University of Texas Press, 1967.

Kendrick, Klaude. *The Promise Fulfilled: A History of the Modern Pentecostal Movement*. Springfield, MO: Gospel Publishing House, 1961.

King, Coretta Scott. *My Life with Martin Luther King, Jr.* New York: Holt, Rinehart and Winston, 1969.

King, Martin Luther, Jr. *Where Do We Go From Here: Chaos or Community?* Boston, MA: Beacon Press, 1994. Originally published 1968.

Klingberg, Frank J., ed. *The Carolina Chronicle of Dr. Francis Le Jau, 1706–1717*. Berkeley, CA: University of California Press, 1956.

Kornweibel, Theodore, Jr. "Bishop C.H. Mason and the Church of God in Christ during World War I: The Perils of Conscientious Objection." *Southern Studies: An Interdisciplinary Journal of the South* 26 (Fall 1987): 261–281.

Lawson, Steven F. *Civil Rights Crossroads: Nation, Community, and the Black Freedom Struggle*. Lexington, KY: University Press of Kentucky, 2003.

Lee, Martha F. *The Nation of Islam: An American Millenarian Movement*. Lewiston, NY: Edwin Mellen Press, 1988.

Lehmann-Haupt, Christopher. "Reverend Ike, Who Preached Riches, Dies at 74." *New York Times*, July 29, 2009.

Lentz, Richard. *Symbols, the News Magazine and Martin Luther King*. Baton Rouge, LA: Louisiana State University Press, 1999.

Levine, Lawrence. *Black Culture and Black Consciousness: Afro-American Folk Thought from Slavery to Freedom*. New York: Oxford University Press, 1977. https://hdl.handle.net/2022/2091.

Lincoln, C. Eric. *The Black Muslims in America*. Boston, MA: Beacon Press, 1961.

Lincoln, C. Eric, and Lawrence H. Mamiya. *The Black Church in the African American Experience*. Durham, NC: Duke University Press, 1990.

Marable, Manning, and Leith Mullings, eds. *Let Nobody Turn Us Around: An African American Anthology*. 2nd ed. New York: Rowman & Littlefield Publishers, 2009.

Masciotra, David. *I Am Somebody: Why Jesse Jackson Matters*. New York: Bloomsbury Publishing, 2020.

Mason, Mary. *The History and Life Work of the Church of God in Christ*. Memphis, TN: Church of God in Christ Press, 1956.

McAfee, Meloynce. "The Nap Bishop is Spreading the Good Word: Rest." *New York Times*, October 13, 2022. www.nytimes.com/2022/10/13/well/live/nap-ministry-bishop-tricia-hersey.html.

McBride, Michael. "Conversion in the Age of Trump." *Journal of Pastoral Theology*, 29, no. 1 (2019): 5–12. doi:10.1080/10649867.2019.1603919.

Michem, Stephanie Y. *Name It and Claim It? Prosperity Preaching in the Black Church*. Cleveland, OH: The Pilgrim Press, 2007.

Minchin, Timothy J. "Beyond the Dominant Narrative: The Ongoing Struggle for Civil Rights in the US South, 1968–1980." *Australian Journal of American Studies* 25, no. 1 (July 2006): 65–86. www.jstor.org/stable/41054007.

Miner, Nancy B. "'All the World Was Shoutin': The Story of the Reverend John Jasper." *Black and Christian*, June 2003. Retrieved from www.Blackandchristian.com/articles/academy/miner-06-03.shtml.

Molina, Alejandra. "Black Lives Matter is 'a spiritual movement,' says co-founder Patrisse Cullors." *Religion News Service*. June 15, 2020. https://religionnews.com/2020/06/15/why-Black-lives-matter-is-a-spiritual-movement-says-blm-co-founder-patrisse-cullors/.

Montgomery, William E. *Under Their Own Vine and Fig Tree: The African-American Church in the South, 1865–1900*. Baton Rouge, LA: Louisiana State University Press, 1993.

Morgan, Philip D. *Slave Counterpoint: Black Culture in the Eighteenth-Century Chesapeake and Lowcountry*. Chapel Hill, NC: University of North Carolina Press, 1998.

Morris, Aldon D. *The Origins of the Civil Rights Movement: Black Communities Organizing for Change*. New York: Free Press, 1984.

Morris, Calvin S. "Reverdy Ransom, the Social Gospel and Race." *The Journal of Religious Thought* 35, no. 1 (1978): 7–21.

Morrison-Reed, Mark D. *Black Pioneers in a White Denomination*. 3rd ed. Boston, MA: Skinner House Books, 1994.

Moses, Wilson Jeremiah, ed. *Classical Black Nationalism: From the American Revolution to Marcus Garvey*. New York: New York University Press, 1996.

Moye, Todd J. *Ella Baker: Community Organizer of the Civil Rights Movement*. Blue Ridge Summit, PA: Blue Ridge Summit, 2013.

Murphy, Joseph M., and J. Gordon Melton, eds. *Encyclopedia of African American Religions*. New York: Garland Publishing, 1993.

Nehuri, Kimani S. *Libation: An Afrikan Ritual of Heritage in Circle of Life*. Lanham, MD: University Press of America, 2015.

Nelson, Jack. "The Civil Rights Movement: A Press Perspective." *The Washington Journalism Review*, April1991.

Newman, Richard, Patrick Rael, and Philip Lapsansky, eds. *Pamphlets of Protest: An Anthology of Early African-American Protest Literature, 1790–1860*. New York: Routledge, 2001.

Oshatz, Molly M. *Slavery and Sin: The Fight Against Slavery and the Rise of Liberal Protestantism*. New York: Oxford University Press, 2011.

Owens, Michael Leo. *God and Government in the Ghetto: The Politics of Church-State Collaboration in Black America*. Chicago, IL: University of Chicago Press, 2007.

Painter, Nell Irvin. *Creating Black Americans: African American History and Its Meanings, 1619 to the Present*. New York: Oxford University Press, 2006.

Parham, Charles F. *The Life of Charles Parham: Founder of the Apostolic Faith Movement*. Baxter Springs, KS: Apostolic Faith Bible College, 1930.

Parker, Kim, and Juliana Menasche Horowitz. "Majority of Workers Who Quit a Job in 2021 Cite Low Pay, No Opportunities for Advancement, Feeling Disrespected." Pew Research Center, March 9, 2022.

Parker, Najia. "Nap Ministry Redefines Resistance by Resting." *The Atlanta Journal-Constitution*, February 27, 2023. www.ajc.com/news/martin-luther-king-jr/nap-ministry-redefines-resistance-by-resting/GJFF2TSLSRHTXHYMSN6X3K6ZO4/.

Parramore, Lynn Stuart. "The Man Behind Moral Mondays: A Conversation with Reverend Doctor William Barber, Who is Leading the Progressive Charge Against Right-Wing Policies in North Carolina." *The American Prospect*, June 18, 2013. https://prospect.org/power/man-behind-moral-mondays/.

Patterson, Charles E., Ray Ross, and Timothy W. Atkins. "History and Formative Years of COGIC." *Charisma*, November 2007.

Payne, Charles M. *I've Got the Light of Freedom: The Organizing Tradition and the Mississippi Freedom Struggle*. Berkeley, CA: University of California Press, 2007.

Payne, Daniel Alexander. "Daniel Payne's Protestation of Slavery." *Lutheran Herald and Journal of the Franckean Synod*, August 1, 1839.

Payton, L'oreal Thompson. "I Called the Nap Ministry Hotline That Encourages Breaks and Here's What Happened." *Fortune*, October 8, 2022. https://fortune.com/well/2022/10/08/tricia-hersey-nap-ministry-hotline/.

Perry, Bruce, ed. *Malcolm X: The Last Speeches*. New York: Pathfinder Press, 1989.

Pinn, Anne H., and Anthony B. Pinn. *Fortress Introduction to Black Church History*. Minneapolis, MN: Fortress Press, 2002.

Pinn, Anthony B. *Introducing African American Religion*. New York: Routledge, 2012.

Pinn, Anthony B. *Terror, and Triumph: The Nature of Black Religion*. Minneapolis, MN: Fortress Press, 2003.

Pinn, Anthony B. *The African American Religious Experience in America*. Westport, CT: Greenwood Press, 2006.

Poole, Thomas G. "What Country Have I? Nineteenth-Century African-American Theological Critiques of the Nation's Birth and Destiny." *The Journal of Religion* 72, no. 4 (1992): 533–548. www.jstor.org/stable/1204618.

Raboteau, Albert J. *A Fire in the Bones: Reflections on African-American Religious History.* Boston, MA: Beacon Press, 1995.

Raboteau, Albert J. *Slave Religion: The "Invisible Institution" in the Antebellum South.* Updated ed. New York: Oxford University Press, 2004.

Randolph, Peter. *Sketches of Slave Life or, Illustrations of the Peculiar Institution.* Boston, MA: published for the author, 1855. Electronic version available at https://docsouth.unc.edu/neh/randol55/randol55.html.

Ransby, Barbara. *Making All Black Lives Matter: Reimagining Freedom in the Twenty-First Century.* Berkeley, CA: University of California Press, 2018.

Ransom, Reverdy C. "Confessions of a Bishop." *Time,* February 13, 1950. Retrieved from https://time.com/archive/6614239/religion-confessions-of-a-bishop/.

Richardson, Harry Van Buren. *Dark Salvation: The Story of Methodism as it Developed among Blacks in America.* Garden City, NY: Anchor Press, 1976.

Richardson, Marilyn, ed. *Maria Stewart, America's First Black Woman Political Writer: Essays and Speeches.* Bloomington: Indiana University Press, 1987.

Robeck, Cecil M. *The Azusa Street Mission and Revival: The Birth of the Global Pentecostal Movement.* Nashville: Thomas Nelson, 2006.

Roberts, Gene, and Hank Klibanoff. *The Race Beat: The Press, the Civil Rights Struggle, and the Awakening of a Nation.* New York: Alfred A. Knopf, 2006.

Roberts, J. Deotis. *Liberation and Reconciliation: A Black Theology.* Louisville, KY: John Knox Press, 2005.

Ross, Rosetta E. "Black Theology and the History of U.S. Black Religions: Post Civil Rights Approaches to the Study of African American Religions." *Religion Compass* 6, no. 4 (2012): 249–261. doi:10.1111/j.1749-8171.2012.00345.x.

Sanders, Cheryl J. *Saints in Exile: The Holiness-Pentecostal Experience.* Oxford: Oxford University Press, 1996.

Sernett, Milton C., ed. *African American Religious History: A Documentary Witness.* Durham, NC: Duke University Press, 1999.

Sernett, Milton C. *Bound for the Promised Land: African American Religion and the Great Migration.* Durham, NC: Duke University Press, 1997.

Sidbury, James. *Becoming African in America: Race and Nation in the Early Black Atlantic.* New York: Oxford University Press, 2007.

Smith, Amanda. *An Autobiography: The Story of the Lord's Dealings with Mrs. Amanda Smith the Colored Evangelist.* New York: Oxford University Press, 1988. Originally published 1893.

Smith, R. Drew, ed. *From Every Mountainside: Black Churches and the Broad Terrain of Civil Rights.* Albany, NY: State University of New York, 2013.

Smith, R. Drew, ed. *New Day Begun: African American Churches and Civic Culture in Post-Civil Rights America.* Durham, NC: Duke University Press, 2003.

Smith, Theophus H. *Conjuring Culture: Biblical Formations of Black America.* New York: Oxford University Press, 1994.

Southern, Eileen. *The Music of African Americans.* 3rd ed. New York: W.W. Norton & Company, 1997.

Squires, Camille, and Alice Markham-Cantor. "The Beginning." *New York Magazine,* January 31, 2022. Accessed from https://nymag.com/article/Black-lives-matter-2022.html.

Standora, Leo. "Luxury-Loving Rev. Ike is Dead." *New York Times,* July 30, 2009.

Stewart, Maria W. *Productions of Mrs. Maria W. Stewart, Presented to the First African Baptist Church & Society of the City of Boston.* Boston, MA: Friends of Freedom and Virtue, 1835.

Synan, Vinson. *The Holiness-Pentecostal Tradition: Charismatic Movements in the Twentieth Century.* Grand Rapids, MI: William B. Eerdmans Publishing Company, 1997.

Tate, Mary Magdalena. *The Constitution Government and General Decree Book of the Church of the Living God, the Pillar and Ground of the Truth*. Chattanooga, TN: New and Living Way, 1924.

Taylor, Clarence. *Black Religious Intellectuals: The Fight for Equality from Jim Crow to the 21st Century*. New York: Routledge, 2002.

Taylor, Mark C., ed. *Critical Terms for Religious Studies*, Chicago, IL: University of Chicago Press, 1998.

Thatcher, Benjamin Bussey. *Memoir of Phillis Wheatley*. Boston, MA, 1834.

Theoharis, Jeanne. *A More Beautiful and Terrible History: The Uses and Misuses of Civil Rights History*. Boston, MA: Beacon Press, 2018.

Thurman, Howard. *Jesus and the Disinherited*. Richmond, IN: Friends United Press, 1981.

Trulear, Harold Dean. "Reshaping Black Pastoral Theology: The Vision of Bishop Ida B. Robinson." *The Journal of Religious Thought* 46, no. 1 (1989): 17–31.

Tucker, David M. *Black Pastors and Leaders: The Organizational History of the Black Church, 1865–1990*. Lanham, MD: University Press of America, 1990.

Tucker, Emma, and Jillian Sykes. "Sonya Massey's Mom Called 911 to Report Her Daughter Was Having a Mental Breakdown the Day Before She Was Killed." CNN, August 1, 2024. Retrieved from www.cnn.com/2024/08/01/us/sonya-massey-mental-health-911-calls/index.html.

Turman, Ebony Marshall. "Black Women's Faith, Black Women's Flourishing." *The Christian Century*, March 13, 2019. Accessed from www.christiancentury.org/article/critical-essay/Black-women-s-faith-Black-women-s-flourishing.

Turner, Richard Brent. *Islam in the African-American Experience*. 2nd ed. Bloomington: Indiana University Press, 2003.

Union Theological Seminary. "Spotlight: Rev. Dr. Liz Theoharis." Accessed September 15, 2024. https://utsnyc.edu/spotlight-liz-theoharis/.

Van der Mass, Ed. *New International Dictionary of Pentecostal and Charismatic Movements*. Grand Rapids, MI: Zondervan, 2002.

Walker-Barnes, Chanequa. "Response to Rev. Michael McBride Plenary, 'Conversions in the Age of Trump.'" *Journal of Pastoral Theology* 29, no. 1 (2018): 13–18.

Walton, Jonathan L. "The Greening of the Gospel (and Black Body): Rev. Ike's Gospel of Wealth and Post-Blackness Theology." *Pneuma* 33 (2011): 181–199.

Walton, Jonathan L. *Watch This! The Ethics and Aesthetics of Black Televangelism*. New York: NYU Press, 2009.

Warnock, Raphael G. *The Divided Mind of the Black Church: Theology, Piety, and Public Witness*. New York: NYU Press, 2014.

Washburn, Patrick S. *The African American Newspaper: Voice of Freedom*. Evanston, IL: Northwestern University Press, 2006.

Washington Informer. "Jesse Jackson Honored for Anti-Apartheid Work." May 1, 2013. Accessed from www.washingtoninformer.com/jesse-jackson-honored-for-anti-apartheid-work/.

Weaver, Elton H. III. *Bishop Charles H. Mason in the Age of Jim Crow: The Struggle for Religious and Moral Uplift*. New York: Lexington Books, 2020.

Weisbrot, Robert. *Father Divine and the Struggle for Racial Equality*. Urbana, IL: University of Illinois Press, 1983.

Weisenfeld, Judith. *New World A-Coming: Black Religion and Racial Identity during the Great Migration*. New York: NYU Press, 2017. doi:10.18574/9781479853687.

Wells-Oghoghomeh, Alexis S. "'She Comes Like a Nightmare': Hags, Witches, and the Gendered Trans-Sense among the Enslaved in the Lower South." *Journal of Africana Religions* 5, no. 2 (2017): 239–274.

Wells-Oghoghomeh, Alexis. *The Souls of Womenfolk: The Religious Cultures of Enslaved Women in the Lower South*. Chapel Hill, NC: University of North Carolina Press, 2021.

West, Cornel. *Prophesy Deliverance!: An Afro-American Revolutionary Christianity*. Louisville, KY: Westminster John Knox Press, 1982.

Wilkinson, Michael, and Steven M. Studebaker, eds. *A Liberating Spirit: Pentecostals and Social Action in North America*. Eugene, OR: Pickwick Publications, 2010.

Williams, Angel Kyodo. *Being Black: Zen and the Art of Living with Fearlessness and Grace*. New York: Penguin Books, 2002.

Williams, Delores S. *Sisters in the Wilderness: The Challenge of Womanist God-Talk*. Maryknoll, NY: Orbis Books, 1993.

Williams, Dennis A., and Elaine Sciolino. "Rebirth of the Nation." *Newsweek* 87, no. 11 (March 15, 1976): 33.

Wilmore, Gayraud S. *Black Religion and Black Radicalism: An Interpretation of the Religious History of Afro-American People*. Maryknoll, NY: Orbis Books, 1983.

Wilmore, Gayraud S., and James H. Cone, eds. *Black Theology: A Documentary History, Volume One: 1966–1979*. Maryknoll, NY: Orbis Books, 1979.

Wilmore, Gayraud S., and James H. Cone, eds. *Black Theology: A Documentary History, Volume Two: 1980–1992*. Maryknoll, NY: Orbis Books, 1993.

Winstead, Kevin C. "Black Catholicism and Black Lives Matter: The Process Toward Joining a Movement." *Ethnic and Racial Studies* 40, no. 11 (2017): 1855–1863. doi:10.1080/01419870.2017.1334932.

Wortham, Robert A. *W.E.B. Du Bois and the Sociology of the Black Church and Religion, 1897–1914*. Lanham, MD: Lexington Books, 2018.

Wright, Richard Robert, Jr. *The Bishops of the African Methodist Episcopal Church*. Nashville, TN: AME Sunday School Union, 1963.

Wright, Richard Robert, Jr. "Social Work and Influence of the Negro Church." *The Annals of the American Academy of Political and Social Science* 30 (1907): 81–93.

Wuthnow, Robert. *Faith Communities and the Fight for Racial Justice: What Has Worked, What Hasn't, and Lessons We Can Learn*. Princeton, NJ: Princeton University Press, 2023.

X, Malcolm. *The Autobiography of Malcolm X, with the assistance of Alex Haley*. New York: Ballantine Books, 2015. Originally published 1964.

X, Malcolm. *February 1965: The Final Speeches*. Edited by Steve Clark. New York: Pathfinder Press, 1992.

X, Malcolm. "God's Judgement of White America." In *End of White World Supremacy: Four Speeches by Malcolm X*. New York: Arcade Publishing, 1971.

X, Malcolm. *Malcolm X Speaks*. Edited by George Breitman. New York: Grove Press, 1966.

X, Malcolm. "Message to the Grassroots." November 10, 1963. Accessed from https://teachingamericanhistory.org/document/message-to-grassroots/.

Yong, Amos and Estrelda Alexander, eds. *Afro-Pentecostalism: Black Pentecostal and Charismatic Christianity in History and Culture*. New York: New York University Press, 2011.

Index

Page numbers in *italics* indicate Figures.

Randolph, A. Philip 93
Randolph, Peter 13
rap music 150
Rauschenbusch, Walter 66
Reagan, Bernice Johnson 150
Reconstruction era 46, 47–50, 137
Redeemers 46
redemptive suffering 101, 113
Refuge Church of Our Lord 66
religion, definition of 1
Render, Michael "Killer Mike" 141–142
Repairers of the Breach 135
respectability politics 46, 48–49, 130
rest, power of; sacredness of *see* Nap Ministry
revivalist preachers 10
revival meetings 11
Ricks, Willie 96–97
ring shout 15
Roberts, Ida E. 50, 90
Roberts, J. Deotis 110
Roberts, Oral 108
Robertson, Carole 98
Robinson, Elizabeth "Lizzie" Woods 57
Robinson, Ida 65, 80–81
Robinson, Jo Ann Gibson 88
Roman Catholic Church 93
Ross, Mary O. 92–93
Rustin, Bayard 93, 95, 120

sacred canopies 1
Sadiq, Mufti Muhammad 73
sanctified Christians 52, 55–56 *see also* Black
  Pentecostalism
Sanders, Cheryl 52
Sanford, Terry 118
Schomburg, Arturo Alfonso 66
Seal, Catherine 72
séances 71
Second Great Awakening 11, 51
Second Vatican Council 93
Seeger, Peter 87
segregation *see* racial segregation
Sernett, Milton 67
sexism, in Black independent churches
  29
Seymour, Jenny Evans Moore 56
Seymour, William H. 52, 56
Sharpton, Al 119–120
Shepard, Mosby 36
Shepherd, Ann 118
Sherman, William Tecumseh 47
Shiloh Association 47
Shrine of the Black Madonna 110
Shuttlesworth, Fred 91
Shuttleworth, Fred 89
Silver Bluff Church 28
Sister Shelly 13

Sitton, Claude 90
slave auction at Richmond, Virginia 7
slavery: biblical evidence justifying 11;
  dehumanization of 5; Europeans
  rationalizing 5; North America rebellions
  35–36; rebellions (*see* insurrections); White
  colonial Americans' debates on Christianity
  and 8–9; White Northerners defending 40
slave trade: domestic 7; transatlantic 5–7
Small, Mary 50
Smith, Amanda Berry 51
Smith, Lewis J. 78
Smith, Lucy Wilmot 49
Smith, Mary Louis 88–89
Smith, Theophus 24, 40
SNCC, SCLC's collaboration with 89
Social Aid Club 72
social justice: advocating for 48–49; altar calls
  and 138; Black Lives Matter and 129–130;
  Black music and 150; community organizing
  approach to 93–96; ecumenical approach to
  91–93; exhaustion as concern 139; freedom
  fighters and 132; Malcolm X's approach to
  99; NAACP and (*see* National Association
  for the Advancement of Colored People
  (NAACP)); spiritual churches advancing
  71–72
Society for the Propagation of the Gospel in
  Foreign Parts (SPGFP) 9
Society of Friends *see* Quakers
soul, definition of 2
Souls of Womenfolk (Wells-Oghoghomeh) 16
Southern Christian Leadership Conference
  (SCLC): Abernathy and 117; Baker and 95,
  96; Clark, and 94–95; classism within 94;
  collaborating with SNCC 89; membership
  decline 117; nonviolent resistance strategy
  88, 89–90; Operation Breadbasket 118;
  sexism within 95–96
Southern migrants 67–68
Southern White Democrats 46
spadework 96
Spann, Jamell 131
Special Field Order No. 15 47
Spencer, Howland 79
spiritual baptism 52–53
spiritual churches 70–72
spiritualism movement 70–71
spirituals 149
spiritual strivings 2
Stevens, Amy 80
Stewart, Maria 32, 34–35
St. George Methodist Episcopal Church 25
Stillwell, William 26
storefront churches 67
Strong, Josiah 66
structural racism 65

For Product Safety Concerns and Information please contact our EU
representative GPSR@taylorandfrancis.com
Taylor & Francis Verlag GmbH, Kaufingerstraße 24, 80331 München, Germany

www.ingramcontent.com/poc-product-compliance
Lightning Source LLC
Chambersburg PA
CBHW081739270326
41932CB00020B/3335